OECD Public Governance Reviews

Optimising Public Infrastructure Investments in Czechia

OECD
BETTER POLICIES FOR BETTER LIVES

The report was funded by the European Union via the Technical Support Instrument, and implemented by the OECD, in co-operation with the European Commission.

Please cite this publication as:
OECD (2024), *Optimising Public Infrastructure Investments in Czechia*, OECD Public Governance Reviews, OECD Publishing, Paris, https://doi.org/10.1787/d4532316-en.

ISBN 978-92-64-32073-4 (print)
ISBN 978-92-64-91767-5 (PDF)
ISBN 978-92-64-38080-6 (HTML)
ISBN 978-92-64-99613-7 (epub)

OECD Public Governance Reviews
ISSN 2219-0406 (print)
ISSN 2219-0414 (online)

Photo credits: Cover © Sergii Figurnyi/Shutterstock.com.

Corrigenda to OECD publications may be found on line at: www.oecd.org/about/publishing/corrigenda.htm.

Foreword

The imperative to swiftly embrace a low-carbon, climate-resilient economy while harnessing the opportunities of digitalisation underscores the urgent need for action. Prioritising quality infrastructure investments is a critical pillar to delivering on these goals and mitigating potential negative impacts, including the risks of increased territorial disparities. Regional and local governments, as major public investors in infrastructure development, alongside central government, are pivotal actors.

However, quality infrastructure investment demands comprehensive, long-term planning and coordination across various sectors and levels of government. This also necessitates robust project selection processes and the implementation of efficient infrastructure financing and delivery methods. Such investment is often sizeable[1], and as government budgets at all levels face increasing pressures, it is important to ensure that limited resources are used effectively to advance economic, social, and environmental goals.

With significant investment expected from the European Recovery and Resilience Facility, Czechia has an opportunity to address its infrastructure gaps, in particular in areas such as transport, digital infrastructure, green and climate-resilient infrastructure and affordable housing. But ensuring effective use of those funds will also require effective decision making and implementation across levels of government, in particular in relation to coherent planning and co-ordination of infrastructure projects, as well stronger institutional national and subnational capabilities on appraisal, and delivery of infrastructure. This report seeks to deliver on those goals. It is structured in three parts. The first provides an overview of the Czech public investment system across levels of government. The second provides analysis and recommendations for the national level, and the third provides analysis and recommendations for the subnational level.

The report is part of the project "Improvements in Governance of Strategic Planning of Public Infrastructure Investments" conducted in Czechia. The project outputs include (i) a benchmarking note that includes good practices from OECD countries, (ii) this assessment and recommendations report; and (iii) guidelines and self-assessment tools to improve governance practices across levels of government. The action was funded by the European Union via the Technical Support Instrument, and implemented by the OECD, in co-operation with the Directorate-General for Structural Reform Support of the European Commission.

This publication was approved for publication by the Regional Development Policy Committee and the Public Governance Committee on April 18, 2024. It was prepared for publication by the Secretariat.

[1] Globally, infrastructure investment needs between 2016 and 2040 are forecasted at USD 94 trillion (Global Infrastructure Hub, 2019[2]) For example, according to the International Energy Agency, in order to meet Net Zero targets, countries will need a more than 4-fold increase in clean energy financing over the period 2026-2030 (for a total of 3.9 TR USD), as compared to investments made over the period 2016-2020. Of this, an estimated 30% will need to come from the public sector (IEA, 2021[1])

Acknowledgements

This report was prepared by the OECD Public Governance Directorate (GOV) led by Elsa Pilichowski and the OECD Centre for Entrepreneurship, SMEs, Regions and Cities (CFE) led by Lamia Kamal-Chaoui. This publication is a result of joint efforts by the Infrastructure and Public Procurement Division (GOV) headed by Edwin Lau and the Regional Development and Multi-level Governance Division (CFE) headed by Dorothée Allain-Dupré. It has been jointly co-ordinated by Matthieu Cahen (GOV) and Isidora Zapata under the supervision of Isabelle Chatry (CFE). Ana Maria Ruiz Rivadeneira (GOV) coordinated the initial phases of the project. Chapter 1 was drafted by Simon Cox, Matthieu Cahen, and Isidora Zapata with inputs from Aleš Pecka. Chapter 2 was drafted by Simon Cox under the guidance of Matthieu Cahen with inputs from Tenzin Dekyi. Chapter 3 was drafted by Isidora Zapata and Yingyin Wu with inputs from Michael Duffy, Charlotte Lafitte, and Brendan Irish.

The OECD expresses its gratitude to the Ministry of Regional Development of Czechia for its co-ordination and leadership throughout this project. In particular, the OECD would like to thank Vojtěch Kubát, who served as the main contact point for the project, Lucie Zapletalová, and Martina Sieber. The OECD would also like to thank the following entities for their participation: the Office of the Government of Czechia, the Ministry of Finance, the Ministry of Transport, the Ministry of the Environment, the Ministry of Industry and Trade, the Ministry of Education, Youth and Sports, the National Development Bank, the State Fund for Transport Infrastructure, Správa železnic, the State Investment Support Fund, the State Environmental Fund, CzechInvest Agency, the National Economic Council of the Government, the Court of Auditors, the Union of Towns and Municipalities, the National Network of Healthy Cities of the Czech Republic, the South Moravian Region, the Moravian-Silesian Region, the Central Bohemia Region, the Ústí Region, the Hradec Králové Region, the City of Prague, the City of Brno, the City of Ostrava, the City of Olomouc, the Town of Žďár nad Sázavou, the Town of Sobotka, the Village of Líský, the Czech Chamber of Commerce, and the Czech Infrastructure Association. The co-operation and commitment of these entities was critical for the successful completion of this project.

This project was funded by the European Union via the Technical Support Instrument and implemented by the OECD in cooperation with the Directorate-General for Structural Reform Support (DG Reform) of the European Commission. The OECD expresses its gratitude to the European Commission for their support to this project, particularly Mr. Daniele Dotto, Deputy Director of DG Reform and Head of Unit, Governance and Public Administration, and Ms. Milena Raykovska, co-ordinator of the project for DG Reform.

The OECD would like to thank Katarzyna Śpiewok from the Association of Polish Cities, Frits Bos from the Netherlands Bureau for Economic Policy Analysis, and Debbie Curtis and Michael Farrington from the Office of Government Procurement, Ireland for their valuable insights. Finally, the Secretariat is also grateful to Aleš Pecka, Consultant, for his contributions to the report.

Table of contents

FIGURES

TABLES

List of Acronyms and Abbreviations

CF	Cohesion Fund
CLLD	Community-led Local Development
CZE	Czechia
CZK	Czech koruna
ERDF	European Regional Development Fund
ESF	European Social Fund
GHG	Greenhouse gas
ICT	Information and communications technology
ITI	Integrated Territorial Investment instrument
JTF	Just Transition Fund
LAG	Local Action Group
MRD	Ministry of Regional Development
NRB	National Development Bank
ORP	Municipality with extended powers
PPP	Public-private partnership
RDS 21+	Regional Development Strategy 21+
RRP	Recovery and Resilience Plan
SFDI	State Fund for Transport Infrastructure
SFPI	State Investment Support Fund
SFŽP	State Environmental Fund
SME	Small and medium-sized enterprise
SUDS	Sustainable Urban Development Strategy
VAM	Voluntary Association of Municipalities

Executive Summary

At a time of increased pressure on government budgets at all levels, improving infrastructure governance can help ensure that scarce resources are used to pursue economic, social, and environmental priorities. Relatively low-cost changes to governance processes and practices and investments in capacity can have outsized effects on the effectiveness and efficiency of large infrastructure investments. Improving governance across sectors and levels of government can help increase the efficiency of investment spending and promote fiscal sustainability.

Infrastructure investment also helps make societies and places more resilient and sustainable. The demographic, green and digital transitions offer opportunities but also raise challenges. Impacts differ across places, and potentially exacerbate existing territorial inequalities, which are already high in Czechia. It is therefore urgent to invest strategically in place-based infrastructure to bridge these territorial disparities.

In Czechia, the importance of good infrastructure governance at all levels of government is underlined in the Recovery and Resilience Plan (RRP). Achieving the RRP's goals of accelerating the transition towards a low-carbon and climate-resilient economy, maximising the benefits of the digital transformation, and improving the quality of public administration depends on sound governance of infrastructure investments.

Below are the main findings and recommendations of this review. Tables in Chapters 2 and 3 provide a list of concrete actions to help Czechia implement these recommendations.

Strengthening the overall infrastructure governance system

Infrastructure planning in Czechia is fragmented along sectoral lines, running the risk of missed synergies and positive spill overs. Although there are areas of good practice in specific sectors and institutions, a more co-ordinated approach to investment could improve value for money and achieve synergies and complementarities among investments. Enhanced cross-sectoral co-ordination through mechanisms such as the new Committee for Strategic Investments could reduce overlap between projects, ensure that investments are mutually reinforcing, and support Czechia's efforts to use infrastructure investment to support a sustainable recovery. It would also help develop a national project pipeline to improve the investment readiness and the absorptive capacity of the public and private sectors.

Czechia does not have a consistent approach to project appraisal and prioritisation across sectors. Some sectors have detailed guidance on project appraisal and rigorous evaluation, but, across the investment system, projects are often prioritised based on their readiness to move forward quickly and their ability to access EU funds. The Ministry of Regional Development could work with other stakeholders to develop a standard approach to project appraisal across sectors, which could be used by subnational governments to support their prioritisation of infrastructure investments and by ministries and state funds to develop funding programmes.

The context and institutional structure of Czechia may exacerbate common public infrastructure procurement challenges. Many contracting authorities do not have regular experience undertaking infrastructure investment nor the resources to build capacity. The overall administrative burden of public procurement and the need to comply with complex requirements is also seen as a significant barrier for accessing EU funds. To address these challenges, the Ministry of Regional Development could work with other stakeholders to increase support for project preparation and facilitate greater use of strategic procurement tools such as framework agreements.

Designing and implementing infrastructure investments across levels of government

Subnational governments in Czechia are key providers of economic and social infrastructure. In 2020, subnational government investment represented 46.4% of total public investment. While regional capital expenditure increased by almost 73% between 2010 and 2020, on average, municipalities are the primary investor, accounting for more than 64% of subnational government investment.

High-quality and effective place-based infrastructure investment is needed to address important regional disparities. In Czechia, regional (TL3) income inequality has increased over the last 20 years. There are significant disparities in infrastructure quality, and the capacity of regions and municipalities to invest also differs across the country. Fine-tuning the multi-level governance system, overcoming sectoral silos, and embedding a territorial perspective in decision making is crucial for place-based infrastructure investments that help reduce territorial inequalities and pursue resilience and environmental objectives. Place-based infrastructure investments also require better co-ordination across levels of government in the design and implementation stages.

Introducing appropriate incentives to encourage inter-municipal co-operation is crucial to ensure adequate scale and capacity to invest. Czechia has the most, and smallest, municipalities among OECD countries: 6 258 municipalities, with 96% having fewer than 5 000 inhabitants. Small municipalities and regions often lack the capacity to plan, fund, and implement infrastructure investments at the right scale that effectively respond to local needs. Establishing financial and non-financial incentives for municipalities to co-operate is necessary to go beyond one-time, single-purpose associations and achieve the scale and capacities needed for long-term infrastructure investment planning.

Strengthening regional and local capacities should remain a priority to increase the quality and efficiency of investments across levels of government. Czechia, notably through the Client-oriented Public Administration 2030 and the RRP initiatives, has set capacity building as a key priority, reflecting the criticality of training, technical assistance, and the provision of guidance documents in areas such as planning, project appraisal, project management, financial management and procurement in the design and delivery of strategic infrastructure projects. A proper diagnosis of capacity gaps in regions and municipalities is required to target and co-ordinate capacity building in a systemic and sustainable way.

Czech regions' and municipalities' dependency on central transfers and limited tax autonomy challenges subnational infrastructure funding and financing. There are different avenues to increase the funding capacities of Czech subnational governments. The OECD has provided recommendations to improve subnational tax revenues, including by revising the tax-sharing formula and making better use of the property tax in Czechia. Strengthening other revenue streams, including via land-value capture, and supporting the use of innovative financing instruments in a prudent manner including green, social, climate and sustainability bonds or loans, could help subnational governments meet the high up-front costs of infrastructure investment and spread those costs across the future beneficiaries. This could also include taking advantage of the renewed momentum for PPPs in Czechia to explore a larger engagement in public-private partnerships by regions and large cities as an option to accelerate infrastructure investments. PPPs can be a means of leveraging private sector resources but also a tool for reforming public procurement and public service delivery.

1 Infrastructure governance and investment trends overview

This chapter provides an overview of the Czech public investment system across levels of government. It depicts the landscape of infrastructure governance at the national and subnational levels and finds that the infrastructure-decision-making process in Czechia is fragmented across sectors and levels of government. Major trends and issues in infrastructure investment are highlighted, including the significant role of EU funds. Finally, it provides an overview of institutions in the transport, housing and energy sectors, as well as cross-sectoral institutions.

Quality infrastructure investment is critical to delivering Czechia's key policy priorities, including facilitating the green transition, building resilience and addressing regional disparities. Yet Czechia is facing infrastructure investment gaps in areas such as transport, digital infrastructure, green and climate transition infrastructure and affordable housing. These gaps are even larger in lagging regions, despite high levels of public investment supported by European Union (EU) Funds. Current national and subnational institutional frameworks also pose challenges to a whole-of-government approach to infrastructure planning, investment and delivery. Improving infrastructure investment outcomes is essential to addressing these long-term challenges, as well as responding to crises such as the COVID-19 pandemic and Russia's war of aggression against Ukraine.

This report focuses on infrastructure governance: the policies, frameworks, processes and tools used by public bodies at all levels to plan, make decisions, implement and monitor infrastructure investments. It considers all the life stages of a public infrastructure asset, starting from planning, prioritisation and funding through to design, procurement, construction, operation, maintenance and decommissioning. The report evaluates the extent to which Czech institutions and decision-making processes at the national and subnational levels foster efficient and effective investment. It makes concrete and actionable recommendations for strengthening Czechia's capacity to prioritise, design and implement sound infrastructure investments.

This first chapter provides an overview of institutions and decision-making processes at various stages of Czechia's infrastructure lifecycle and supports the analysis in Chapter 2 (national infrastructure investment) and Chapter 3 (subnational infrastructure investment). It provides an overview of the government structure and infrastructure decision-making processes, followed by a description of trends, issues and institutions in three key sectors (transport, housing and energy), as well as cross-sectoral institutions.

1.1 Infrastructure governance in Czechia

National governance involves ministries and state funds

The Government of Czechia is appointed by the President and consists of the Prime Minister and ministers. There are currently 18 members of the government: the Prime Minister, 14 ministers in charge of the respective 14 ministries and another 3 ministers with special portfolios (Science, Research and Innovation; European Affairs; Legislation and Chair of the Legislative Council) (Government of Czechia, n.d.[1]).

Although the government shares the legislative initiative with Parliament, the Senate and regional councils, it is the government which most often submits draft proposals, especially those of a complex nature. All draft legislation is sent to the Government Legislative Council for review and scrutiny for compliance with Czechia's constitutional principles, international treaties, EU law, other laws in force and the rules of the legislative process (Government of Czechia, n.d.[2]).

Ministries' competences and mandates are defined in the 1969 Competency Law.[1] The Competency Law also defines the mandates of an additional 17 central state administration bodies, such as the Czech Statistical Office, the Office of the Government, and the Czech Telecommunications Office (Czechia, 1969[3]). The Competency Law has been subject to several amendments creating, changing or abolishing institutions.

As competences are defined by legislation, infrastructure investment takes place in a rather rigid framework in which it can be difficult to respond and adapt to changes in interrelations among government activities, and to address issues which cross ministerial competences. Responding to emerging or newly important issues – such as crisis management, the green transition and climate change – which require effective horizontal co-ordination and planning between ministries and where roles are not always clearly assigned by the Competency Law can be particularly challenging (OECD, 2023[4]).

Alongside the ministries which directly oversee infrastructure investments within their competences, another set of stakeholders in Czechia have a significant bearing on public infrastructure investment: the states funds. State funds are independent legal entities established by law. The framework for their establishment is enshrined in the Budget Rules, which define state funds as "legal entities established for the financial security of specially defined tasks and the management of funds earmarked for them." Individual funds are based on dedicated laws which define their operating parameters and characteristics. There are currently six state funds, and their revenue and expenditure in 2022 are shown in The state funds most involved in infrastructure investment – the State Fund for Transport Infrastructure, the State Environmental Fund and the State Investment Support Fund – were three of the four largest funds by revenue and expenditure in 2022.

Figure 1.1:

1. State Fund for Transport Infrastructure (SFDI)
2. State Agricultural Intervention Fund (SZIF)
3. State Cinematography Fund (SFKi)
4. State Culture Fund (SFK ČR)
5. State Investment Support Fund (SFPI)
6. State Environmental Fund (SFŽP)

The state funds most involved in infrastructure investment – the State Fund for Transport Infrastructure, the State Environmental Fund and the State Investment Support Fund – were three of the four largest funds by revenue and expenditure in 2022.

Figure 1.1. The State Fund for Transport Infrastructure is the largest of the six funds

State funds revenues and expenditures in 2022, CZK billions

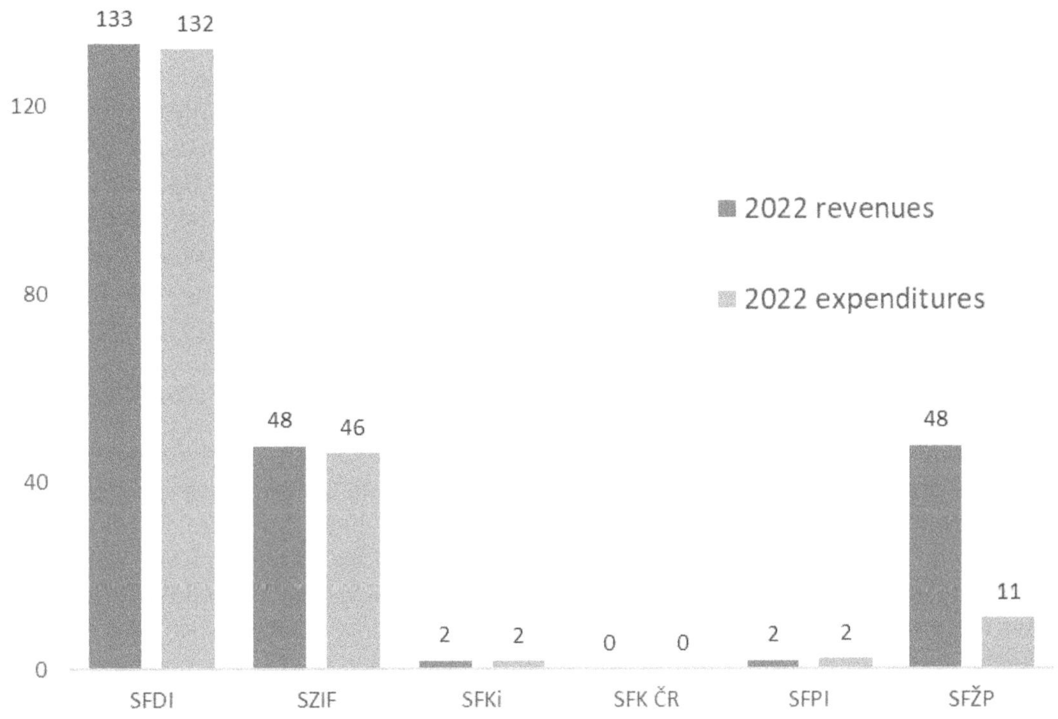

Note: SFDI: State Fund for Transport Infrastructure; SZIF: State Agricultural Intervention Fund; SFKi: State Cinematography Fund; SFK ČR: State Culture Fund; SFPI: State Investment Support Fund; SFŽP: State Environmental Fund.
Source: (Ministry of Finance, 2023[5]), *State Final Account of Czechia for the Year 2022*. https://www.mfcr.cz/cs/rozpoctova-politika/statni-rozpocet/plneni-statniho-rozpoctu/2022/statni-zaverecny-ucet-za-rok-2022-51132

State funds play a significant role in infrastructure investment. For example, the approved 2023 state budget included CZK 84 billion (approximately EUR 3.4 billion) in investment transfers to state funds, compared to only CZK 41 billion (approximately EUR 1.6 billion) in direct state acquisitions of tangible assets and CZK 10 billion (approximately EUR 410 million) in investment transfers to municipalities and regions (Ministry of Finance, 2023[6]). Similarly, in the transport sector, investment expenditure by the State Fund for Transport Infrastructure (SFDI) represented on average 88% of total annual investment expenditure on transport infrastructure between 2010 and 2022 (Ministry of Transport, 2010-2022[7]) (State Fund for Transport Infrastructure, 2010-2022[8]).

The government plays a strategic role in identifying investment priorities, strengthening the capacities of the various levels of government involved in managing public investment, and ensuring sound framework conditions for the governance of public investment (OECD, 2017[9]). Line ministries are then responsible for infrastructure policy and strategic planning in their respective sectors. There are limited high-level co-ordination mechanisms; this role is fulfilled by ad hoc inter-ministerial councils or committees on specific topics. There are a number of these temporary and permanent councils and advisory bodies, most of which are under the Office of the Government (OECD, 2023[4]). While some of these councils are established to provide visibility and representation to minority groups or to address specific issues (e.g. the Council for Roma Minority Affairs, the Council for Gender Equality), others are tasked with steering and co-ordinating cross-cutting issues (e.g. the Government Council for Sustainable Development, the Research, Development and Innovation Council) (Government of Czechia, n.d.[10]).

In June 2023, the government created the Committee for Strategic Investments, a permanent co-ordinating, initiating and advisory body. The committee will facilitate the implementation and support of strategic investments in the areas of transport, housing, energy, education and science, research and innovation. It will monitor and facilitate the implementation of existing strategies and help co-ordinate new strategies in its areas of responsibility; co-ordinate cross-cutting legislative proposals to accelerate their adoption and coherence; evaluate options and proposals to finance strategic investments; and identify opportunities to promote best practices. The committee is chaired by the Prime Minister and its membership includes a number of ministers with infrastructure-focused portfolios, the Chairs of the Association of Regions and the Union of Towns and Municipalities, the Presidents of the Chamber of Commerce and the Confederation of Industry and Transport, the National Security Advisor and the committee's Secretary. The committee has the power to establish temporary or permanent working groups which can be tasked with conducting analysis and preparing proposals and recommendations on specific issues. The committee will be supported by a secretariat under the Office of the Government (Government of Czechia, 2023[11]; Government of Czechia, n.d.[12]).

Subnational governance involves regions and multiple small municipalities

Successive reforms since 1989 have seen Czechia transition from a centralised system towards a system with two tiers of self-governing territorial entities. In 1990, the Constitution recognised local communities' right to self-government and designated municipalities as the basic structure for this new local self-government, with their own budgets and assets. In 1991, Law No. 367/1990 Coll., on Municipal Administration established self-governing municipalities with a high level of independence and simplified the process for creating new municipalities (by removing constraints or limits, such as a minimum number of inhabitants, or territory size). As a result, between 1990 and 1993, the number of municipalities increased by 50% (OECD, 2023[4]). The legal framework, organisation and responsibilities of municipalities was revised in 2000 with the adoption of the Law on Municipalities 128/2000, and the Law on the Capital Prague 131/2000 that gives a special status to the capital city. As of 2021, the municipal level comprised 6 258 municipalities of several categories, 604 cities/towns (*město*), 26 statutory cities (*statutarní město*) and 223 market towns (*městys*). Of these, 95.7% of municipalities had fewer than 5 000 inhabitants, and 88.6% had fewer than 2 000, with a median size of 442 inhabitants (OECD, 2023[4]). Czechia's average municipal size of 1 710 inhabitants per municipality is the smallest among OECD countries (Figure 1.2), and well below the OECD average of 10 250 (OECD-UCLG, 2022[13]).

Figure 1.2. Czechia has an above-average share of small municipalities

Municipalities by population class size, % of municipalities, 2022-2023

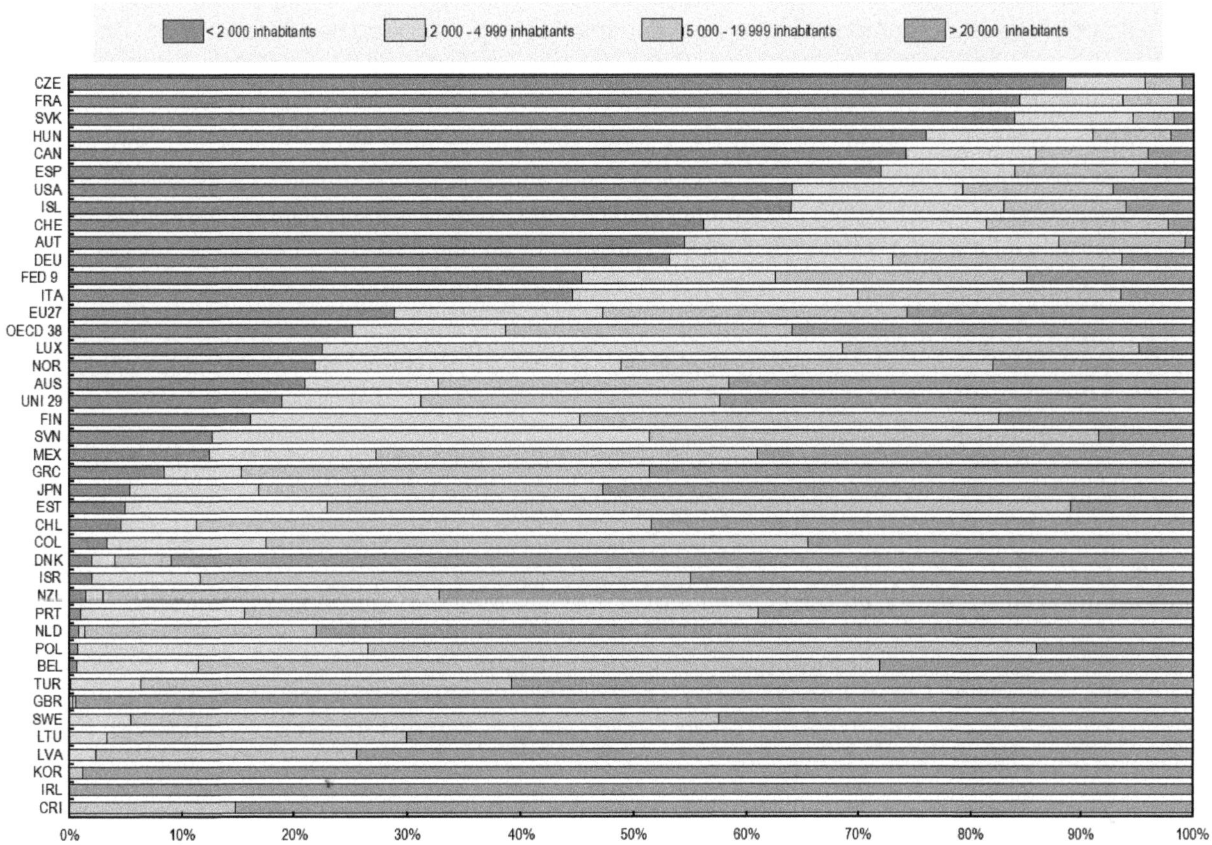

Note: Earlier years may have been used for some countries (based on last available census). The United States' size-classes are slightly different: less than 2 499 inhabitants, 2 500 to 4 999, 5 000 to 24 999, 25 000 or more. For Türkiye, metropolitan municipalities are not included to avoid double counting.

Source: (OECD, 2023[14]), *Subnational Governments in OECD Countries: Key data*. https://www.oecd.org/regional/multi-level-governance/NUANCIER%202023-3.pdf.

Reforms have also led to the progressive establishment of regions and the transfer of competences from the central government to regions and municipalities. The 14 self-governing regions were created in 1997 but were only effectively established in 2000 through Regional Act No. 129/2000 Coll., which transferred a series of responsibilities to the new entities. The act entered into force in 2003 after creating the conditions for the regions to function effectively (OECD, 2023[4]). Decentralisation continued with the replacement of 77 district offices (former administrative divisions executing state administration at the local level) by municipalities with extended competences, which became effective from January 2003. Since then, districts exist solely as territorial units and remain the seats for some offices, notably the courts, police and archives. The Act on Territorial Division of the State, in effect since 2021, aims to simplify the system of state territorial administration by completing the transition from the system of districts to the delegation of functions at the municipal level (OECD, 2023[4]). With this, Czechia finalised its transformation into a combined or mixed model of public governance involving a two-tier system of territorial self-government, i.e. a model with municipalities and regions carrying out both their own self-governmental or autonomous competences and competences delegated by the central state administration.

Municipalities differ in the extent of their delegated competences:

- At the upper level, 205 municipalities have "extended powers" to fulfil several administrative functions delegated by the central government on behalf of smaller surrounding municipalities (e.g. maintaining civil registers, issuing identity cards and driving licences, co-ordinating social services).
- At the intermediate level, 388 municipalities (including the 205 municipalities with "extended powers") have an "authorised municipal authority" to perform delegated functions, but on a smaller scale (e.g. operating the building authority and registry office, offering social assistance, administering war graves), and with a specific agenda for environment and agriculture.
- At the primary level, all municipalities have basic delegated powers (e.g. holding elections, maintaining population records, managing water management). Smaller municipalities can also delegate additional functions to the intermediate and upper-level municipalities through public law contracts if they are unwilling or unable to provide them due to a lack of capacity (OECD, 2023[4]).

Regional governments also have autonomous and delegated competences. Regions are responsible for several functions related to the development of their own territory: for example, they approve planning and zoning documents and are responsible for regional economic development and environmental protection. They are also responsible for regional transport.

As a result of these successive reforms, regions and municipalities in Czechia have significant responsibilities for infrastructure and service delivery in the areas of education, health, utilities, social protection and economic affairs (Table 1.1). Regarding infrastructure, municipalities are responsible for building utility networks in their territory (e.g., sewerage, including connection to wastewater treatment plants; gas, water and heat supply); constructing local roads, parking spaces, pavements; building leisure facilities (e.g. playgrounds and sports grounds, facilities for cultural and social activities in larger municipalities); and maintaining local public and green spaces. Meanwhile, regions are responsible for building and maintaining Class II and III roads. They are also in charge of establishing and managing the regional hospitals, as well as establishing social service centres, homes for the elderly, shelters, residential homes and other social service institutions.

Table 1.1. Municipalities and regions have specific roles related to infrastructure

Local government	Public utilities/transport	Social services	Health	Education
Municipalities				
Infrastructure	Municipal roads and streets	Asylum housing, residential services for the elderly	--	Pre-school facilities and primary schools
Competences	Maintenance, construction and repairs	Provision of social services	--	--
Source of funds and their use	Municipal budgets, and grants	Municipal budgets, subsidies and grants	--	Financing operating costs and investments for construction and renovation of facilities
Regions				
Infrastructure	Class II and Class III roads	Building social service centres, homes for the elderly, shelters, residential homes, etc. as contributory organisations	Building and managing regional hospitals and medical rescue services	Building and managing secondary schools and higher vocational schools
Competences	Management, maintenance and repair	Maintenance of the register and quality control of the services provided	Authorisation of provision of health services	Allocating funds from the state budget for pedagogical and non-teaching staff salaries

				in the region's schools
Source of funds and their use	Regional budgets, state subsidies (SFDI), EU Funds (Regional Operational Programme)	Subsidies from the Ministry of Labour and Social Affairs. Allocation of funds	Operating costs and investments for constructing and renovating facilities	Regional budgets and subsidies. Operating costs and investments for constructing and renovating facilities

Source: Authors, based on (OECD, 2023[4]). *OECD Public Governance Reviews: Czech Republic: Towards a More Modern and Effective Public Administration*. https://doi.org/10.1787/41fd9e5c-en.

The infrastructure decision-making process in Czechia is fragmented

Given infrastructure's cross-cutting nature, multiple institutions and arrangements are responsible for and contribute to ensuring that investment achieves policy objectives. The governance arrangements and scope of action of these institutions vary from country to country, depending on history, constitutional arrangements and government capacities. Furthermore, these institutions often have complementary and sometimes overlapping responsibilities, creating an additional level of complexity (Ruiz Rivadeneira and Mcmaster, 2023[15]).

In Czechia, the national government takes a sectoral approach to infrastructure governance and decision making. Each line ministry is primarily responsible for infrastructure policy and for making decisions on planning and investing in their sector. With each ministry generally planning and prioritising projects related to their own sectoral remits, the roles of infrastructure planning, financing and delivery are spread across a number of institutions. This sectoral approach is mirrored at the subnational level. As a result, processes can differ significantly depending on the sector and whether responsibility lies primarily with the central government or with regions and municipalities. This approach has the advantage that line ministries and other sectoral bodies or local governments often have specialised technical, sectoral or local knowledge that can contribute to more efficient and effective infrastructure planning and delivery. However, the increasing number of cross-sectoral policy challenges can create potential responsibility overlaps, gaps and co-ordination issues (Ruiz Rivadeneira and Mcmaster, 2023[15]). This siloed approach also reduces opportunities for understanding the territorial impact of infrastructure investments. Place-based infrastructure planning requires a cross-sectoral approach that understands the territory and the complementary investments that are needed.

The Spatial Development Policy of Czechia (Ministry of Regional Development, 2021[16]) is a national spatial planning document prepared by the Ministry for Regional Development[2]. It serves mainly as a tool for co-ordinating spatial development at the national level, as well as spatial planning activities by regions and municipalities. It defines nationally relevant areas, axes and corridors (for example, for high-speed rail lines, motorways, or large water works). It does not include project details or constitute project approval, but only requires that the identified areas, axes and corridors be reflected in subsequent regional and municipal spatial planning documentation.

Regions develop their own regional spatial plans, which define the areas and corridors which require a more thorough examination. Where appropriate, they set out the sequence of development for the region and requirements for municipal planning. Municipalities also develop strategic development and spatial plans. Strategic development plans set the direction and priorities for the municipality's development. While such plans are not mandatory, they are important when applying for grants and other support from the state budget and EU funds. Larger municipalities are more likely to have strategic development plans; a 2015 survey found that more than 90% of municipalities with over 10 000 inhabitants had a strategic plan (Ježek, 2015[17]). Municipal spatial plans are mandatory, and function primarily as a regulatory tool that sets direction and limits on land use. The Ministry of Regional Development currently operates a web application, ObcePRO,[3] to support municipalities and associations of municipalities in preparing their development programmes. The application also allows for monitoring and evaluating implementation.

Table 1.2 provides an overview of the roles and responsibilities of the various institutions throughout Czechia's infrastructure lifecycle. Given the diversity of processes across sectors, this is only illustrative.

Table 1.2. Roles and responsibilities in Czechia's infrastructure lifecycle are fragmented

Infrastructure lifecycle stage	Process and institutions responsible
Strategic planning	At the national level, line ministries are responsible for developing strategic plans for specific sectors. These plans set objectives, identify priority areas and outline the strategic direction for infrastructure projects. The consultation process includes formal commentary from other ministries, as well as consultation with stakeholders (e.g. regions and municipalities) and the public. Municipalities and regions are responsible for spatial planning at the local level, as well as local planning for the infrastructure and services they provide (e.g. public transport).
Prioritisation and funding	Line ministries are responsible for project appraisal and prioritisation within their sector. Different prioritisation and appraisal methodologies are used to select projects aligned with available funding and strategic plans. Line ministries and state funds operate grant and loan programmes to fund municipal and regional infrastructure. The Ministry of Finance is responsible for budget allocations for line ministries, regions and municipalities (including co-financing from EU funds) and for reviewing ministries' multi-year plans and major projects. State funds allocate funding for infrastructure investments, as well as providing loans and guarantees for national and subnational entities. The National Development Bank can provide project financing and advice in certain circumstances, including for subnational governments (e.g., for public-private partnerships).
Design, procurement and construction	Depending on the sector, projects may be delivered by ministries, regions and municipalities, or other public bodies (e.g. Railway Administration). Depending on the size and nature of the project, planning and construction permissions are the responsibility of municipalities and regions, or the Transport and Energy Construction Authority. Environmental impact assessments are similarly the responsibility of municipalities and regions or the Ministry of the Environment. The Ministry of Regional Development is responsible for procurement policy at the national level.
Operations, maintenance and decommissioning	Throughout the maintenance and operating phase, relevant institutions, for example the Roads and Motorways Directorate in the case of highways, are responsible for undertaking maintenance and operations, while line ministries establish policies and the Ministry of Finance and state funds finance operations, maintenance and renewal. Municipalities and regions are responsible for the operation and maintenance of the infrastructure assets they own.

1.2 Trends in infrastructure investment in Czechia

COVID-19 and the Russian war of aggression have affected Czechia's fiscal position

Czechia's post-COVID recovery was disrupted by the Russian war of aggression against Ukraine. Increases in energy and commodity prices and disruptions to oil and gas imports from Russia triggered a cost-of-living crisis. High uncertainty and energy price increases resulted in declines in consumer and business sentiment and real wages fell steeply. Growth in gross domestic product (GDP) slowed to 2.5% in 2022, with core inflation among the highest in the EU. The OECD's 2023 Economic Survey forecasts that economic growth will be subdued in 2023, before picking up in 2024 (OECD, 2023[18]).

Czechia is making progress towards all the United Nations Sustainable Development Goals (SDGs), but is lagging behind the EU average for some targets, mainly those related to environmental sustainability. It performs extremely well on SDG targets related to equity such as zero poverty (SDG 1), decent work and economic growth (SDG 8), and reduced inequalities (SDG 10) (European Commission, 2023[19]).

While Czech public debt is low (44.1% of GDP in 2022 compared to the EU average of 85.3%), the structural deficit and medium-term risks have increased in the last three years. Expansionary fiscal policy, especially in 2020 and 2021, weakened the public finance position as Czechia responded to the challenges of the COVID-19 pandemic and the energy crisis resulting from Russia's invasion of Ukraine (European Commission, 2023[19]). To address these fiscal pressures, the government has committed to measures aimed at reducing the deficit by at least CZK 70 billion (approximately EUR 2.9 billion) in 2024 (Ministry of Finance, 2023[20]).

Czechia's challenging fiscal position may limit the near-term scope for significant new infrastructure investments funded through the national budget. This difficult environment increases the importance of strong infrastructure governance, which can improve outcomes from existing levels of investment rather than requiring expenditure increases. By improving the efficiency and effectiveness of infrastructure spending at all levels of government, Czechia can maximise the value of the investments it is able to make at a time of fiscal consolidation.

EU funds are a significant source of historical and planned infrastructure investment in Czechia

Before its accession to the EU, Czechia drew from three pre-accession instruments (Phare, SAPARD and ISPA programmes), which provided technical, economic and infrastructural expertise and assistance to support accession, as well as a focus on financing infrastructure projects in the areas of environment and transport (European Commission, n.d.[21]). Upon accession in May 2004, Czechia joined the 2000-2006 programming period, during which it accessed over EUR 1.69 billion overall from 2004 to 2006 across 13 programmes (Ministry of Regional Development, n.d.[22]).

In the next programming period (2007-2013), Czechia was allocated approximately EUR 26 billion under the cohesion policy through the European Regional Development Fund (ERDF), European Social Fund (ESF) and Cohesion Fund (CF). In this period, infrastructure investment through the cohesion policy represented over 40% of total public investment, indicating its major role in Czech public investment[4] (European Commission, 2022[23]). Investment focused on the European Union cohesion policy objectives for the 2007-2013 programming period:

Convergence: aimed at promoting the economic and social development of regions with GDP per capita of less than 75% of the EU average. This objective was financed by the ERDF, ESF and CF and covered all Czech regions except the City of Prague.

Regional competitiveness and employment: this supported regions with GDP per capita of more than 75% of the EU average. This objective was financed by the ERDF and ESF, and only covered the City of Prague.

European territorial co-operation: this promoted cross-border, interregional and transnational co-operation between regions located along Member States' internal and certain external borders. This objective was financed by the ERDF (Ministry of Regional Development, n.d.[24]).

In the 2014-2020 period, EUR 22.7 billion were available to Czechia under the cohesion policy. Including national financing, the total investment amounted to EUR 29.6 billion, approximately 2.2% of GDP for 2014-2020 (European Commission, 2023[19]). Funding was delivered through the European Regional

Development Fund, Cohesion Fund, European Social Fund and Youth Employment Initiative. Infrastructure investments through the cohesion policy funds in this programming period still played a significant role in infrastructure investment, representing approximately one-third of national public investment (European Commission, 2022[23]).

Major infrastructure programmes included the Transport Programme, which invested in sustainable transport modes and removing bottlenecks on key network infrastructure; the Integrated Regional Programme, which sought to improve regional connectivity through investments in regional roads and the development of public transport; and the Environment Programme, whose priorities included improving water quality, reducing flood risks and enabling public sector energy savings (European Commission, 2023[25]).

Planned investments during the current programming period are significant

Czechia will benefit from sizeable EU cohesion policy funds over the 2021-2027 period. The country's total allocation is EUR 26.7 billion (including both the EU share and national co-financing), divided among the European Regional Development Fund (EUR 13.8 billion), European Social Fund+ (EUR 3.2 billion), Cohesion Fund (EUR 29.2 billion), and Just Transition Fund (EUR 7.2 billion) (European Commission, 2023[26]). This funding is divided into five themes, with the Just Transition Fund and technical assistance making seven overall (see Figure 1.3 for the overall amounts for each):

- Greener Europe: investing in low-carbon transitioning towards a net zero carbon economy, the circular economy, climate change mitigation and adaptation, risk prevention and sustainable urban mobility.
- Social Europe: investing in a more social and inclusive Europe through the implementation of the European Pillar of Social Rights.
- Connected Europe: investing in enhanced sustainable mobility, including Trans-European Transport Network priorities.
- Smarter Europe: investing in a more competitive and smarter Europe by promoting innovative and smart economic transformation and regional ICT connectivity.
- Europe closer to citizens: fostering the sustainable and integrated development of all types of territories and supporting local initiatives.
- Just Transition Fund: The JTF supports regions most affected by the transition towards climate neutrality through the shift away from coal. In Czechia, this includes the regions of Karlovarský, Ústecký, and Moravskoslezký.
- Technical assistance: Investing in administrative capacity to manage complex investments and ensure quality governance.

Figure 1.3. Greener Europe accounts for Czechia's largest share of Cohesion Policy funds

Cohesion policy funds in Czechia by theme, EUR billions (2021-2027)

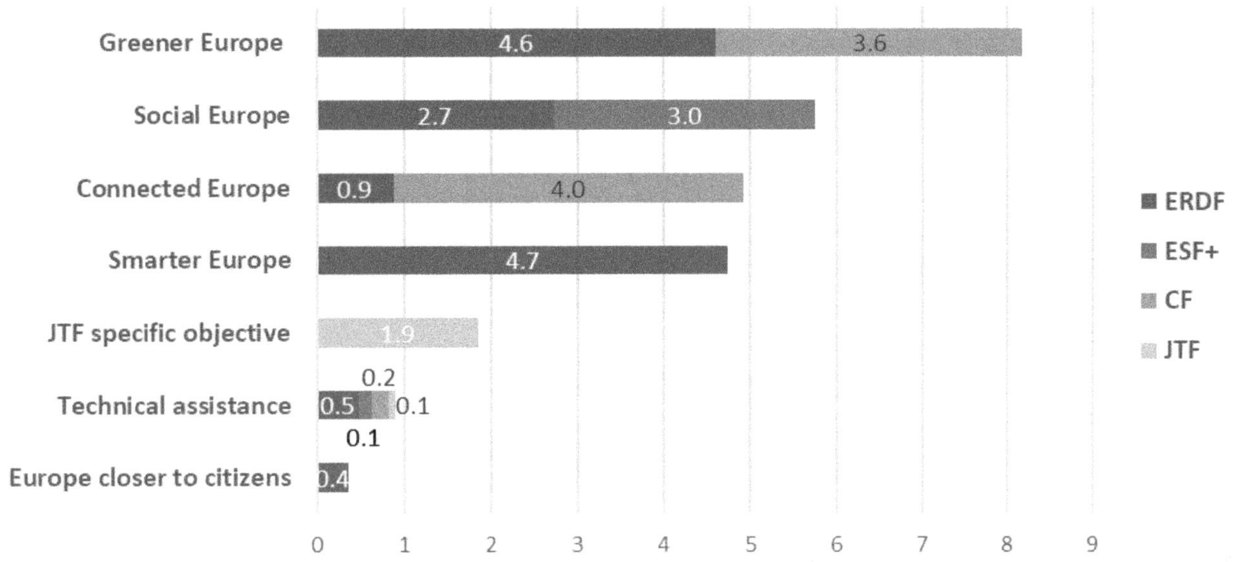

Note: Refresh date: 19 July 2023
Source: European Commission, Cohesion Open Data Platform, https://cohesiondata.ec.europa.eu/

Within the cohesion policy funds, investments in the green transition total EUR 14.1 billion. This amount includes: 1) investments through the ERDF to promote energy efficiency and help to improve the energy performance of around 750 000 square meters of public buildings; and 2) through the Cohesion Fund to support climate adaptation measures enhancing water retention, resulting in over 2 000 hectares of green infrastructure being built or upgraded. Across themes, investments in digital transformation total EUR 1.7 billion, and include measures to accelerate the building of very high-capacity networks to close deep digital divides between urban and rural areas in terms of coverage and exploitation (European Commission, 2023[19]).

Investments across themes are also aimed at addressing significant, though stable, regional disparities. While more developed regions suffer from unaffordable housing and pressures on transport networks, less developed regions face issues arising from demographic pressures, social exclusion and insufficient focus on areas such as the energy transition and digitalisation. The City of Prague is Czechia's most developed region, with a GDP per capita that was 203% of the EU-27 average in 2020. There are six moderately developed regions,[5] with 2020 GDP per capita ranging between 73% and 85% of the EU average. The poorest region (Severozápad) had a GDP per capita that was 61% of the EU average in 2020. While all the other Czech regions are converging on the EU average, Severozápad has persistently lagged behind (European Commission, 2023[19]).

Czechia is also benefiting from other EU programmes in the 2021-2027 programming period, notably the Connecting Europe Facility, which has allocated EU funding of EUR 462.6 million to 17 specific projects on strategic transport networks to date. The Public Sector Loan Facility under the Just Transition Mechanism also makes EUR 125 million of grant support available for projects over 2021-2027, which will be combined with European Investment Bank loans to support investments by public sector entities in just transition regions (European Commission, 2023[19]).

Czechia's Recovery and Resilience Plan includes a significant focus on physical infrastructure and the green transition

The Recovery and Resilience Facility is part of the EU's broader NextGenerationEU package and runs concurrently with the EU cohesion policy funding instruments. It will support Member States' investments and reform measures aimed at allowing them to emerge stronger from the COVID-19 pandemic. Czechia will receive grants totalling EUR 7 billion (2.9% of 2021 GDP) through this facility, to be disbursed by 2026 (OECD, 2023[18]).

Czechia's Recovery and Resilience Plan (RRP) details its approach to the use of Recovery and Resiliency Facility funds and was officially adopted on 17 May 2021 by Government Resolution No. 467. The plan was formally submitted to the European Commission on 1 June 2021, and approved by the Council of the European Union on 31 August 2021 (Council of the European Union, 2021[27]). The RRP has six main pillars (Figure 1.4).

Figure 1.4. Czechia's Recovery and Resilience Plan rests on six pillars

EUR billions

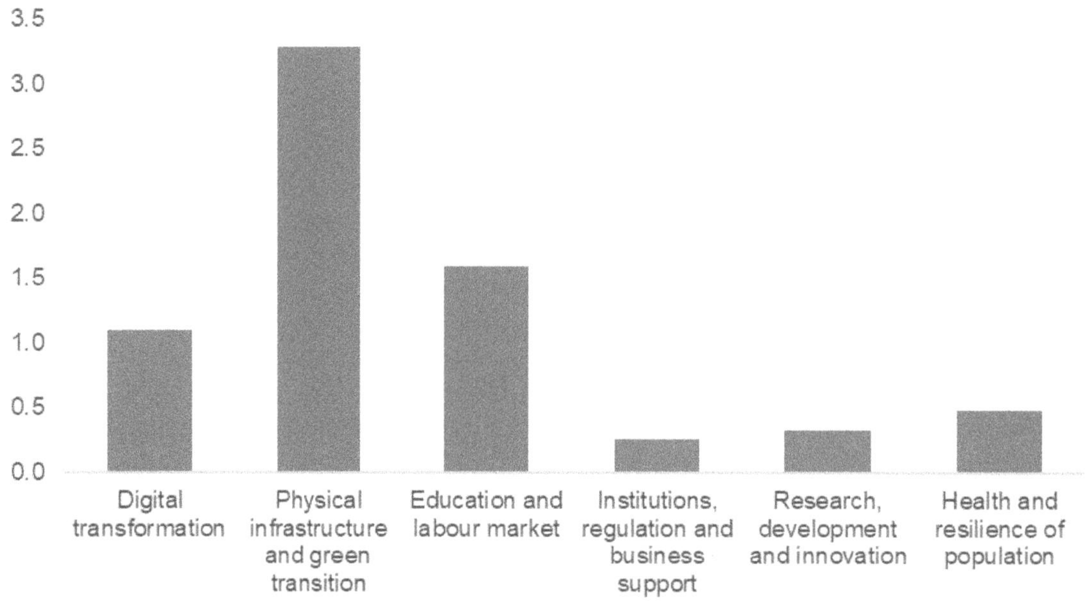

Source: Adapted from (European Commission, 2021[28]), *Analysis of the Recovery and Resilience plan of Czechia.*

As part of the physical infrastructure and green transition pillar, the RRP includes EUR 1.4 billion to finance large-scale renovation programmes to increase the energy efficiency of residential and public buildings, including childcare and long-term care facilities. This pillar also includes investments of EUR 1.1 billion in sustainable mobility, notably in low-emission vehicles for the public and business sector, improving railway infrastructure, and promoting electric charging stations and cycling pathways. Key infrastructure investments will also include EUR 227 million in very high-capacity networks (VHCN) as part of the digital transformation pillar. These allow for expanded and faster internet connectivity, particularly in less developed or rural regions that would benefit from better provision of digital services and business opportunities. The component also foresees the development of 5G networks, particularly in rural areas, both through reforms and investment. The plan also includes EUR 130 million to support the regeneration of brownfield sites owned by municipalities and regions (European Commission, 2021[28]) (European Commission, 2021[29]).

The RRP also includes measures to strengthen the capacity of the public administration and increase the efficiency of investment. Recently adopted amendments to the Building Act (152/2023 Coll.) are expected to shorten the length of time it takes to issue construction permits. Measures aimed at building administrative capacity are planned to support the delivery of public investment projects by providing methodological assistance to strengthen investment readiness and increase the use of public-private partnerships (PPP). The plan also intends to increase the use of non-price criteria in public procurement (European Commission, 2021[28]).

Finally, the EU launched the REPowerEU Plan after Russia's invasion of Ukraine to scale up renewable energy sources, boost energy efficiency measures and reduce dependence on Russian fossil fuels. The plan adds additional grants totalling EUR 20 billion to accelerate Member States' implementation of their climate and energy saving plans (European Commission, 2023[30]). Czechia will receive approximately EUR 680 million in additional funding for initiatives supporting energy security, an increase in the uptake of renewables and energy efficiency, an increase of energy storage capacities and a reduction in dependence on fossil fuels (Ministry of Finance, 2022[31]).

The size of planned investments makes strong infrastructure governance critical

Over the next decade, Czechia is expected to absorb approximately EUR 40 billion of EU funds (European Commission, 2023[19]). The Recovery and Resilience Facility and cohesion policy funds will require greater implementation capacity and efficient procedures to prepare and successfully deliver public sector investment projects. Absorption rates in Czechia remain above the European average, but were lower in the most recent programming period. In the 2004-2006 programming period, Czechia absorbed almost all its allocated financing (99.5%), falling slightly to 96% in the 2007-2014 period, and further to 84% for the 2014-2020 programming period (Ministry of Regional Development, n.d.[22]; Ministry of Regional Development, n.d.[32]; European Commission, 2023[33])

Sufficient implementation capacity is also needed to address the green and digital transitions and successfully seize the opportunities created by the European Green Deal and the Digital Europe Programme. The European Commission's 2023 country report found that low absorption capacity is a contributing factor to the growing disparities between the Severozápad region and other Czech regions (European Commission, 2023[19]).

1.3 Overview of key infrastructure sectors

This section provides a short overview of trends and challenges in three critical infrastructure sectors: transport, energy and housing. It also provides a brief description of the most important institutions (ministries, state funds, etc.) in these sectors, as well as cross-sectoral institutions involved in infrastructure investment.

Transport investment is important for Czechia's green transition and regional equity

Transport is one of the sectors in Czechia with the highest emissions growth (European Commission, 2021[34]). It is therefore a key target for investment to support energy efficiency and reduce carbon emissions and air pollution (OECD, 2020[35]). Car ownership in Czech cities increased significantly after the fall of communism: in Prague it doubled – from 276 per 1 000 inhabitants in 1990 up to 550 in 2014 (Huerta Melchor and Gars, 2020[36]). The uptake of zero-emission road mobility has been modest, with the share of new electric vehicle registrations at only 3.8%, and only one-third of the railway network electrified (European Commission, 2023[19]). The European Commission's analysis of Czechia's RRP noted that upgrades to key areas of the transport infrastructure could boost the shift towards more climate-friendly and sustainable modes of transport. A modernised passenger rolling stock could increase the attractiveness and service quality of rail transport, while at the local level, modern and attractive public transport should help to reduce emissions (European Commission, 2021[28]).

After falling in the wake of the global financial crisis, public investment in transport infrastructure grew again during the second half of the 2010s (Figure 1.5). The 2022 Programme Statement of Czechia commits to creating an investment plan for transport and increasing the efficiency of funds spent on transport construction. The government has also committed to considering the use of public-private partnerships (PPPs) in transport infrastructure projects (see Section 2.4 in Chapter 2), while improving procurement practices more generally (e.g. ensuring transparent and fair selection procedures) (Government of Czechia, 2022[37]).

Figure 1.5. Public investment in rail and road infrastructure is increasing

CZK millions

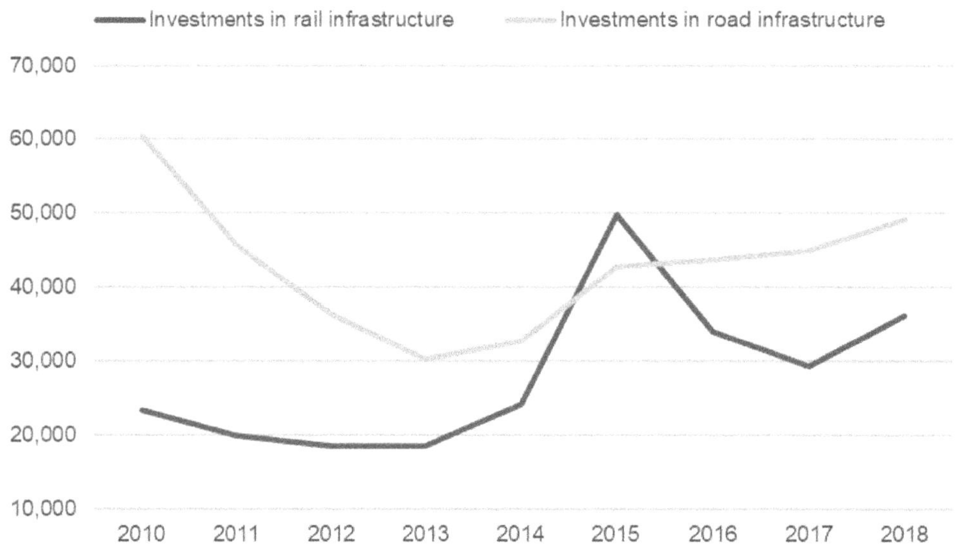

Notes: Includes investment in motorways and Class I, II and III roads, but not in urban roads. Does not include investment in vehicles or rolling stock.
Source: (ITF, 2023[38]), "Transport infrastructure investment and maintenance", ITF Transport Statistics (database), https://doi.org/10.1787/g2g55573-en

Greater regional connectivity can help to advance economic development (ITF, 2023[39]). Connectivity in Czechia, including access to the country's transport network, is still relatively uneven and limits the development prospects of less developed regions. In 2018, more than 88.7% of the population of Prague lived within a radius of 120 km that could be reached in less than 90 minutes (on average). In Jihozápad and Severovýchod, two moderately developed regions, this share was only just over 50% (European Commission, 2023[19]). Infrastructure investment in transport connectivity through the RRP is aimed at levelling out these regional inequalities. The investment in public transport networks is particularly relevant for structurally disadvantaged regions, where the modernisation of rail infrastructure and investment in sustainable transport links are expected to help connect remote regions to economic centres, improving labour market outcomes (European Commission, 2021[28]).

Key transport sector institutions include the Ministry of Transport and the State Fund for Transport Infrastructure (Table 1.3).

Table 1.3. Four key institutions are involved in the transport sector

Institution	Description
Ministry of Transport (Ministerstvo dopravy, MD)	The Ministry of Transport is responsible for the state transport strategy and, within the scope of its competence, for its implementation. This includes developing the Transport Policy and associated sector strategies. The ministry works with the Ministry of Finance to determine the expenditure framework for transport investment. It also works with the State Fund for Transport Infrastructure (SFDI) in preparing the available financial resources and drafting the outlook for the infrastructure financing framework for future years. The planning is typically done with a one-year perspective, in which concrete financial resources are granted by the government to transport. The outlook for future years is for information purposes.
State Fund for Transport Infrastructure (Státní fond dopravní infrastrukury, SFDI)	The State Fund for Transport Infrastructure's objectives are the development, construction, maintenance, and modernisation of roads, motorways, railways, and inland waterways. The SFDI has the largest budget of all Czechia's state funds. In 2023, its budget totalled CZK 150.9 billion (approximately EUR 6.4 billion), of which CZK 46.6 billion (approximately EUR 2.0 billion) was allocated for operational expenditures and CZK 104.3 billion (approximately EUR 4.4 billion) for capital investment. Of this total, CZK 65.5 billion (approximately EUR 2.8 billion) was allocated to the Motorway Directorate and CZK 70.4 billion (approximately EUR 3.0 billion) to the Railway Administration. A further CZK 6.0 billion (approximately EUR 250 million) per year (for the 2023 budget year and the medium-term outlook for 2024 and 2025) were allocated to Class II and III roads, which are under the competence of the regions. SFDI revenues are provided from a road tax, a percentage of the excise duties on hydrocarbon fuels and mineral oils, and motorway tolls and charges. In addition, EU funds provide complementary funding, totalling CZK 27.6 billion (approximately EUR 1.2 billion) in 2023 (State Fund for Transport Infrastructure, 2022[40]). The SFDI is administered by a committee chaired by the Minister of Transport and composed of members selected by the government. A supervisory board is elected by the Chamber of Deputies to oversee its operation and management (State Fund for Transport Infrastructure, n.d.[41]).
Road and Motorway Directorate (Ředitelství silnic a dálnic ČR, ŘSD)	The mission of the Road and Motorway Directorate (ŘSD) is primarily the construction of roads and motorways, as well as the maintenance and repair of motorways and Class I roads.[6] The ŘSD undertakes activities for the preparation and implementation of construction, upgrading and repair, including the proper handover of the works to the subsequent administrators in the case of Class II and III roads. The ŘSD is also responsible for implementing the approved transport policy and strategy for Class I roads and motorways. Currently, more than 7,127 kilometres of motorways and Class I roads are under the management of the ŘSD, of which more than 1,360 kilometres are motorways. The ŘSD will become a state enterprise in 2024. In its current legal form, it is bound by general government regulations on salaries and hiring. Becoming a state-owned enterprise is expected to improve how it hires and retains technical experts, and allow it to insource currently outsourced functions (Ministry of Transport, 2021[42]).
Railway Administration (Správa železnic, SŽ)	As the manager of state-owned railway assets (over 9,400 kilometres of track, over 2,500 stations and stops and over 6,00 bridges), the Railway Administration's main activities include maintaining existing infrastructure and preparing and implementing projects to modernise and expand the network. It also manages the Czech and foreign carriers operating on its network (Railway Administration, n.d.[43]). In 2022, the Railway Administration's total budget was CZK 66.9 billion (approximately EUR 2.8 billion), including CZK 42.5 billion (approximately EUR 1.8 billion) in capital investments (Railway Administration, 2023[44]). It is overseen by a Supervisory Board whose members are appointed by the government on the recommendation of the Minister of Transport.

Energy investments can help reduce Czechia's high emissions

Czechia has some of the highest per-capita greenhouse gas (GHG) emissions in the EU, and the emissions intensity of its GDP is also above the EU average. This is largely due to its significant reliance on coal, large transport sector and inefficient energy use (European Commission, 2021[28]). In 2019, coal accounted for one-third of total energy supply, 46% of electricity generation and over 25% of residential heating (IEA, 2021[45]). Energy intensity per unit of GDP is also considerably higher than in many other OECD countries, driven in part by the energy-inefficient stock of residential buildings. Energy use in Czech dwellings, per square metre, is among the highest in the EU, partly because of the large share of older buildings. Nevertheless, Czechia has made headways in reducing its GHG emissions over the past three decades, including significant reductions in the share of coal in the primary energy supply (OECD, 2023[18]).

The International Energy Agency's (IEA) 2021 Energy Policy Review of Czechia found that more efforts are needed to reach the target set out in its National Energy and Climate Plan of reducing GHG emissions by 30% compared to 2005 levels by 2030. After declining noticeably from 2005 to 2015, total greenhouse gas emissions have remained relatively stable at approximately 17% lower than 2005 (IEA, 2021[45]). Along with the GHG impacts, a reliance on coal and emissions from road transport and residential housing means that more than 75% of the population is exposed to harmful levels of air pollution (OECD, 2021[46]). Czechia's high reliance on fossil fuels calls for a faster roll-out of renewables and energy efficiency investments, as well as a diversification of energy supply sources. As Czechia reduces its use of coal, a broad range of technologies, including solar, wind, geothermal, hydrogen and biomethane, could be developed further to substitute for natural gas imports, particularly in households and industry (European Commission, 2023[19]). Intermediate plans to reduce GHGs, which relied on switching from coal to natural gas for energy general and heating, have been delayed by the Russian aggression against Ukraine, which led to a significant increase in the price of natural gas.

GHG emissions per capita differ across regions. The per-capita emissions in the majority of large regions are below 10 tons of carbon dioxide equivalent (tCO_2e) per capita. Only the Central Bohemian Region, Moravia-Silesia and Severozápad exceed the OECD average per-capita emissions of 11.5 tCO_2e. Severozápad's estimated per-capita emissions are more than 12 times higher than those of Prague (OECD, 2021[47]). All regions use coal in electricity generation, with Prague depending exclusively on coal for electricity.

Initiatives being undertaken under the RPP are designed to contribute to the ambitious EU targets of reducing GHG emissions by 30% by 2030 compared to 2005, and of achieving carbon neutrality by 2050, through an optimal energy mix and the use of renewable energy sources (European Commission, 2021[28]). For example, they seek to tackle the regulations and lengthy construction processes that have been barriers to green investment in Czechia. The new Building Act (No. 283/2021 Coll.) has made important changes aimed at reducing waiting times for renovations or new construction projects. In addition, an amendment to the Energy Act (No. 458/2000 Coll.) has increased the threshold for the obligation to hold a licence for electricity generation from 10 kW to 50 kW. The same threshold will also apply to building permits for renewables projects, shortening construction lead times and reducing the barriers to investing in renewables (OECD, 2023[18]). Czechia's main energy sector institution is the Ministry of Industry and Trade (Table 1.4).

Table 1.4. The Ministry of Industry and Trade is Czechia's main energy sector institution

Institution	Description
Ministry of Industry and Trade (Ministerstvo průmyslu a obchodu, MPO)	The Ministry of Industry and Trade (MPO) is the central state administrative body for state industrial policy, trade policy, foreign economic policy and energy policy. It is also the central body for promoting entrepreneurship and investment in manufacturing and industrial R&D, technology and engineering, including the use of European funds in this

area. The MPO is tasked with developing and implementing energy policies, including the State Energy Policy – the main strategic document guiding energy policy in Czechia (IEA, 2021[48]).

The MPO consults with municipalities and regions on project investment plans during their preparation and implementation. It works with the Ministry of Finance on a broad range of aspects related to the conditions and parameters of subsidy programmes, the approval of budgets, and the approval of applications for subsidies and the evaluation of subsidy programmes. For example, the government regularly publishes calls to support energy management projects as well as for technical assistance with the application documentation through the State Programme for Support of Energy Savings and Use of Renewable Secondary Energy Sources (EFEKT). This includes a network of energy consultation and information centres which provide free advice to SMEs and municipalities to support the uptake of energy-saving measures and renewable energy sources (IEA, 2021[48]). The MPO is also responsible for the overall National Recovery and Resilience Plan, while the preparation and delivery of specific components of the plan are the responsibility of individual ministries (Ministry of Industry and Trade, n.d.[49]).

Housing investment is needed to increase supply

Housing is, on average, the largest expenditure for OECD households, and its share in household spending has risen over time (OECD, 2021[50]). In Czechia, the share of housing related items in total spending is higher than the OECD average (28% compared with 23%) (OECD, 2023[51]). House prices have doubled over the past six years (Figure 1.6) (OECD, 2023[18]). Average property price growth has exceeded 12% in recent years, significantly exceeding growth in average household income in the same period (Czech National Bank, 2022[52]). The high and growing demand for housing in Czech cities has not been met by a sufficient increase in housing supply. Construction activity has not kept up with its pre-2009 levels, and zoning and land-use planning do not steer housing development to where it is most needed. The shortage of qualified construction workers and the complexity of the building permit process pose further constraints to private sector housing supply (OECD, 2021[53]).

However, while the cost, quality and affordability of housing are major concerns in many Czech cities, there are regional differences. For instance, in 2016 only 30% of Prague residents considered it to be easy to find good housing at reasonable prices, compared to 65% of people in Ostrava. Similarly, the average price per square metre of an apartment in Prague was 30% higher than in Brno (Huerta Melchor and Gars, 2020[36]).

Figure 1.6. Housing prices have doubled over the past six years

2008 = 100

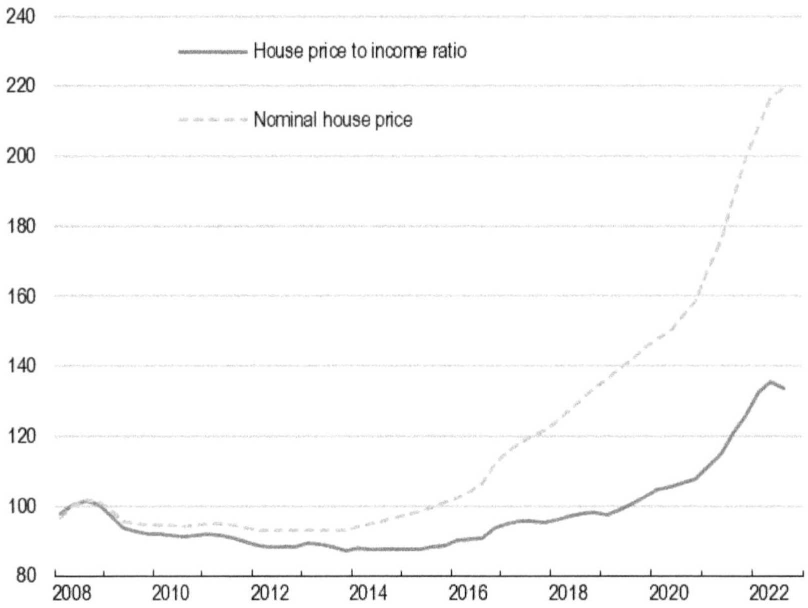

Source: (OECD, 2023[18]), OECD Economic Surveys: Czech Republic 2023, https://doi.org/10.1787/e392e937-en

According to a 2020 survey of municipalities, the main constraints for private developers were the costs of infrastructure provision, the lack of available land and the lack of infrastructure capacity. Municipalities tend to lack a local housing policy framework and inter-municipal co-ordination on housing policy remains limited (OECD, 2021[53]). Municipal rental stock is also very limited and there are no incentives for increasing rental or co-operative housing in order to increase the supply of affordable housing. Moreover, the integration of people fleeing from Ukraine could put further pressure on housing demand (European Commission, 2023[19]).

The private rental market offers few alternatives to ownership due to rising rents and relatively limited supply, while the social housing stock is too small to meet the demand from low-income and vulnerable households (OECD, 2021[53]). The housing stock was largely privatised in the 1990s and government expenditures on social housing are very low (Figure 1.7). The number of co-operatively owned dwellings declined from 700 000 in 1991 to 140 000 in 2021 and rentals declined from 1 465 000 to 890 000 (Czech Statistical Office, 2021[54]). The combined share of outright owners (58.9%) and those with mortgages (16.6%) is higher than the OECD averages (48.2% and 23.3%, respectively), while the combined share of private renters (17.8%) and subsidized renters (1.2%) is lower (16.8% and 6.7% respectively across the OECD) (OECD, 2023[55]; OECD, 2023[56]).

Figure 1.7. Public spending on supporting social rental housing is negligible in Czechia

Government spending as percentage of GDP in selected OECD countries, 2020 or latest year available

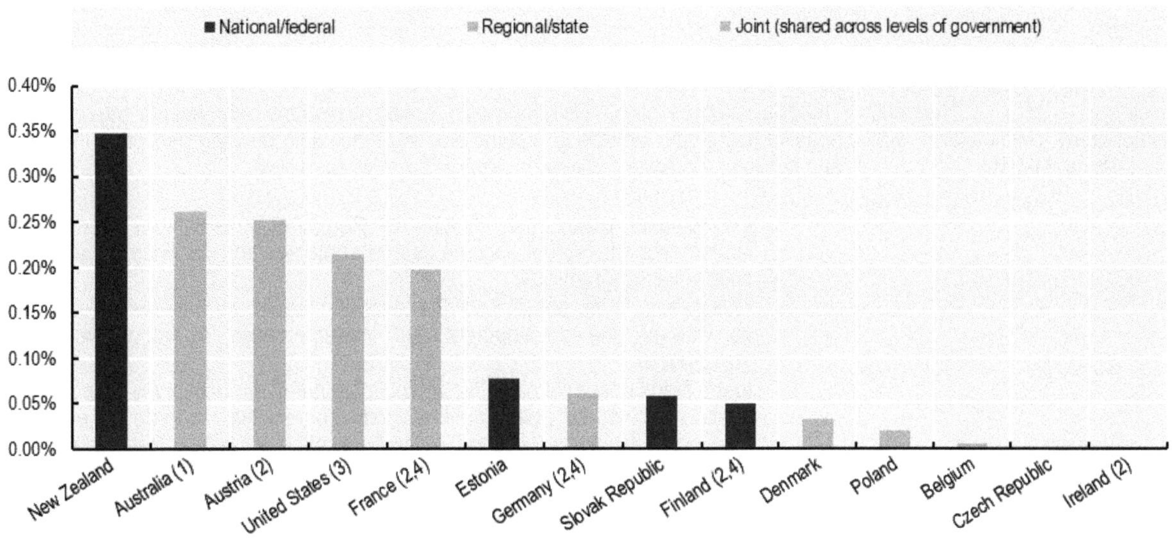

Note:
1. Data for Australia are based on the 2019/2020 fiscal year. GDP is adjusted to reflect this.
2. Data refer to 2020, with the exceptions of Austria and Ireland, where they refer to 2019; France, where they refer to 2018; and Finland and Germany, where they refer to 2017.
3. Data for the United States are based on the 2020/2021 fiscal year. GDP is adjusted to reflect this, based on OECD projections for 2021.
4. For Finland, France and Germany data are based on responses to previous QuASH rounds.
Source: (OECD, 2023[57]), OECD Questionnaire on Affordable and Social Housing (QuASH), 2019, 2021.

The government's 2022 Programme Statement highlights housing as a key issue and commits to supporting both owner-occupied and rental housing, including social housing. This includes accelerating the building process in co-ordination with local governments, as well as creating new tools for municipalities and new financial instruments for affordable housing construction. The Programme Statement also commits to supporting programmes for renovating buildings and replacing existing heating sources with greener options (Government of Czechia, 2022[37]). In 2023, a new Rental Housing Programme was announced with a total allocation of CZK 800 million (approximately EUR 33 million), of which CZK 500 million (approximately EUR 21 million) is intended for municipalities. Under the scheme, applicants can receive grants for up to 25% of eligible expenditure and loans for up to 90% of eligible expenditure. Support can be obtained, inter alia, for constructing apartment buildings containing rental flats, or for renovating unfit family or apartment buildings (State Investment Support Fund, n.d.[58]). The RRP also includes measures related to housing investment, including investing in the energy efficiency of housing stock and modernising district heating distribution networks.

Key housing sector institutions include the Ministry of Regional Development and the State Investment Support Fund (

Table 1.5). Effective co-ordination between the various public bodies will be key for providing affordable and quality housing (European Commission, 2021[28]).

Table 1.5. There are two key housing sector institutions in Czechia

Institution	Description
Ministry of Regional Development (Ministerstvo pro místní rozvoj, MMR)	The Ministry of Regional Development's areas of responsibility include regional policy, housing policy and legislation, spatial planning (including building and permitting rules), and public procurement (Ministry of Regional Development, n.d.[59]): • On regional policy, the Ministry of Regional Development prepares and implements conceptual documents and strategies and provides grants through supportive programmes. • The ministry is responsible for the legal and regulatory framework for housing, as well as the development and implementation of supportive housing instruments. • In the fields of spatial planning and building rules, the ministry is responsible for spatial development policy, maintaining planning activity records and overseeing the work of the Advisory Board for the Application of Building Regulations. It also assesses draft development principles developed by the regions, and generally supervises spatial planning matters. • Finally, the ministry is the National Coordination Authority for implementing programmes co-financed by EU funds.
State Investment Support Fund (Státní fond podpory investic, SFPI)	The State Investment Support Fund supports the development of housing in Czechia and the sustainable development of municipalities, cities, and regions. The main pillars of the SFPI's housing policy are ensuring the availability of adequate housing, helping create a stable environment for housing and supporting the improvement of housing quality. The SFPI therefore aims at regenerating the existing housing stock, reducing the energy consumption of housing, and the construction of housing (State Investment Support Fund, n.d.[60]). In 2022, SFPI revenues totalled CZK 1.9 billion (approximately EUR 75 million). This included CZK 650 million from the state budget (approximately EUR 27 million), CZK 350 million in EU funds (approximately EUR 15 million), and CZK 820 million (approximately EUR 35 million) in loan repayments and interest. The SFPI disbursed CZK 1.0 billion in grants (approximately EUR 42 million) and offered CZK 1.2 billion (approximately EUR 51 million) in loans over the same period (State Investment Support Fund, 2023[61]). The governing body of the SFPI is the Fund Committee, chaired by the Minister for Regional Development and made up of representatives from the Ministry of Regional Development, the Ministry of Finance, the Ministry of Industry and Trade and independent experts. The Fund Committee is responsible for developing the fund's draft. A second body, the fund's Supervisory Board, is appointed by the Chamber of Deputies and is responsible for approving the fund's financial statements and overseeing the fund's activities (Government of Czechia, 2020[62]).

Cross-sectoral institutions are also important for infrastructure governance

This section describes a number of other institutions that play an important role in infrastructure governance.

Ministry of Finance

The Ministry of Finance (Ministerstvo finance) is responsible for fiscal policy, macroeconomic and fiscal forecasts, financial market regulation and preparing the state budget (approved annually) and the budgets for the state funds. The main regulatory framework and rules for these competences are anchored in the Act No.218/2000 Coll., on Budget Rules, which governs the preparation of the mid-term state budget outlook, financial control mechanisms, and the framework for managing the state treasury and state debt.

The ministry has further responsibilities for financial management, financial control, reviewing the management of local self-government units and decisions on co-financing from EU funds. As regards infrastructure governance, the role of the ministry is primarily limited to the budgeting process and reviewing individual projects (Ministry of Finance, n.d.[63]).

CzechInvest

CzechInvest's activities include attracting high value-added investment into Czechia, supporting municipalities in attracting investors, and supporting small and medium enterprises. CzechInvest's 2022 expenditures totalled CZK 250 million (approximately EUR 10.5 million), funded primarily by the Ministry of Industry and Trade and European Funds (CzechInvest, 2023[64]).

CzechInvest has 13 regional offices whose activities include working with municipalities or regions to identify investment needs and provide support in areas such as brownfield regeneration. For example, the industrial zone support programme "Smart Parks for the Future" provides for the development of existing industrial zones and improving their infrastructure, including measures to reduce negative climate impacts and regenerate brownfield sites. CzechInvest also operates a database of business real estate in Czechia, enabling it to offer suitable land, offices and business parks directly to investors (CzechInvest, n.d.[65]).

National Development Bank

The National Development Bank (Národní rozvojová banka, NRB) is a specialised state-owned banking institution. It is the main provider of financial instruments funded from public and European sources, as well as from its own resources and in co-operation with private capital. Its shareholder, Czechia, is represented by the Ministry of Industry and Trade, the Ministry of Regional Development and the Ministry of Finance. The NRB has primarily focused on providing support to SMEs through bank guarantees and preferential loans. The bank has also introduced programmes for financing housing development and municipal infrastructure and served as a manager of infrastructure loans from the European Investment Bank. The bank has assumed the role of manager of EU funds' financial instruments.

Its activities are anchored in three main pillars:

1. Financing the investment and operational needs of Czech enterprises through guarantees, loans, equity and quasi-equity instruments.
2. Supporting specific segments of the Czech economy in co-operation with ministries, regions or municipalities. This includes programmes for enterprises as well as loans for municipalities.
3. Project financing of public infrastructure, particularly transport, social, energy, environmental and digital infrastructure. This pillar is covered by the NRB (loans, subordinated loans, guarantees) and its two subsidiary companies: the National Development Investments (equity or mezzanine financing) and the National Development Fund (mezzanine and junior financing, PPP financing).

The NRB also offers advisory services for clients. Currently, advisory services are available for social enterprises, energy efficiency and energy performance contracting projects, and project financing of public infrastructure (National Development Bank, n.d.[66]).

Ministry of the Environment

The Ministry of the Environment (Ministerstvo životního prostředí, MŽP) co-ordinates the activities of ministries and other central state administrative authorities in environmental matters. It oversees strategy implementation on climate change and produces annual evaluation reports on the state of the environment in Czechia.

The ministry is responsible for developing the Czech State Environmental Policy, which outlines overarching environmental priorities, objectives and strategies, as well as the Climate Protection Policy, which sets emission reduction targets and defines climate protection objectives (Ministry of the Environment, n.d.[67]). The MŽP oversees the implementation of the Strategic Framework Czechia 2030, the overarching strategy for sustainable development in Czechia (OECD, 2023[4]), and ensures alignment with other strategies crucial for climate change, particularly the State Energy Policy and the National Energy and Climate Plan. The MŽP is also the administrator of the State Environmental Fund and appoints the fund's board (State Environmental Fund, n.d.[68]).

State Environmental Fund

The State Environmental Fund (Státní fond životního prostředí, SFŽP) provides direct financial support through subsidies, and indirect financial support through loans or contributions towards interest on loans, to environmentally focused projects (e.g. to improve water quality, use of renewable energy sources, buildings' energy performance). The SFŽP is also responsible for administering EU funds, funds from the state budget, and revenues from fees collected from polluters (State Environmental Fund, n.d.[69]). The fund has a nationwide network of consultants and project managers located in 13 offices in Czechia's major regional cities (State Environmental Fund, n.d.[70]).

In 2022, SFŽP revenues totalled CZK 47.5 billion (approximately EUR 2.0 billion; see The state funds most involved in infrastructure investment – the State Fund for Transport Infrastructure, the State Environmental Fund and the State Investment Support Fund – were three of the four largest funds by revenue and expenditure in 2022.

Figure 1.1), including CZK 2.2 billion (approximately EUR 93 million) from environmental charges (for pollution and resource use) and CZK 43.3 billion (approximately EUR 1.8 billion) from EU funds and the state budget. Expenditures totalled over CZK 10 billion, including CZK 10.2 billion (approximately EUR 430 million) in grants and CZK 66 million (approximately EUR 3 million) in loans from the fund budget. The fund also administered 10.3 billion (approximately EUR 430 million) in project funding on behalf of the Ministry of the Environment (State Environmental Fund, 2023[71]).

The Minister of the Environment appoints the SFŽP board, which assesses major matters related to the development and use of the fund, as well as the annual budget. As of 2022, the board included members of the Chamber of Deputies and the Senate, representatives of the Ministries of the Environment, Finance, Industry and Trade and Regional Development, representatives from regions and municipalities, and civil society organisations (State Environmental Fund, n.d.[72]).

Notes

1 Act No. 2/1969 Coll., on Establishment of Ministries and Other Central Authorities of the State Administration of Czechia ("the Competency Law").

2 Note that this report refers throughout to the 2021 version of the Spatial Development Policy. Subsequent to the drafting of the report, a new version of the Spatial Development Policy came into effect on March 1st, 2024

3 https://www.mmr.cz/cs/ministerstvo/regionalni-rozvoj/regionalni-politika/koncepce-a-strategie/rozvoj-obci

4 Note that this comparison takes the ERDF and Cohesion Fund as proxies for public investment, though some ERDF expenditures finance businesses.

5 The NUTS 2 regions of Moravskoslezko, Střední Morava, Střední Čechy Jihovýchod, Severovýchod, and Jihozápad.

6 In Czechia, motorways and Class I roads are owned by the state while Class II and Class III roads are owned by the regions. Local roads are owned by municipalities.

References

Council of the European Union (2021), *Council implementing decision on the approval of the assessment of the recovery and resilience plan for Czechia*, https://data.consilium.europa.eu/doc/document/ST-11047-2021-INIT/en/pdf. [27]

Czech National Bank (2022), *Financial Stability Report: Spring 2022*, Czech National Bank, Prague, https://www.cnb.cz/export/sites/cnb/en/financial-stability/.galleries/fs_reports/fsr_2022_spring/fsr_2022_spring.pdf. [52]

Czech Statistical Office (2021), *Ownership structure of houses (database)*, Czech Statistical Office, Strašnice, https://www.scitani.cz/ownership-structure-of-houses#skupina-54463. [54]

Czechia (1969), *Act No. 2/1969 Coll., on the Establishment of Ministries and Other Central Authorities of the State Administration of Czechia*, https://www.zakonyprolidi.cz/cs/1969-2# (accessed on 10 June 2023). [3]

CzechInvest (2023), *Annual Report 2022*, CzechInvest, Prague, https://www.czechinvest.org/getattachment/03a24875-7757-4fe8-bc6e-ddbd6516aed7/Vyrocni-zprava-2022. [64]

CzechInvest (n.d.), *Services for Municipalities (in Czech)*, CzechInvest, Prague, https://www.czechinvest.org/cz/Sluzby-pro-municipality/Uvod (accessed on 10 June 2023). [65]

European Commission (2023), *2014-2020 Cohesion Policy Overview*, European Commission, Brussels, https://cohesiondata.ec.europa.eu/cohesion_overview/14-20 (accessed on 22 July 2023). [33]

European Commission (2023), *2023 Country report - Czechia*, European Commission, Brussels, https://economy-finance.ec.europa.eu/system/files/2023-05/CZ_SWD_2023_603_en.pdf. [19]

European Commission (2023), *Cohesion Open Data Platform*, https://cohesiondata.ec.europa.eu/countries/CZ/14-20 (accessed on 22 July 2023). [25]

European Commission (2023), *Cohesion Open Data Platform*, European Commission, Brussels, https://cohesiondata.ec.europa.eu/countries/CZ/21-27 (accessed on 21 July 2023). [26]

European Commission (2023), *NextGenerationEU: Questions and Answers on REPowerEU and on the revision of national recovery plans*, European Commission, Brussels, https://ec.europa.eu/commission/presscorner/detail/en/qanda_23_2489 (accessed on 7 July 2023). [30]

European Commission (2022), *Cohesion in Europe towards 2050: Eighth report on economic, social and territorial cohesion*, European Commission, Brussels, https://ec.europa.eu/regional_policy/information-sources/publications/communications/2022/cohesion-in-europe-towards-2050-8th-cohesion-report_en. [23]

European Commission (2021), *Analysis of the recovery and resilience plan of Czechia*, European Commission, Brussels, https://eur-lex.europa.eu/legal-content/EN/TXT/PDF/?uri=CELEX:52021SC0211. [28]

European Commission (2021), *Analysis of the recovery and resilience plan of Czechia*, https://eur-lex.europa.eu/legal-content/EN/TXT/PDF/?uri=CELEX:52021SC0211. [34]

European Commission (2021), *NextGenerationEU: European Commission disburses €915 million in pre-financing to Czechia*, https://ec.europa.eu/commission/presscorner/detail/en/ip_21_4912. [29]

European Commission (n.d.), *Cohesion Policy Instruments*, European Commission, Brussels, https://www.dotaceeu.cz/en/evropske-fondy-v-cr/programove-obdobi-2004-2006-(1)/nastroje-politiky-soudrznosti (accessed on 19 July 2023). [21]

Government of Czechia (2023), *Resolution of the Government of Czechia No 448*, Government of Czechia, Prague, https://www.odok.cz/portal/services/download/attachment/2023/448/pdf/. [11]

Government of Czechia (2022), *Policy Statement of the Government of Czechia*, Government of Czechia, Prague, https://www.vlada.cz/assets/jednani-vlady/policy-statement/Policy-Statement-of-the-Government.pdf. [37]

Government of Czechia (2020), *Statute of the State Investment Support Fund*, Government of Czechia, Prague, https://sfpi.cz/zakladni-dokumenty/. [62]

Government of Czechia (n.d.), *Advisory and Working Bodies*, Government of Czechia, Prague, https://www.vlada.cz/en/pracovni-a-poradni-organy-vlady/ (accessed on 10 June 2023). [10]

Government of Czechia (n.d.), *Annex to the Government Resolution of 21 June 2023 No 448*, Government of Czechia, Prague, https://vlada.gov.cz/assets/ppov/strategicke-investice/priloha_usneseni_2023_448_1_statut.pdf. [12]

Government of Czechia (n.d.), *Members of the Government*, Government of Czechia, Prague, https://www.vlada.cz/en/vlada/ (accessed on 10 June 2023). [1]

Government of Czechia (n.d.), *Working Committees*, Government of Czechia, Prague, https://www.vlada.cz/cz/ppov/lrv/pracovni-komise/ (accessed on 10 June 2023). [2]

Huerta Melchor, O. and J. Gars (2020), "Planning mobility in a fragmented metropolitan area: The case of Prague and its suburbs", *OECD Regional Development Papers*, No. 08, OECD Publishing, Paris, https://doi.org/10.1787/4cdf2d31-en. [36]

IEA (2021), *Czech Republic 2021 Energy Policy Review*, IEA Energy Policy Reviews, OECD Publishing, Paris, https://doi.org/10.1787/fd01b443-en. [48]

IEA (2021), *Czech Republic 2021 Energy Policy Review*, IEA Energy Policy Reviews, OECD Publishing, Paris, https://doi.org/10.1787/fd01b443-en. [45]

ITF (2023), *ITF Transport Outlook 2023*, OECD Publishing, Paris, https://doi.org/10.1787/b6cc9ad5-en. [39]

ITF (2023), "Transport infrastructure investment and maintenance", *ITF Transport Statistics* (database), https://doi.org/10.1787/g2g55573-en (accessed on 7 July 2023). [38]

Ježek, J. (2015), *Critical analysis of strategic planning of municipalities, cities and regions in Czechia*, Vydala Západočeská univerzita v Plzni, https://dspace5.zcu.cz/handle/11025/22570. [17]

Ministry of Finance (2023), *Approved Sort Budget for Expenditures: Central Government*, Ministry of Finance, Prague, https://monitor.statnipokladna.cz/statni-sprava/schvaleny-rozpocet/vydaje-druhovy?rad=t&obdobi=2312 (accessed on 7 September 2023). [6]

Ministry of Finance (2023), *Convergence Programme of the Czech Republic*, Ministry of Finance, Prague, https://commission.europa.eu/system/files/2023-04/Czechia-CP-2023_EN.pdf. [20]

Ministry of Finance (2023), *State Final Account of Czechia for the Year 2022*, Ministry of Finance, Prague, https://www.mfcr.cz/cs/rozpoctova-politika/statni-rozpocet/plneni-statniho-rozpoctu/2022/statni-zaverecny-ucet-za-rok-2022-51132. [5]

Ministry of Finance (2022), *Ministers agree on the distribution of EUR 20 billion from the RePowerEU package, the Czech Republic will get about CZK 16.7 billion*, Ministry of Finance, Prague, https://www.mfcr.cz/en/news/press-releases/2022/ministers-agree-on-the-distribution-of-e-48940/ (accessed on 7 July 2023). [31]

Ministry of Finance (n.d.), *About the ministry*, Ministry of Finance, Prague, https://www.mfcr.cz/cs/o-ministerstvu/zakladni-informace/hlavni-cinnosti (accessed on 10 October 2022). [63]

Ministry of Industry and Trade (n.d.), *Authority of the Ministry*, Ministry of Industry and Trade, Prague, https://www.mpo.cz/dokument1926.html (accessed on 10 October 2022). [49]

Ministry of Regional Development (2021), *Spatial Development Policy of the Czech Republic (as amended, in effect on 1 September 2021)*, Ministry of Regional Development, Prague, https://mmr.gov.cz/getmedia/d081772b-2d7e-4454-9fef-478a70c788e6/Spatial-Development-Policy-of-the-CR_recent-version-from-September-2021.pdf.aspx?ext=.pdf. [16]

Ministry of Regional Development (n.d.), *Ministry of Regional Development*, Ministry of Regional Development, Prague, https://www.mmr.cz/cs/ministerstvo (accessed on 5 July 2023). [59]

Ministry of Regional Development (n.d.), *Programming period 2004-2006*, Ministry of Regional Development, Prague, https://www.dotaceeu.cz/en/evropske-fondy-v-cr/programove-obdobi-2004-2006-(1) (accessed on 21 July 2023). [22]

Ministry of Regional Development (n.d.), *Programming period 2007-2013*, https://www.dotaceeu.cz/en/evropske-fondy-v-cr/programove-obdobi-2007-2013 (accessed on 22 July 2023). [24]

Ministry of Regional Development (n.d.), *Programming period 2007-2013*, Ministry of Regional Development, Prague, https://www.dotaceeu.cz/en/evropske-fondy-v-cr/programove-obdobi-2007-2013 (accessed on 22 July 2023). [32]

Ministry of the Environment (n.d.), *Climate Policy of the Czech Republic*, Ministry of the Environment, Prague, https://www.mzp.cz/en/climate_policy_of_the_czech_republic (accessed on 3 July 2023). [67]

Ministry of Transport (2021), *ŘSD will turn into a state-owned enterprise, the government approved savings and speeding up construction*, Ministry of Transport, Prague, https://mdcr.cz/Media/Media-a-tiskove-zpravy/RSD-se-zmeni-na-statni-podnik,-uspory-a-urychl-(1). [42]

Ministry of Transport (2010-2022), *Transport Yearbooks Czechia*, Ministry of Transport, Prague, https://www.sydos.cz/cs/rocenky.htm. [7]

National Development Bank (n.d.), *About the bank*, https://www.nrb.cz/en/about-the-bank/ (accessed on 10 October 2022). [66]

OECD (2023), *Housing Sector Country Snapshot: Czech Republic*, https://www.oecd.org/housing/policy-toolkit/country-snapshots/housing-policy-czech-republic.pdf. [51]

OECD (2023), *Housing Tenure Distribution*, https://www.oecd.org/els/family/HM1.3-Housing-tenures.xlsx (accessed on 18 December 2023). [55]

OECD (2023), *OECD Economic Surveys: Czech Republic 2023*, OECD Publishing, Paris, https://doi.org/10.1787/e392e937-en. [18]

OECD (2023), *OECD Public Governance Reviews: Czech Republic: Towards a More Modern and Effective Public Administration*, OECD Publishing, Paris, https://doi.org/10.1787/41fd9e5c-en. [4]

OECD (2023), *Public spending on support to social rental housing as % GDP*, https://www.oecd.org/els/family/PH4-1-Public-spending-social-rental-housing.xlsx (accessed on 18 December 2023). [56]

OECD (2023), *Public spending on support to social rental housing as % GDP*, https://www.oecd.org/els/family/PH4-1-Public-spending-social-rental-housing.xlsx (accessed on 18 December 2023). [57]

OECD (2023), *Subnational governments in OECD countries: key data, 2023 Edition*, https://www.oecd.org/regional/multi-level-governance/NUANCIER%202023-3.pdf. [14]

OECD (2021), *Brick by Brick: Building Better Housing Policies*, OECD Publishing, Paris, https://doi.org/10.1787/b453b043-en. [50]

OECD (2021), *Economic Policy Reforms 2021: Going for Growth: Shaping a Vibrant Recovery*, OECD Publishing, Paris, https://doi.org/10.1787/3c796721-en. [46]

OECD (2021), *Housing Affordability in Cities in the Czech Republic*, OECD Urban Studies, OECD Publishing, Paris, https://doi.org/10.1787/bcddcf4a-en. [53]

OECD (2021), *OECD Regional Outlook 2021: Addressing COVID-19 and Moving to Net Zero Greenhouse Gas Emissions*, OECD Publishing, Paris, https://doi.org/10.1787/17017efe-en. [47]

OECD (2020), *OECD Economic Surveys: Czech Republic 2020*, OECD Publishing, Paris, https://doi.org/10.1787/1b180a5a-en. [35]

OECD (2017), *The Governance of Land Use in the Czech Republic: The Case of Prague*, OECD Regional Development Studies, OECD Publishing, Paris, https://doi.org/10.1787/9789264281936-en. [9]

OECD-UCLG (2022), *World Observatory on Subnational Government Finance and Investment*, https://www.sng-wofi.org/country-profiles/. [13]

Railway Administration (2023), *Annual Report 2022*, [44]

https://www.spravazeleznic.cz/documents/50004227/156465524/V%C3%BDro%C4%8Dn%C3%AD+zpr%C3%A1va+2022/06df59a1-94fa-4360-85b7-a0c7dc6bc129.

Railway Administration (n.d.), *Company profile*, https://www.spravazeleznic.cz/web/en/about-us/our-activities. [43]

Ruiz Rivadeneira, A. and P. Mcmaster (2023), "Mapping institutional arrangements for infrastructure governance in OECD countries", *OECD Working Papers on Public Governance*, No. 62, OECD Publishing, Paris, https://doi.org/10.1787/31825d0d-en. [15]

State Environmental Fund (2023), *Management Report of the State Environmental Fund of Czechia for 2022*, State Environmental Fund of the Czech Republic, Prague, https://www.sfzp.cz/o-sfzp-cr/vyrocni-zpravy/detail-vyrocni-zpravy/?id=55. [71]

State Environmental Fund (n.d.), *About us*, State Environmental Fund of the Czech Republic, Prague, https://www.sfzp.cz/en/about-us/ (accessed on 3 July 2023). [68]

State Environmental Fund (n.d.), *Advisory Board*, State Environmental Fund of the Czech Republic, Prague, https://www.sfzp.cz/en/about-us/advisory-board/ (accessed on 4 July 2023). [72]

State Environmental Fund (n.d.), *What we do*, https://www.sfzp.cz/en/about-us/what-we-do/ (accessed on 4 July 2023). [69]

State Environmental Fund (n.d.), *What we do*, State Environmental Fund of the Czech Republic, Prague, https://www.sfzp.cz/en/about-us/what-we-do/ (accessed on 3 July 2023). [70]

State Fund for Transport Infrastructure (2022), *Budget of the State Fund for Transport Infrastructure for 2023 and the medium-term outlook for 2024 and 2025*, State Fund for Transport Infrastructure, Prague, https://www.sfdi.cz/soubory/obrazky-clanky/rozpocet/2023_rozpocet_text-rozpoctu.pdf. [40]

State Fund for Transport Infrastructure (2010-2022), *Annual Reports and Financial Statements*, State Fund for Transport Infrastructure, Prague, https://www.sfdi.cz/rozpocet/vyrocni-zpravy-a-ucetni-zaverky/. [8]

State Fund for Transport Infrastructure (n.d.), *General information*, State Fund for Transport Infrastructure, https://www.sfdi.cz/en/ (accessed on 4 July 2023). [41]

State Investment Support Fund (2023), *2022 Annual Report and Financial Statements for 2022*, State Investment Support Fund, Prague, https://sfpi.cz/vyrocni-zpravy/. [61]

State Investment Support Fund (n.d.), *Rental housing*, State Investment Support Fund, Prague, https://sfpi.cz/najemni-bydleni/ (accessed on 30 June 2023). [58]

State Investment Support Fund (n.d.), *SFPI*, State Investment Support Fund, Prague, https://sfpi.cz/sfpi/ (accessed on 10 June 2023). [60]

2 Improving national infrastructure planning, prioritisation and delivery

This chapter analyses challenges in Czechia's infrastructure governance system at the national level and makes recommendations to address them. It considers whether national institutions and processes foster efficient and effective investment decisions and good governance practices in infrastructure investment. It focuses on three critical, interlinked phases in the infrastructure governance cycle: 1) long-term strategic planning and co-ordination across sectors; 2) project selection, appraisal and prioritisation; and 3) the procurement and delivery of infrastructure. Across these phases, it explores the mobilisation of private investment, stakeholder engagement and the monitoring and evaluation of outcomes. The analysis and recommendations are supported by concrete international examples, references and data from selected OECD and European Union countries.

Summary of recommendations

Given the challenges of implementing a full suite of reforms simultaneously, Czech authorities could consider sequencing concrete actions under broader recommendations. By grouping actions according to the time horizon (short term, and medium to long term) needed to implement them effectively, Czech authorities could allocate resources to reforms in a way which would provide incremental benefits. However, it should be noted that the concrete actions listed below, irrespective of their time horizon, are complementary and interconnected.

Table 2.1. Summary of recommendations and concrete actions to support their effective implementation

	Short term	Medium to long term
National level recommendation 1: Increase co-ordination in planning and enhance stakeholder engagement		
Concrete actions to support the implementation of recommendation 1	**1.1. Make greater use of co-ordinating bodies and newly formed institutions to improve the planning and delivery of infrastructure investments.** Greater co-ordination will allow for a bottom-up approach to strategic planning and ensure synergies between projects.	**1.2. Develop and maintain a cross-sectoral short-list of projects.** A short-list would help to improve investment readiness and absorptive capacity of the public and private sectors and focus financing from various sources on the most impactful projects. **1.3. Standardise stakeholder consultation processes at the national level.** This would make stakeholder consultation more transparent, helping stakeholders better understand methods of engagement, sources of information, and how inputs will be considered in decision-making. **1.4. Improve the alignment between infrastructure investment planning and national strategies and priorities.** A long-term strategic vision could align infrastructure planning with national strategies and priorities and help to ensure that investments are planned and delivered in a way that supports broader national objectives. This could help to provide a longer term strategic orientation beyond electoral cycles and European programming periods.

	Short term	Medium to long term
National level recommendation 2: Standardise national project appraisal and prioritisation		
Concrete actions to support the implementation of recommendation 2	**2.1. Improve the quality and sharing of data.** Evidence-informed decision making on infrastructure investment can be supported by data ranging from the condition of existing assets, the use of infrastructure (e.g., traffic and ridership data), and demographic trends and distributions.	**2.2. Introduce a consistent and transparent evaluation appraisal of project costs and benefits across sectors.** A standard, transparent approach to project appraisal could support consistent prioritisation and the efficient use of resources across sectors. **2.3. Standardise and expand the use of ex-post evaluations of infrastructure investments.** A common methodology and guidelines for ex-post evaluations across sectors and undertaking them systematically would improve future investment decisions and enhance accountability.
National level recommendation 3: Improve infrastructure delivery capacity		
Concrete actions to support the implementation of recommendation 3	**3.1. Improve investment efficiency by increasing the use of framework agreements.** For frequently purchased services and works, a framework agreement can secure required expertise, generate savings and reduce administrative burdens for contracting authorities and suppliers. **3.2. Develop a consistent, evidence-informed approach to decisions on infrastructure delivery models.** There should be no institutional, procedural or accounting bias either in favour of or against PPPs.	**3.3. Increase funding and direct support for project preparation to improve infrastructure delivery.** Smaller entities face challenges in project preparation, which is a particular issue for the housing sector as many municipalities lack long-term experience in undertaking investment or the resources to invest in capacity. **3.4. Develop the procurement capacity of the public sector to improve value for money in project delivery.** Infrastructure procurement requires sophisticated legal, financial, technical and operational expertise.

Introduction

Even in decentralised systems like Czechia's, the national government has a strategic role – identifying investment priorities, strengthening the capacities of the various levels of government involved in managing public investment, and ensuring sound framework conditions for the governance of public investment (OECD, 2017[1]). In Czechia, the importance of strong national infrastructure governance is critical in the context of the recovery from the COVID-19 pandemic and the implementation of the Recovery and Resilience Plan (RRP). Achieving the RRP's goals of accelerating the transition towards a low-carbon and climate-resilient economy, maximising the benefits of the digital transformation, and improving the quality of public administration depends on strong long-term planning, co-ordination across sectors, robust project appraisal and prioritisation processes, and ensuring value for money, including the appropriate use of public private partnerships (PPPs). With a total of EUR 7 billion to be invested by 2026 through the RRP alone, Czechia will need to ensure that national institutions are working collectively to make the right investments; this is also an opportunity to put in place the governance institutions that can support strong value for money over the long term. While Czechia's absorption rate of EU funds for the 2014-2020 programming period was relatively high (84% through 2022; see Chapter 1), directing this funding to the best projects was consistently raised as a challenge by Czech officials and stakeholders (European Commission, n.d.[2]).

The massive increase in infrastructure investment planned across many sectors reinforces the need for enhanced co-ordination. Major investments are planned in areas such as the expansion and electrification of rail infrastructure, the transition to clean energy sources, the renovation of energy efficient buildings, and climate adaptation. Although there are areas of good practice in specific sectors and institutions, a more co-ordinated approach to investment has the potential to improve outcomes and value for money, and achieve synergies and complementarities among investments. This could be achieved by disseminating existing good practices across sectors and levels of government and standardising approaches to infrastructure delivery and data sharing.

At a time of increased pressure on government budgets, improving infrastructure governance can help to maximise the use of scarce resources to advance economic, social, and environmental priorities. The average infrastructure efficiency gap, defined as the deficit between the average and best performers, has been estimated at 15% for advanced economies (Baum, Verdier and Mogues, 2020[3]). Relatively low-cost changes to governance processes and practices and investing in capacity can have outsized effects on large infrastructure budgets. Improving co-ordination across sectors, project appraisal and selection, and project delivery provides an opportunity to increase the efficiency of investment spending, promoting fiscal sustainability and preserving fiscal space for future projects.

As well as advancing broader policy objectives, better governance of infrastructure has a direct and significant impact on downstream productivity growth. A recent study found that sound governance of infrastructure investment is associated with stronger productivity growth in firms operating downstream, with a gain in average annual productivity growth of 0.24 percentage points over ten years. The study identified long-term planning and co-ordination across different levels of government as particularly relevant for productivity increases (Demmou and Franco, 2020[4]). This chapter focuses on reforms Czechia can make in three critical, interlinked phases in the infrastructure governance cycle: 1) long-term strategic planning and co-ordination across sectors; 2) project selection, appraisal and prioritisation; and 3) the procurement and delivery of infrastructure. Each of these themes are explored in the sections which follow.

2.1 Strengthening strategic planning and cross-sectoral co-ordination

Infrastructure planning in Czechia is fragmented along sectoral lines; a lack of co-ordination risks missing opportunities for synergies and positive spillovers. Line ministries are responsible for infrastructure policy and strategic planning in their respective sectors, but high-level co-ordination mechanisms are limited (Chapter 1). Although high-level government priorities are set out in documents such as the Policy Statement of the Government and the Resilience and Recovery Plan, translating and co-ordinating these priorities across sectors have proven more challenging. In addition, Czechia has more than 300 sectoral strategies, adding to the coherence and implementation challenge (OECD, 2023[5]). Co-ordination between sectors on infrastructure planning and investment does take place, but generally on an informal working level. While state funds generally have clearly defined responsibilities and close working relationships with partner ministries, their significant role in financing investment increases the number of bodies involved in infrastructure governance, heightening the need for co-ordination.

The Policy Statement of the Government commits to close co-operation on climate and the environment between the Ministries of Environment, Agriculture, Industry and Trade, Transport and Regional Development. This includes supporting significant infrastructure development for electro-mobility and other clean alternative vehicles to help improve air quality (Government of Czechia, 2022[6]). These commitments are also reflected in Pillar II of the RRP, which foresees investment in approximately 4 700 charging stations for electric vehicles and the acquisition of electric public transit vehicles (European Commission, 2021[7]). In the past, however, the implementation of these types of long-term, cross-sectoral commitments and strategies has suffered from the absence or weakness of institutional structures and co-ordination mechanisms to translate them into long-lasting concrete actions.

For example, in 2019 the Czech government published the National Investment Plan 2020-2050, its unified national investment strategy (Government of Czechia, 2019[8]). Despite the intention to consolidate long-term investment planning and co-ordinate public investors, the National Investment Plan has not succeeded in providing a long-term strategic vision. Challenges reported in the development of the plan included a lack of prioritisation or systematic assessment of projects, resulting in a plan without overarching guiding principles or a co-ordinated cross-sectoral approach. Instead of creating a shared vision leading to co-ordinated activity and ongoing monitoring of implementation, it lacked a strong articulation of priorities and raised expectations that were incompatible with available funding.

The Strategic Framework Czechia 2030 and the Regional Development Strategy of Czechia 2021+ have been more durable, but also do not appear to play a prominent role in directing infrastructure investment. The Strategic Framework Czechia 2030, published in 2017, set out a framework for long-term development in six priority areas: people and society, the economy, resilient ecosystems, regions and municipalities, global development, and good governance (Government of Czechia, 2017[9]). Based on Czechia 2030, the Regional Development Strategy of Czechia 2021+ establishes the main objectives of regional development over a seven-year period. It does not take precedence over other national strategies and plans, but should be reflected in their approach to regional development issues (Ministry of Regional Development, 2019[10]). Czechia 2030 and the Regional Development Strategy both acknowledge the importance of quality infrastructure and identify specific challenges, such as improving connections to the broader European transportation network, but do not appear to be clear points of reference in the development of sector-specific infrastructure policies and strategies.

Co-ordination between sectors can reduce the risk of duplication and promote complementarities between investments (OECD, 2020[11]). As infrastructure services become increasingly interdependent across sectors such as housing, energy and transport, siloed infrastructure planning, prioritisation and delivery can limit the effectiveness and efficiency of public investment (OECD, 2017[12]). For example, investments in housing need to be complemented by the right investments in transport networks, which are generally planned and implemented by different sectoral ministries or levels of government (OECD, 2017[1]). Co-ordinating housing and transport investments can ensure more attractive housing options that provide greater access to employment and other services. To maximise these benefits, infrastructure entities need to co-ordinate the location and capacity of transport routes with decisions about where and how to invest in housing, as well as related social infrastructure like schools and hospitals. This type of long-term strategic planning needs to be aligned with a country's development aims and economic conditions across sectors (OECD, 2023[13]).

Technological advances further increase the benefits of a cross-sectoral approach to infrastructure planning as they blur sectoral boundaries in areas such as energy, transport and communications. To respond to these changes, planning frameworks need to address infrastructure needs in a holistic and integrated way (OECD, 2021[14]). For example, the de-carbonisation of end-use sectors such as transport and buildings can have interactions with the planning and implementation of energy infrastructure. The widespread adoption of electric vehicles is a challenge for the transport sector but will also require the large-scale expansion of charging stations and will affect patterns of demand on the electricity grid.

The OECD Recommendation on the Governance of Infrastructure provides guidance on developing and implementing a successful cross-sectoral approach to infrastructure investment. The Recommendation advises countries to develop a long-term strategic vision for infrastructure which articulates shared cross-sectoral ambitions and priorities (OECD, 2020[15]). Breaking down sectoral silos requires the active participation of multiple stakeholders, whose perspectives and inputs should be gathered through a structured process. A strategic vision should be informed by a broad-based stakeholder engagement process and implemented through an institutional framework which provides clear mandates (OECD, 2021[14]). An example from the Australian state of Victoria demonstrates how the development of a long-term vision can progressively inform a medium-term cross-sectoral plan and a pipeline of specific projects (see Box 2.1).

Box 2.1. Victoria, Australia: from a comprehensive 30-year infrastructure strategy to a project pipeline

In the Australian state of Victoria, the independent advisory body Infrastructure Victoria prepares a 30-year infrastructure strategy that is presented to the State Parliament. The 30-year infrastructure strategy, which must be reviewed and updated every three to five years, provides the basis for the government's five-year infrastructure plan.

In developing the most recent 2021 strategy, Infrastructure Victoria undertook extensive modelling, examined the complementarities between infrastructure and spatial planning, and conducted wide-ranging consultations. This included forecasting growth and development; commissioning research on housing and density targets; a broad social, environmental and economic assessment; and consideration of distributional impacts. The strategy draws on existing land-use plans to inform better infrastructure planning, and will act as an important input to future spatial planning. Infrastructure Victoria released a draft strategy which was subject to rigorous collaboration and consultation with community and industry stakeholders. This included surveys, roundtables and sector dialogues, and a deliberative engagement process.

Following the release of the strategy, the government is required to prepare a five-year infrastructure plan which responds to the 30-year strategy and the state's infrastructure needs and priorities across all infrastructure sectors. The government's plan must identify specific major priority infrastructure projects and a rationale for their selection, including an explanation of how they will achieve the objectives of the 30-year strategy. The current plan takes an integrated approach to spatial and infrastructure planning that seeks to identify key locations for employment and housing growth and the transport, health and education infrastructure that is required to support that growth.

The government also maintains a major projects pipeline to make it easier for businesses, suppliers, and contractors to contribute to major projects. The pipeline is updated as new major projects are announced and budgeted.

Source: (Infrastructure Victoria, 2021[16]; Office of Projects Victoria, n.d.[17]; Department of Treasury and Finance Victoria, 2021[18])

The OECD Recommendation also highlights the need to inform, consult and engage to ensure that infrastructure planning and investments meet citizens' needs. Stakeholder participation can lead to better investments from an environmental, economic, and social perspective by providing decision makers with better information. It can also help avoid conflicts later in the implementation process. Effective participation enables stakeholders to express, and decision makers to take account of, relevant needs and concerns, thereby increasing the accountability and transparency of the decision-making process and building support for the decisions taken (OECD, 2023[19]).

Better national co-ordination of infrastructure investments and strategies has the potential to improve investment outcomes in Czechia. The following recommendations are designed to achieve this at the national level by strengthening strategic planning and the co-ordination of strategies, plans, priorities, and activities among sectors. Implementing these recommendations is expected to improve infrastructure quality by allowing for better integrated and more effective investments, maintaining a clear focus on the most pressing infrastructure needs and linking investments to broader national priorities. Failure to implement them, by contrast, could lead to decision-making processes that fail to capitalise on the potential for Czechia's large, planned infrastructure investments, including over EUR 40 billion in EU funds, to drive economic growth and the green and digital transitions.

Improve co-ordination for more efficient planning and delivery of infrastructure investments

Czechia could improve co-ordination among infrastructure investment bodies at the national level. Czechia's approach to infrastructure investment, with line ministries responsible for overseeing policy in their respective sectors and state funds playing a significant investment role, can create challenges for effective co-ordination. While this approach provides clarity for accountability and responsibility, it can limit the ability of ministries to co-operate on holistic solutions (Huerta Melchor and Gars, 2020[20]). However, an institutional structure where sector or line ministries are collectively responsible for infrastructure policy is not uncommon in OECD member countries. A recent OECD study found that 13 of 38 member countries have institutional structures in which line ministries are collectively responsible for infrastructure policy, making it the second most common set of infrastructure governance institutional arrangements (Ruiz Rivadeneira and Mcmaster, 2023[21]).

These co-ordination challenges could be addressed by improving the instruments and mechanisms for strategic planning between sectors to enhance the consistency and alignment of infrastructure investment. In Czechia, institutions and mechanisms for co-ordination between ministries and other entities with infrastructure responsibilities are currently limited at the national level. While infrastructure investment comes from both EU funds and the state budget, there is no institution that jointly co-ordinates decision-making on both sources of funding.

Previous co-ordination efforts have had limited success. The Council for Public Investment was established by Government Resolution No. 61 of 21 January 2019 to prepare recommendations for the approval of important strategic projects and create draft rules for effective public investment. However, after a period of inactivity, the Council was abolished in June 2023. It was described by some officials as largely unsuccessful in providing strategic direction, potentially due to a lack of formal decision-making powers. Other mechanisms exist but are limited in their scope. The Ministry of Finance is involved in both the development of the state budget and decisions on co-financing from EU funds, but its role is largely restricted to the budgeting process and reviewing individual projects, rather than overarching infrastructure strategy and co-ordination. Inter-ministerial co-ordination generally takes place on a working level and through the formal inter-ministerial comment process on strategies and plans. The OECD's Public Governance Review of Czechia found that the lack of convening power or capabilities of some councils, or their insufficient integration into decision-making processes, made alignment on cross-cutting topics, like infrastructure, more difficult (OECD, 2023[5]).

The government has recently sought to address these co-ordination challenges by creating the Committee for Strategic Investments (see Chapter 1). With an appropriate mandate and support, it could help to ensure alignment across sectors and drive a co-ordinated approach to infrastructure investment. While the committee is not a decision-making body, high-level political representation[1] means it can play a crucial role in setting policy direction, mobilising support and facilitating dialogue between stakeholders. To play this role successfully and ensure its decisions are informed by evidence, the committee will need to be supported by strong technical analysis and expertise. It offers several opportunities:

- To allow ministries, agencies, state funds and subnational governments to communicate their sector-specific challenges and priorities to decision makers and inform the assessment of long-term infrastructure needs.
- To oversee the infrastructure lifecycle from the development of sectoral plans and strategies to the monitoring and evaluation of outcomes.
- To identify opportunities for co-operation across sectors and between levels of government and establishing high-level priorities, the committee could help to facilitate collaboration and a coherent approach to investment.

- To play a role in monitoring the implementation of sector strategies and related infrastructure investments.

The importance of strong implementation and monitoring is underlined by the challenges faced by other Czech government strategies for reasons such as a lack of capacity or funding, misalignment with the current priorities of the government, or a lack of focus on implementation (OECD, 2023[5]). For example, Czechia's Strategy Database is an online register of strategic and conceptual documents where ministries and regions upload strategic and conceptual documents. The Database was created to allow for the connection of objectives from international, national and local levels and to help avoid duplication and find synergies. At the same time, the number of strategies in the Database suggests they may be overlapping in their themes and objectives: there are nearly 2,000 active strategies and another 1,000 archived, including almost 300 from the national level (Ministry of Regional Development, n.d.[22]).

The OECD's Public Governance Review of Czechia found that the lack of convening power or capabilities of some councils or their insufficient integration into decision-making processes made alignment on horizontal topics, like infrastructure, more difficult (OECD, 2023[5]). As it is chaired by the Prime Minister and includes the Ministers of large infrastructure ministries, the Committee for Strategic Investments has significant convening power.

While the Committee's statutes indicate that it will make maximum use of existing ministerial and inter-ministerial working groups and forums, this will need to be operationalised carefully. It will also be important to clearly define its roles and divisions of responsibility with existing bodies (e.g., the Council for Sustainable Development, the Council for Regional Development). Carrying out a co-ordination and monitoring function will require the committee's secretariat, planned to be part of the Office of the Government, to be adequately resourced with staff with the necessary knowledge and competences. The new committee's working group structure could also be leveraged to prioritise key issues such as project appraisal and delivery while ensuring sufficient representation and involvement from key ministries and other stakeholders. The secretariats of the United Kingdom's National Infrastructure Commission, the Netherlands' Council for the Environment and Infrastructure and the Irish National Economic and Social Council – all with similar mandates – have approximately 15 to 50 staff. The government could consider using secondments from infrastructure ministries or other bodies to staff the secretariat rapidly with experts with the necessary skills and knowledge.

Coordination could also be improved at an operational level. As a component of its RRP, Czechia has proposed the creation of a Housing Investment Advisory Hub and Housing Investment Support Centres to provide support and expertise in the housing sector. The main objective is to increase housing affordability in the medium and long term by supporting investment in rental housing. This would involve providing support to municipalities through eight regional Support Centres in the form of methodological guidance, connecting them with local experts, facilitating the co-ordination of local housing policies, and the preparation of projects intended for support by national financial instruments. Two central Support Centre Units, one focused primarily on the housing sector and the other focused on other public infrastructure, would provide additional direct support where required. Along with this support through the Support Centres, the Housing Investment Advisory Hub would provide methodological, information and data support as well as serving as a hub for disseminating good practices and innovations. Both the Housing Investment Advisory Hub and the Housing Investment Support Centres would be part of the State Investment Support Fund.

Given their direct relationship with municipal stakeholders, there may be opportunities for the Housing Investment Support Centres and the Housing Investment Advisory Hub to play a co-ordinating role with national bodies in other sectors that are not focused on housing. The establishment of the Housing Investment Support Centres could be strengthened by a review of existing service offerings from other ministries, state funds and agencies to avoid overlap and identify complementarities and opportunities to co-ordinate efforts (e.g. with the regional offices of CzechInvest).

Create a cross-sectoral short-list of projects

A pipeline (or short-list) of projects can help to ensure that the public sector does not contribute to construction cost inflation and can encourage investment in private sector capacity. Major infrastructure investments involve the participation of the private sector throughout the lifecycle, including during the planning, design, engineering, financing, construction, and maintenance phases. A predictable pipeline of projects can give the private sector the confidence to invest in the necessary people and equipment (OECD, 2023[13]). A strong project pipeline can also allow governments and the public to track progress on the implementation of its overall infrastructure vision. To help co-ordinate investment and promote transparency, a pipeline or short-list of priority projects should be accompanied by a rationale for their selection and an explanation of their alignment with the overall strategy or vision for infrastructure (OECD, 2017[1]). In the 2020 OECD Survey on the Governance of Infrastructure, 47% of respondents indicated that their country had a cross-sectoral short list of priority projects at the national level and 34% reported having a short list of projects at a sector level; Czechia was only one of six countries that reported not having a priority projects short-list (Figure 2.1) (OECD, 2020[23]).

Figure 2.1. Czechia is one of only six OECD countries that reported a lack a short-list of priority projects

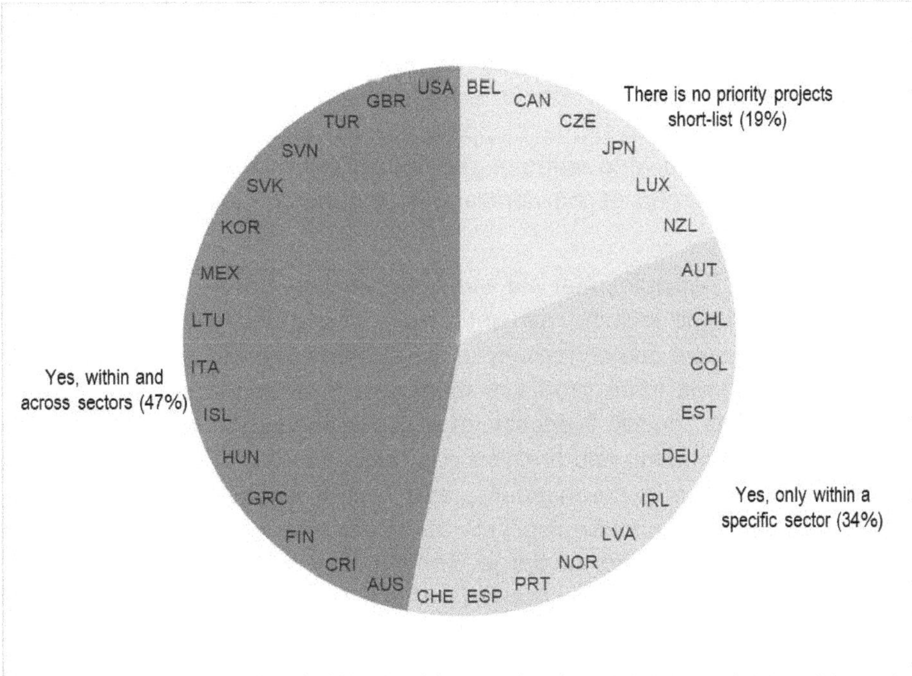

Note: Data for 2020 for Denmark, France, Israel, Netherlands, Poland and Sweden are not available. The 2020 data for Belgium are based on the responses from Flanders only.
Source: (OECD, 2020[23]), Survey on the Governance of Infrastructure.

A national project pipeline in Czechia would improve the investment readiness and absorptive capacity of the public and private sectors. The process of developing a cross-sectoral list of priority projects, based on common priorities and a shared vision for infrastructure, would also provide an opportunity to identify potential synergies and complementarities between projects. However, it will be important to ensure that the process of developing a short-list of priority projects does not unnecessarily slow the decision-making process and project delivery process. Establishing a threshold based on project value or national significance would help to avoid this by ensuring that large, significant projects went through the prioritisation process while allowing the flexibility for smaller projects to advance more quickly.

The Committee for Strategic Investments, supported by the Ministry of Regional Development, could be a decision-making venue for identifying projects to be included in the pipeline. The process could be modelled on the Ministry of Transport's Central Committee, which is made up of deputy ministers and directors of relevant departments who appraise, evaluate, and make budgetary decisions about planned projects. It is also supported by the State Fund for Transport Infrastructure, which provides expert opinions on materials prepared for the committee. Before each formal central committee meeting, projects are consulted, developed and appraised at a working expert level, with only sufficiently mature projects discussed by the central committee. If given appropriate decision-making powers and resources, the Committee for Strategic Investments could play a similar role in developing and maintaining a pipeline of projects across sectors. As it is not a technical body, projects would need to be appropriately appraised and prioritised before reaching the committee, however.

Standardise national stakeholder consultation processes

Stakeholder and citizen participation can take many forms in infrastructure governance. In the 2020 OECD Survey on the Governance of Infrastructure, countries reported varying levels of stakeholder participation in the development of national infrastructure plans (Figure 2.2). The appropriate approach will depend on the project and the stage of the infrastructure lifecycle. Effective consultation requires that processes are proportionate to the particular characteristics of the project or strategy (e.g., size, political sensitivity and population affected). For example, larger, longer-lasting public investments that impact a wide range of people may need a more structured, systematic approach, involving many different methods of gathering information, to accurately capture a wide range of perspectives. A more specific public investment with a direct impact on only a small group of individuals may require more in-depth, targeted engagement (OECD, 2023[13]).

Nevertheless, there are broad principles that are widely applicable. Consultation processes should cover the full infrastructure lifecycle and include relevant groups in decision making, while at the same time remaining proportionate to the size and complexity of the strategy or project. This can range from sharing information (both on-demand and more proactive measures to disseminate information), to a two-way exchange in which stakeholders provide feedback, to active collaboration in design and delivery (OECD, 2023[24]). Upfront stakeholder mapping and analysis can help ensure that input is sought early enough in the process to influence decisions meaningfully, and that it continues throughout the life of the infrastructure asset. Governments should also provide stakeholders with the most relevant and timely information available, expressed in clear language, and should explain how stakeholder input has been assessed and incorporated in the decisions reached. There should be clear objectives for participation, and sufficient time for stakeholders to contribute meaningfully (OECD, 2020[11]; OECD, 2017[25]). The stakeholders can include infrastructure delivery entities (line ministries, agencies and state funds, state-owned enterprises, municipalities, and regions), private infrastructure businesses, membership organisations that represent particular professions (e.g., institutes of engineers), and the general public.

Figure 2.2. Mechanisms for participation in national infrastructure plans vary across the OECD

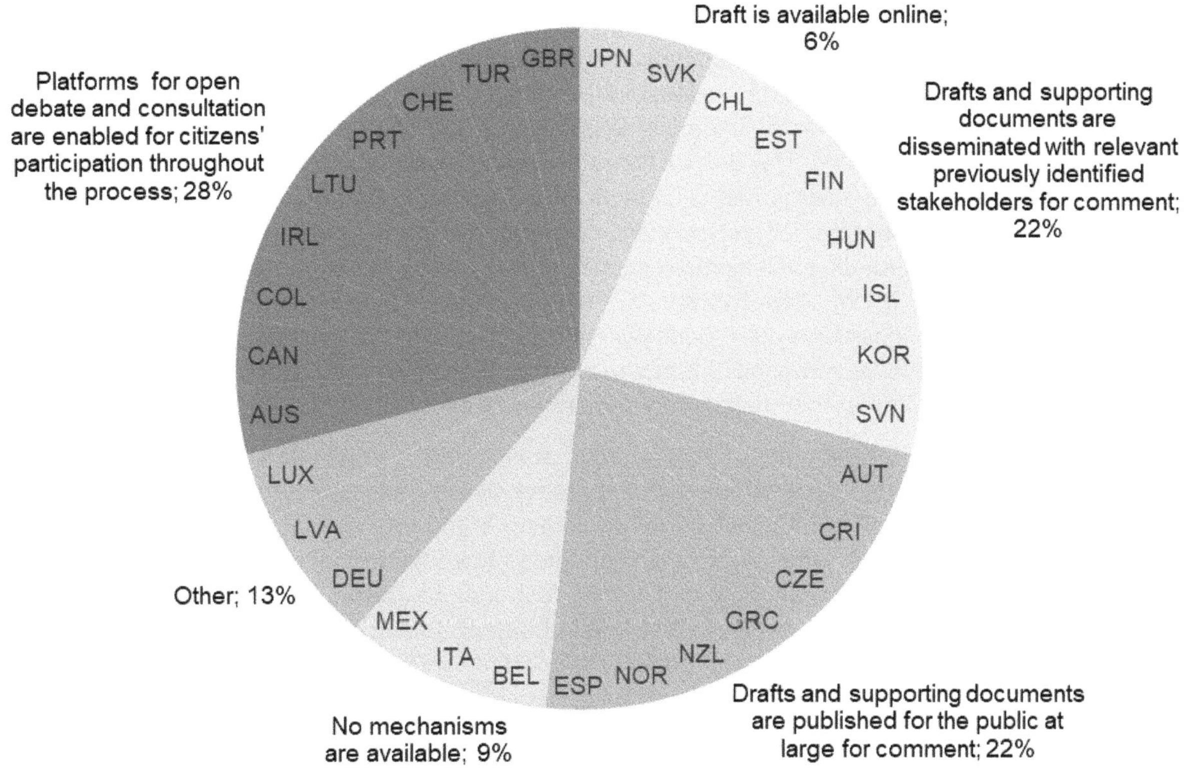

Note: Data for 2020 for Denmark, France, Israel, Netherlands, Poland and Sweden are not available. The 2020 data for Belgium are based on the responses from Flanders only. Australia's data on long-term strategic vision for infrastructure are based on the 2021 Australian Infrastructure Plan. The 2021 Australian Infrastructure Plan is a practical and actionable roadmap for infrastructure reform, developed by Infrastructure Australia, an independent advisory agency. The plan is not a politically sanctioned document.
Source: (OECD, 2020[23]), Survey on the Governance of Infrastructure.

Mechanisms for stakeholder participation in infrastructure planning and delivery exist in Czechia but are inconsistent between ministries and sectors. While Czechia has general guidelines on consultation in place, they are not universally used across infrastructure delivery entities. An exception is for environmental impact, with infrastructure projects and plans subject to the Law on Environmental Impact Assessment and on Amendments to Certain Related Acts (No. 100/2001 Coll.), which sets requirements for consultation on environmental policy making (OECD, 2023[5]). The Law on Environmental Impact Assessment requires details on the environmental impact of projects and strategic plans to be published and provides opportunities for the public to comment on assessments and participate in public hearings.

However, other than for environmental impacts, national level bodies responsible for infrastructure in Czechia can sometimes struggle to effectively gather inputs, including stakeholder comments, for planning, programme design and decision making, leading to challenges in identifying local needs. Drafts of strategies and plans are published for public comment, but engagement by the broader public can be limited. In the 2020 OECD Survey on the Governance of Infrastructure, Czechia indicated that consultation guidance addressed the long-term planning and project appraisal phases of the infrastructure lifecycle, but not subsequent phases such as procurement, construction and operations. Ministries do not always co-ordinate their engagement with stakeholders, particularly regions and municipalities. Information provided by ministries is not always clear, and engagement is impacted by staff turnover. These gaps between subnational and national levels can lead to a lack of responsiveness, or the perception of a lack of responsiveness, to local challenges. For example, effective stakeholder participation in the development of housing programmes could make them more attractive for municipalities and raise awareness and understanding of funding opportunities. Nevertheless, officials indicated that there is currently limited communication between the State Investment Support Fund and municipalities on housing issues.

Information on infrastructure projects and plans is currently provided to the public through a central portal linked to the environmental impact assessment process, the Environmental Impact Assessment Information[2]/Strategic Environmental Impact Assessment[3] (EIA/SEA) system, and the website of the National Coordination Authority[4]. The EIA/SEA system provides information on public comment periods as well as evaluations of the environmental impacts of projects and strategies, as required by the Law on Environmental Impact Assessment. The National Coordination Authority provides basic project information for projects funded by EU funds, such as the responsible entity, the project budget, the location and a brief description. Finally, the Information System of Project Plans[5] collects together the project plans of municipalities, regions and national institutions (with the exception of the Moravian-Silesian Region). In the 2020 OECD Survey on the Governance of Infrastructure, Czechia indicated a focus on sharing information on impact assessments, rather than risks, procurement and project execution.

The Ministry of Regional Development could improve stakeholder participation in infrastructure planning and implementation by promoting a standardised approach across ministries, agencies and state funds. It could consider developing a centralised portal containing comprehensive information on infrastructure plans, strategies and projects. Most other OECD countries have taken this approach: in the 2020 OECD Survey on the Governance of Infrastructure, 19 of 33 respondents (58%) reported having a government-wide digital platform to provide information on infrastructure projects (Figure 2.3). This information could extend beyond environmental impacts and projects supported by EU funds to include information on risks, procurement and project status. This could build on or supplement the EIA/SEA system, the website of the National Coordination Authority and the Information System of Project Plans, creating a single point of reference for interested citizens and stakeholders. A consolidated system could also be used to communicate with project stakeholders, for example through targeted messages about financing opportunities (as is currently planned for the Information System of Project Plans).

The housing sector could provide a model for a more comprehensive and cross-institutional approach to stakeholder participation. The Ministry of Regional Development's proposed Housing Investment Support Centres could play a role in facilitating the bottom-up aggregation of housing needs and identifying challenges faced by municipalities in planning and implementing housing projects. By aggregating the needs and challenges of local stakeholders, the Housing Investment Support Centres could help the Ministry of Regional Development, the State Investment Support Fund and other national infrastructure bodies develop strategies, supports, and financing mechanisms that better target the barriers to affordable housing development. Identifying challenges such as land availability, regulatory constraints, and funding gaps could help to develop sustainable housing plans and facilitate smoother project implementation.

Figure 2.3. A majority of OECD countries have a national digital platform on infrastructure projects

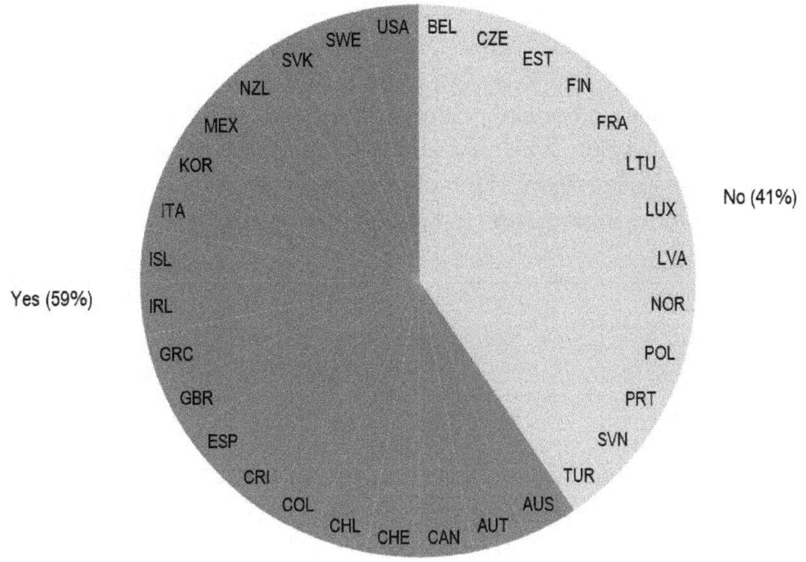

Note: Data for Belgium based on the survey responses from Flanders only.
Source: (OECD, 2022[26]), *Survey on the Governance of Infrastructure* - Part I: Ensure transparent, systematic and effective stakeholder participation.

Develop a national vision for infrastructure that aligns with national policies and strategies

Aligning long-term infrastructure plans with other government plans and strategies can increase the efficiency of investments and help ensure that projects are not working at cross purposes. The OECD Recommendation on the Governance of Infrastructure includes a pillar on developing a strategic infrastructure vision (OECD, 2020[15]). A consistent long-term vision for infrastructure investments can help governments establish an appropriate institutional framework, implement clear governance arrangements, define needs and targets and co-ordinate with stakeholders. A cross-sectoral vision can help to identify long-term commitments and challenges and ensure that individual investments are aimed at common goals. A long-term perspective is particularly important given the long lifespan of infrastructure assets (OECD, 2021[14]).

For example, spatial planning can protect existing and new infrastructure from future legal challenges or competing land uses. Spatial plans often signal new corridors or zones for infrastructure development while projects are still in the conceptual phase, providing greater certainty over the future location and timing of infrastructure, which helps send positive investment signals to the private sector (OECD, 2023[13]). Aligning infrastructure investment decisions with long-term climate and development objectives is also critical to avoiding lock-in of emissions-intensive infrastructure (OECD, 2021[14]). For example, Ireland's National Development Plan 2021-2030 (NDP) sets out an overarching strategy to guide investment worth EUR 165 billion. The NDP is aligned with Ireland's Recovery and Resilience Plan and will receive significant support from the European Union's Recovery and Resilience Facility (Box 2.2).

Box 2.2. Co-ordinating Ireland's National Development Plan with climate and environmental ambitions

Ireland's National Development Plan 2021-2030 (NDP) sets out an overarching investment strategy to make Ireland a better country for all and to build a more resilient and sustainable future. The EUR 165 billion NDP has a particular focus on housing, climate, transport, healthcare and regional jobs growth. As part of the development of the plan, a climate and environmental assessment of the NDP initiatives was undertaken, along with an assessment of the plan's overall alignment with Ireland's green recovery plan. When developing measures for inclusion in the NDP, seven climate and environmental outcomes were considered:

1. Climate mitigation
2. Climate adaptation
3. Water quality
4. Air quality
5. Waste and the circular economy
6. Nature and biodiversity
7. Just transition

The NDP includes a number of environmental and climate initiatives, including providing EUR 5 billion in additional carbon tax receipts to increase capital investment levels in energy efficiency; committing to increasing the share of renewable electricity to 80% by 2030; and improving the energy efficiency of homes through the upgrade of at least 500 000 homes to a Building Energy Rating of B2/cost optimal or carbon equivalent by 2030, and the installation of 400 000 heat pumps in existing homes. It also includes commitments to further reforms of the Public Spending Code (the rules and procedures governing public expenditures) to ensure compatibility with Ireland's climate ambition.

Ireland's NDP is aligned with its Recovery and Resilience Plan, with relevant projects rooted in advancing the green transition, accelerating and expanding digital reforms and transformations, and recovery and job creation. Ireland will receive approximately EUR 990 million in grants from the European Union's Recovery and Resilience Facility, which will be used to support investments under the NDP.

Source: (OECD, n.d.[27]; Department of Public Expenditure, NDP Delivery and Reform, 2021[28])

Defining a national vision for infrastructure in Czechia could improve the alignment and co-ordination between sectoral infrastructure planning and other national policies and priorities. Existing sector-specific infrastructure plans provide sector-specific strategies, but a siloed approach can threaten cross-sectoral policy objectives such as regional development or climate change adaptation and can overlook synergies between sectors. Improved cross-sectoral co-ordination could reduce the potential for overlap between projects, ensure that investments are mutually reinforcing, and support Czechia's efforts to harness infrastructure investment to support a sustainable and green recovery.

Unlike many OECD countries, Czechia's responses to the 2020 OECD Survey on the Governance of Infrastructure indicated a lack of co-ordination between infrastructure planning and broader policy goals and plans. Czechia indicated that its long-term sectoral infrastructure plans do not explicitly consider how to align the infrastructure strategic vision with other policies and strategies. This was reinforced in discussions with Czech officials and stakeholders held as part of this project, who indicated that despite the many strategies across sectors and ministries, there is a limited overarching vision or focus on prioritisation and implementation.

Czechia could build on its existing sectoral infrastructure plans, its Recovery and Resilience Plan, the National Investment Plan 2020-2050, and the Regional Development Strategy in aligning infrastructure investment with its overall strategic goals. As noted above, Czechia has a number of sector-specific long-term plans (see Box 2.3 for examples in key sectors). This is similar to many of its peers: responses to the 2020 OECD Survey on the Governance of Infrastructure indicated that long-term sectoral plans are in place in approximately half of OECD (56%) and EU (47%) countries. While these plans are critical for effective investment within a sector, lack of co-ordination may result in missed opportunities to benefit from synergies among investments in different sectors. In the 2020 Survey, Czechia indicated it had not used co-ordination mechanisms in the formulation of the National Investment Plan 2020-2050. This was confirmed with discussions with Czech officials and stakeholders held as part of this project, who indicated that co-ordination at the national level is challenging, both generally and in the development of the National Investment Plan 2020-2050. This contrasts with the majority of surveyed countries, more than half of which (18 out of 31 OECD countries or 58%; 10 out of 17 EU countries or 59%) indicated that they had used mechanisms for cross-sector co-ordination during the formulation (or revision) of their most recent long-term national infrastructure plan.

Box 2.3. Sectoral plans in Czechia

Czechia has a large number of sector-specific plans and strategies, many of which have a significant infrastructure component. The main strategic documents in the housing, transport and energy sectors are summarised here.

Housing Concept of Czechia 2021+

The Housing Concept of Czechia 2021+ sets out the national housing policy from 2021. It articulates a vision for the housing sector built around four primary objectives:

- increasing the availability of affordable, quality housing
- creating a stable legislative and institutional environment for housing investment
- ensuring sustainable housing development
- developing an innovative and productive housing sector.

These objectives are supported by detailed measures (e.g., establish an institutional and legal framework for social housing, improvement of energy performance) and further broken down into clearly assigned tasks (e.g., assess the functionality of the current benefit system, identify new energy-efficient project types) with estimated costs in some cases. The Housing Concept is supported by a monitoring and implementation plan.

Transport Policy of Czechia

The Transport Policy of Czechia is the highest-level transport sector planning document. The Transport Policy is built around three strategic objectives: (1) sustainable mobility, (2) territorial cohesion and (3) the use of automation and information technology. These are supported by specific objectives, such as adaptation to climate change and the balanced provision of transport infrastructure across regions, which are further supported by specific measures (e.g., set quantitative and qualitative standards in the planning of transport services, support the development of cross-border rail transport projects). The most recent version of the Transport Policy was published in 2021.

The objectives contained in the Transport Policy are outlined further in other plans, concepts, strategies and processes. For example, specific transport sector strategies constitute the main plans for the financing and development of rail, road, and waterway transport infrastructure. These transport sector strategies create a list of known projects; assess projects based on multi-criteria and cost-benefit evaluation; and prioritise and schedule projects based on the order of importance and the availability of financial resources. The Transport Policy refers to other strategic documents such as the Strategic Framework Czechia 2030, the State Energy Concept, and the Regional Development Strategy.

State Energy Policy of Czechia

The State Energy Policy aims to ensure a reliable, secure and environmentally friendly supply of energy, reflected in its three strategic objectives of security, competitiveness and sustainability. These objectives are supported by strategic priorities such as establishing a balanced energy mix, increasing energy efficiency, and strengthening international co-operation and the integration of regional electricity markets. The State Energy Policy provides the basis for further strategic documents, such as the National Action Plans for Smart Grids, the Action Plan for Biomass, and the National Action Plans for Energy Efficiency. The most recent version of the State Energy Policy was published in 2015.

The National Energy and Climate Plan, published in 2020, further expands on Czechia's contribution to European climate and energy objectives, which relate to the reduction of greenhouse gas emissions, efforts to increase the share of renewable energy sources and increases in energy efficiency.

Source: (Ministry of Regional Development, 2021[29]) (Ministry of Transport, 2021[30]) (Ministry of Industry and Trade, 2020[31]) (Ministry of Industry and Trade, 2015[32])

Summary of key recommendations

Given the challenges of implementing a full suite of reforms, Czech authorities could consider sequencing the recommendations made above. By grouping recommendations according to the time horizon needed to implement them effectively (short term, and medium to long term), Czech authorities could allocate resources to reforms in a way which would provide incremental benefits. A potential sequencing is included below.

Short-term reforms

1. **Make greater use of co-ordinating bodies and newly formed institutions to improve the planning and delivery of infrastructure investments.** Greater co-ordination will allow for a bottom-up approach to strategic planning and ensure synergies between projects.

- Given its mandate and responsibilities, the Committee for Strategic Investments could serve to ensure alignment across sectors and drive a co-ordinated approach to infrastructure investment. It could help communicate sector-specific challenges and priorities, and inform the assessment of cross-sectoral needs, thereby improving strategic planning.
- Ensure that relevant stakeholders are well represented in the committee and its working parties and that the supporting secretariat is adequately resourced with experts with the necessary skills and knowledge.
- Focus on the committee's role in monitoring the implementation of sector strategies and related infrastructure investments to provide greater insight into their effectiveness.
- Increase co-ordination for the delivery of infrastructure investments. The Ministry of Regional Development's proposed Housing Investment Advisory Hub and Housing Investment Support Centres could play a co-ordinating role between national bodies and municipalities in housing-related investments, for example.

Medium to long-term reforms

2. **Develop and maintain a cross-sectoral short-list of projects.** A short-list or project pipeline would help to improve the investment readiness and absorptive capacity of the public and private sectors and focus financing from various sources on the most impactful projects.

- Develop the short-list using objective and transparent criteria. This would clarify the decision-making process and foster trust by helping stakeholders and the public understand why certain projects are prioritised and how they align with broader objectives.
- Ensure the short-list is cross-sectoral to promote the efficient use of available funding and reduce the risk of disproportionately targeting investment towards a single sector.
- The new Committee for Public Investments could be a decision-making venue for identifying projects to be included on the short-list. As a high-level body with representation from multiple sectors, the committee would provide legitimacy and would attach political commitment to the short-list, sending clear signals to the market.

3. **Standardise national stakeholder consultation processes.** This would make stakeholder consultation more transparent, helping stakeholders better understand methods of engagement, sources of information, and how inputs will be considered in decision making.

- Create a standardised approach to stakeholder consultation that covers the full infrastructure lifecycle. Develop central guidance on consultation that is proportional to the characteristics of the project or strategy (e.g. size, political sensitivity, environmental aspects, population affected) and to the overall public interest.

- To support this standardised approach, Czechia could consider providing comprehensive project and strategy information to stakeholders in one location, such as a central portal. Information should cover the infrastructure lifecycle from planning to regulatory approvals and construction for all projects, regardless of funding source. This improved access to information for stakeholders could increase the breadth and quality of their inputs.

4. **Improve the alignment between infrastructure investment planning and national strategies and priorities.** A long-term strategic vision could align infrastructure planning with national strategies and priorities and help to ensure that investments are planned and delivered in a way that supports broader national objectives. This could help to provide a longer-term strategic focus beyond electoral cycles and European programming periods.

- Ensure the long-term infrastructure vision outlines desired investment outcomes, identifies priority sectors and defines the role of infrastructure in achieving broader goals. It could be developed based on the detailed existing national and sectoral plans and strategies.
- Requiring that infrastructure planning and project selection explicitly consider key national priorities as articulated in the long-term vision could create coherence between strategic priorities and individual investments.

2.2 Improving project appraisal and prioritisation

Strong project prioritisation and appraisal are critical elements of infrastructure governance. Governments face a significant challenge in determining which of the many investment possibilities are best able to achieve their policy goals and strategies. Strong appraisal ensures that potential projects are rigorously evaluated based on their feasibility; their economic, social and environmental impacts; and their alignment with broader policy goals and development strategies. To ensure that limited resources are allocated efficiently while maximising benefits, governments require infrastructure investment selection processes based on a sound understanding of the expected returns (OECD, 2021[14]). If assumptions and findings are made public, appraisal and prioritisation processes can also play an important role in ensuring transparency in decision-making processes.

Czechia lacks a consistent approach to project appraisal and prioritisation across sectors. In some sectors, such as transport, there is detailed guidance on project appraisal and rigorous evaluation. For example, the Departmental Guideline for the Evaluation of Economic Effectiveness of Transport Construction Projects provides detailed methodological guidance for evaluating transport infrastructure investments (Ministry of Transport, 2018[33]). Originally developed for the EU funds programming period 2014-2020, the guideline is used to evaluate transport projects with costs of over CZK 30 million (approximately EUR 1.3 million). However, across the investment system as a whole, projects are often prioritised based on their readiness to move forward quickly and their ability to access European funds rather than conducting a standardised appraisal of the costs and benefits of the investment. In the 2020 OECD Survey on the Governance of Infrastructure, Czechia indicated that while project benefit estimates in the transport and energy sectors are based on international benchmarks, in other sectors such as social or water infrastructure they are not. The difficulty of prioritising across sectors was also reported by officials as a factor in the challenges in implementing the National Investment Plan 2020-2050.

The fragmentation of decision making and responsibility for infrastructure investment across sectors in Czechia makes a consistent approach to project prioritisation and appraisal challenging. In each sector, different entities are responsible for developing their own prioritisation criteria. Prioritisation is often based on eligibility under EU Funds, with funding reallocated to less efficient projects due to timing challenges. A lack of structured analysis can also contribute to inconsistent prioritisation across the electoral cycle: the focus is often on quick wins where spending can align with political and programme timelines, rather than projects with the greatest return.

Another issue for Czechia is that high-quality data are not readily available for project analysis, and capacity challenges can limit the ability of the public sector to generate and use data to inform decision making. Fragmentation can also limit the availability of data on infrastructure performance, making it difficult to assess how future investments could be optimised. Existing decision-making frameworks are not always suitable for accommodating a more diverse set of policy goals, such as the green transition and digital transformation. However, these issues are not unique to Czechia: while many countries do collect data, most of the data required to compare the overall cost and performance of projects across sectors are not systematically aggregated or used (OECD, 2017[1]).

Effective prioritisation and appraisal should be informed by data-based evidence. Governments should put in place systems that ensure the systematic collection, analysis, dissemination, and use of relevant data for project prioritisation and appraisal (OECD, 2017[1]). Specific sectors require more targeted data: for example, evaluating transport projects often requires data on topics such as traffic patterns and congestion, while energy infrastructure decision making requires data on trends in consumption and planned production. However, these data requirements are often interlinked: housing investments, for example, can impact both traffic patterns and energy consumption. A lack of systematic data collection on investment performance can therefore undermine decision making by limiting governments' ability to identify strengths and weaknesses. The limited availability of data can also make it difficult to assess the potential impacts and estimated costs of infrastructure projects. Ex-post evaluations can be a valuable means of producing data and evidence for future decision making. The OECD Recommendation on the Governance of Infrastructure advises adherents to ensure that ex-post value-for-money evaluations are carried out and that the results are used in the decision-making process for future investment projects (OECD, 2020[15]).

Standardising project appraisal and prioritisation processes has the potential to improve the effectiveness of infrastructure investment. The sections which follow make recommendations for how Czechia could make the appraisal of project costs and benefits more consistent and improve the availability of evidence on which to base those evaluations. Implementing these recommendations is expected to increase the consistency and transparency of decision making, reduce investment risks and allow resources to be allocated more efficiently. While estimates will vary depending on the national context, one study found that choosing the right combination of projects and eliminating wasteful ones could save 7% of total infrastructure investment on a global basis (Dobbs et al., 2013[34]). While this is necessarily a high-level estimate, it indicates the scale of the potential fiscal impact of better project appraisal and prioritisation: 7% of planned investments of EU funds in Czechia alone over the next decade would total EUR 2.8 billion.

Standardise the evaluation of project costs and benefits across sectors

The Ministry of Regional Development could work with other stakeholders to develop a standard approach to project appraisal across sectors. The standardised methodology could be used by ministries and state funds when developing funding programmes, and also be made available to subnational governments to support their prioritisation of infrastructure investments. As noted above, it is not unusual among OECD countries for line ministries to have responsibility for infrastructure investment in their sector. However, it is less common for line ministries to set their own prioritisation criteria – this occurs in only 7 of 33 countries (including Czechia) responding to the 2020 OECD Survey on the Governance of Infrastructure (Figure 2.4) (Ruiz Rivadeneira and Mcmaster, 2023[21]).

Figure 2.4. Most OECD countries have a single institution that prioritises infrastructure projects

Primary institution for setting the criteria to prioritise infrastructure projects in OECD countries, 2020

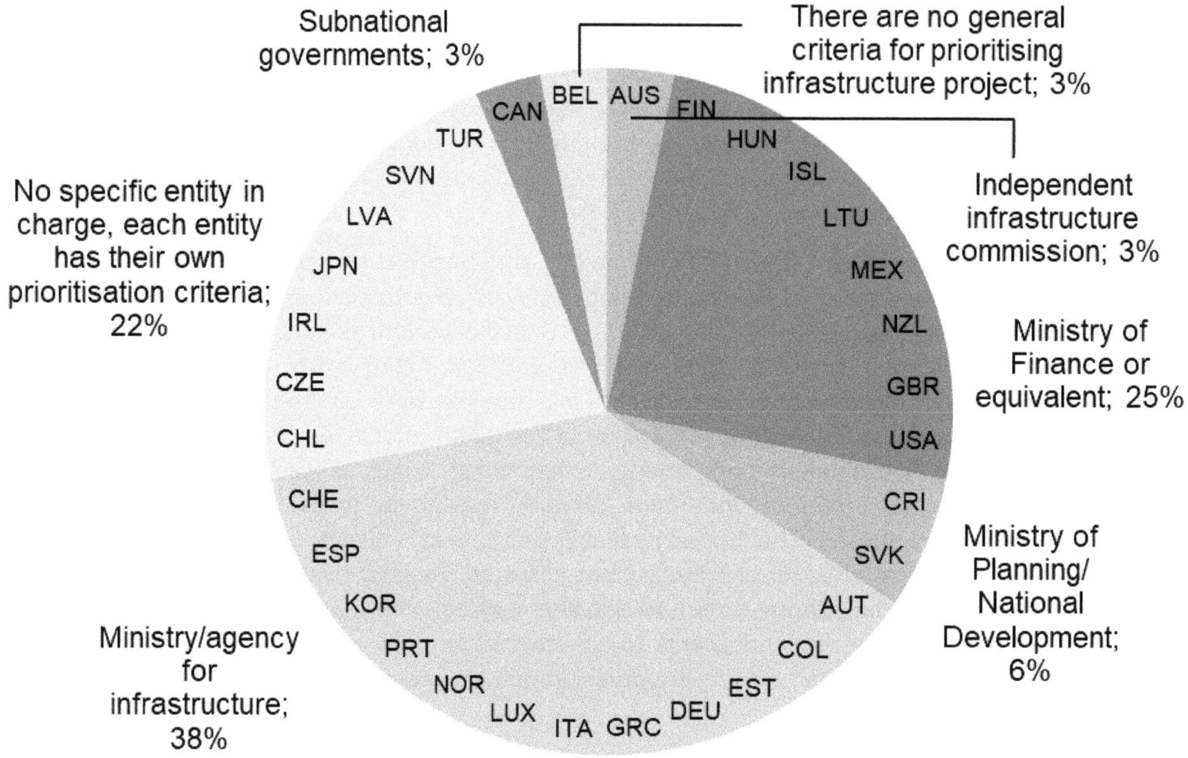

Note: Data for 2020 for Denmark, France, Israel, Netherlands, Poland and Sweden are not available. The 2020 data for Belgium are based on the responses from Flanders only.
Source: OECD (2020), Survey on the Governance of Infrastructure.

Project selection should be based on a rigorous appraisal of costs and benefits, driven by factors such as forecast demand or need, economic efficiency, and environmental and social sustainability. As highlighted by the OECD Recommendation on the Governance of infrastructure, it is especially important to provide for an independent and impartial assessment of the costing, risk management and governance for projects that exceed a high investment threshold (OECD, 2020[15]). When processes for identifying priority projects and choosing delivery modes are not sufficiently formalised, political dynamics can undermine sound decision making (OECD, 2021[14]).

To be applied widely, project appraisal methodologies need to be flexible to reflect differences in project size and complexity and differences between sectors. Countries take different approaches to setting a threshold for full project appraisal (see Box 2.4 for examples). However, a standardised approach could involve (OECD, 2020[35]; World Bank, 2021[36]):

- A holistic cost-benefit analysis, including the evaluation of economic, environmental, and social dimensions (see Box 2.5). This could include a set of common assumptions and a methodology for evaluating common project elements across sectors (e.g., carbon impact) and a consistent approach to cost estimation.
- A calculation of lifecycle costs or total cost of ownership, which is critical for ensuring that projects enable the most efficient use of funds and minimise sustainability risks.

- An assessment of whether the project is feasible and deliverable, and a review of elements such as risk, the capacity of the implementing agency, the quality of project governance and whether the supplier market has been tested and the procurement strategy is well developed.
- An evaluation of strategic alignment with major policy objectives, as well as alignment with other government policy tools (such as spatial planning and regional development plans). This should include establishing the rationale for the project and placing it in the overall strategic context, along with identifying potential linkages and alignment with other infrastructure projects and sectors.

Czechia does already have a standardised methodology for presenting business cases for data, digital and information technology projects developed by the Office of Chief Architect of eGovernment of the Ministry of the Interior. The Information Concept of Czechia includes general principles on planning, procurement and operations and is accompanied by the forms which central institutions need to complete to present business cases for information and communication technology projects (OECD, 2023[5]). These may act as a model for the type of guidance materials that could support stronger project appraisal across sectors.

Box 2.4. OECD country examples of thresholds for applying the project appraisal system

- In Chile, all investment initiatives financed by the government are subject to technical and economic analysis. This includes municipal projects financed with capital transfers from the central government, provided the transfers cover more than 50 percent of project costs.
- In Korea, the threshold is KRW 50 billion (EUR 35 million) for central government projects, and KRW 30 billion (EUR 21 million) for subnational government projects or projects with private participation receiving a central government contribution equal to or greater than that amount.
- In Norway, the threshold is NOK 750 million (EUR 65 million) for central government projects.
- In Ireland, the appraisal methodology depends on the type, scale, and complexity of the project:
  - For project proposals below EUR 10 million, approving authorities (government department with the ultimate responsibility for the project) should decide with sponsoring agencies (primary responsibility for evaluating, planning, and managing projects) as to whether an economic appraisal is required and what type of economic appraisal is appropriate.
  - For project proposals over EUR 10 million, approving authorities and sponsoring agencies should engage on the choice of the appropriate appraisal methodology in line with sectoral guidance. Wherever possible, cost-benefit analysis should be used. In cases where this may not be possible or desirable, cost-effectiveness or multicriteria analysis may be used.
  - As a general rule, cost-benefit analysis is required for all major projects with an estimated cost over EUR 200 million, as well as a mandatory assurance process involving independent expert reviews.

Source: (Baum, Verdier and Mogues, 2020[3]), (Department of Public Expenditure, NDP Delivery and Reform, 2023[37]) (OECD, 2023[38])

Infrastructure investment is increasingly expected to address multiple economic, social, and environmental objectives beyond a narrow definition of user needs. This creates challenges for decision makers, who are required to weigh and balance different (and sometimes competing) goals in selecting and prioritising projects (OECD, 2021[14]). The OECD Recommendation on the Governance of infrastructure advises adherents to ensure that methodological tools accommodate multiple objectives (OECD, 2020[15]). Supplementing cost-benefit analysis with other methodological tools to accommodate multiple objectives and uses can establish the overall societal return on investments and support the allocation of resources to the best projects. A standardised approach to project appraisal and prioritisation can help address these challenges but should also be flexible to account for differences across sectors in terms of needs, timelines, stakeholders and decision-making processes. Applying rigorous project appraisal and selection processes that take into account economic, social, and environmental costs and benefits can help with this challenge. In Italy, for example, new guidelines were introduced for the ex-ante valuation of projects, along with a new investment scoring system that evaluates dimensions of sustainability. To support this new approach, the Italian government created a Centre for Innovation and Sustainability in Infrastructure and Mobility (Box 2.5).

Box 2.5. Greening the planning and evaluation of Italy's infrastructure projects

In 2021, the Italian Ministry for Sustainable Infrastructure and Mobility (MIMS) introduced an innovative approach to planning and evaluating projects which integrates sustainability considerations. The initiative sought to provide methodological tools to strengthen the ministry's decision-making capacity with a focus on economic, environmental, social and governance dimensions. Moreover, the new approach aligns with the requirements for funding under the Next Generation EU plan, including the Recovery and Resilience Facility, and other international sustainability principles and guides, such as the EU taxonomy for sustainable activities and the Sustainable Development Goals.

The tools introduced include new guidelines for the ex-ante valuation of projects, together with related operational sector-specific guidelines and a new scoring system that evaluates dimensions of sustainability to help define project prioritisation. A further reform is the introduction of new guidelines for evaluating the technical and economic feasibility of projects financed through Italy's Recovery and Resilience Plan. These new guidelines seek to simplify the process for investing in green and digital technologies; ensuring compliance with energy and environmental responsibility criteria when awarding public contracts, including through the definition of minimum environmental criteria; including measures to encourage the inclusion of SMEs in the construction phase; and introducing digitisation for the public investment process.

To develop the skills and expertise needed to ensure that the new approach is effective, the Centre for Innovation and Sustainability in Infrastructure and Mobility was also created within MIMS. The centre will collaborate with other ministries and academia, both at the national and international level, to carry out research and promote innovation in the field of infrastructure sustainability.

Source: (OECD, 2023[38])

Following a common, structured format for project appraisal can also facilitate independent review and provide a transparent record of decisions. A consistent approach can be reinforced through the systematic publication of ex-ante and ex-post appraisals, which enables review by external stakeholders. This can also support expanded centralised review to verify assumptions and ensure projections are realistic. In the United Kingdom, for example, the Infrastructure and Projects Authority manages independent assurance reviews of the government's most complex and high-risk projects (Box 2.6).

Box 2.6. Centralised project governance to ensure value for money in the United Kingdom

Strong governance arrangements include appropriate checks and balances to ensure that there is an ongoing assessment of whether a project offers value for money as it evolves throughout its lifecycle. Large projects entail fiscal risks that that can affect the overall public investment programme. For this reason, the United Kingdom has made central agencies responsible for the oversight of public investment programmes part of the governance structure for major projects.

The UK Infrastructure and Projects Authority (IPA) arranges and manages independent assurance reviews of major government projects each year. These reviews are mainly for the government's most complex and high-risk projects within the Government Major Projects Portfolio (GMPP). The IPA also publishes an annual public report on the progress made on projects within the GMPP. The IPA reports to the Cabinet Office and the Treasury and is led by a Chief Executive who reports jointly to the Chancellor of the Exchequer and the Minister for the Cabinet Office. It employs approximately 180 people in roles such as policy advisors, project delivery professionals, and project finance professionals.

Assurance is an essential part of successful project delivery. The IPA has established a Major Projects Review Group (MPRG) comprised of a pool of experts from which panels are put together to scrutinise the largest and most complex major government projects. It is co-chaired by the Chief Executive of the Civil Service and the Second Permanent Secretary to the Treasury. The MPRG panels challenge projects on deliverability, affordability and value for money at key points in the project life cycle. The MPRG aims to improve the performance of projects and programmes and advise HM Treasury ministers on which projects within the GMPP are ready to proceed through the next stage-gate. Projects are selected for MPRG review according to the following criteria: projects with a whole life cost of over GBP 1 billion; projects that are high risk and complex in their procurement and delivery of benefits; projects that set a precedent or are highly innovative; and other projects 'of concern' (as recommended by HM Treasury or the IPA and agreed by the MPRG Chair).

Source: (OECD, 2020[39]; Infrastructure and Projects Authority, 2021[40]; Infrastructure and Projects Authority, 2020[41])

According to the 2020 OECD Survey on the Governance of Infrastructure, 71% of OECD countries (22 out of 31) reported conducting regular independent and impartial expert assessments (19% for all projects, 29% for projects above a threshold and 23% for projects of special relevance). Within the EU, the share was 63% (10 out of 16)[6] (Figure 2.5). Data for Czechia are not available for this survey question, but it appears that the independence and quality of project assessments varies depending on the sector and institutional structure. For transport projects worth over CZK 1.8 billion (approximately EUR 75 million), project appraisals must include an evaluation provided by the State Fund for Transport Infrastructure. The State Fund for Transport Infrastructure co-operates with external entities such as the Transport Research Centre and the Institute of Construction Economics and Management at the Brno University of Technology to select appropriate evaluators. Through the budgeting process, the Ministry of Finance plays a role in reviewing projects worth over CZK 300 million (approximately EUR 12 million); however, a significant proportion of Czech infrastructure investment is undertaken by state funds over which the Ministry of Finance has more limited influence. For example, officials indicated that approximately 40% of the government's infrastructure budget is approved through a small number of decisions related to transfers into state funds, with limited oversight of project selection.

Figure 2.5. The majority of OECD countries require independent and impartial expert assessment of infrastructure projects

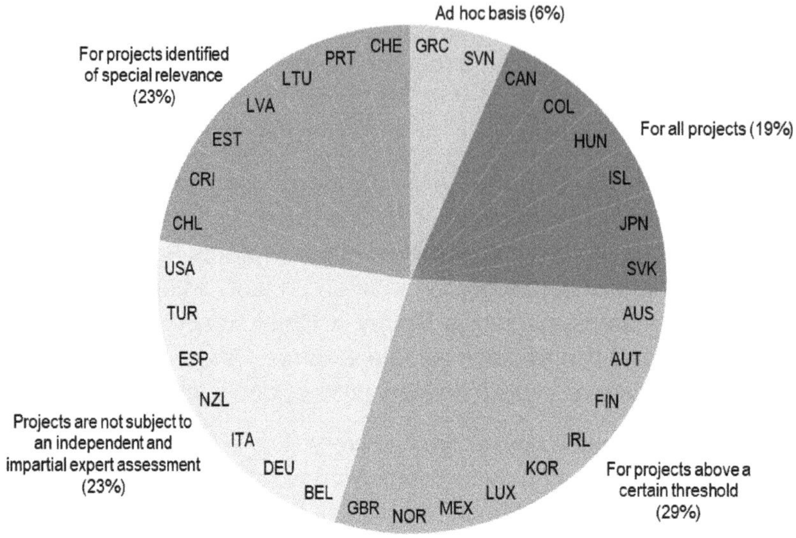

Note: Data for Belgium are based on the survey responses from Flanders only. In Austria, independent and impartial expert assessments are conducted for projects above a certain threshold as well as for projects identified of special relevance.
Source: 2020 OECD Survey on the Governance of Infrastructure

Czechia could consider expanding the role of independent review of infrastructure investment at the national level. An independent and impartial expert assessment can test factors such as project costing, fiscal sustainability, timelines, risk management and governance and help to identify flaws or gaps. Independent reviews can also provide a mechanism for monitoring and evaluating project performance over time, helping to identify issues as they arise. In Norway, for example, an external quality assurance process is compulsory for projects with an expected budget over EUR 100 million. The quality assurance process is refined through an independent process of ex-post evaluations of completed projects. In Czechia, this could be achieved by applying the approach used by the State Fund for Transport Infrastructure to other sectors, or increasing the role and capacity of the Ministry of Finance. Publishing independent assessments would also increase transparency in infrastructure appraisal and selection by providing stakeholders and the wider public with access to objective evaluations of project feasibility, costs and benefits. This could promote accountability and help build public trust in the investment system.

Box 2.7. Norway's quality assurance process and Concept Research Programme

The Norwegian quality assurance process is compulsory for land based public investment projects with an expected budget of over NOK 750 million (approximately EUR 100 million). Analysis and decision documents are prepared by ministries according to a common format issued by the Ministry of Finance and reviewed by external quality assurers pre-qualified by the Ministry of Finance.

Funded by the Ministry of Finance and led by the Norwegian University of Science and Technology, the Concept Research Program organises ex-post evaluation of completed projects that have been through the quality assurance process. The lessons learned are seen as crucial for improving knowledge and practices in the development and implementation of projects and in the quality assurance process itself.

Results are openly available and published in a series of scientific reports, in addition to textbooks, working papers, scientific papers in journals and conference proceedings, etc.

Source: (Kim, Fallov and Groom, 2020[42])

Improve data quality and sharing across sectors

Evidence-informed infrastructure decision making requires a broad range of data. Data on existing infrastructure and its condition can help identify areas where upgrades and maintenance may be necessary. For example, linking strategic objectives – such as increased mobility – with indicators such as congestion hotspots, traffic flows and journey time maps can help to identify areas where there is a case for investment. Traffic data can help identify areas where highway or public transit investments could improve mobility. Data can also be used to identify disparities in access to infrastructure: for example, data on housing affordability across regions can help identify where new affordable housing projects may be needed. Demographic data, including insights into population trends and distribution, are necessary for needs analysis and can provide insights into distributional impacts. Economic data, such as employment rates and industry sector trends, can be used to evaluate the potential economic impacts of projects, while data on air quality, water resources, and land-use patterns are necessary to evaluate environmental impacts. Technical data such as construction cost indices, maintenance requirements, and asset conditions are critical for developing cost estimates, assessing feasibility and prioritising.

Governments with a strategic approach to the use of data across the entire public sector are better able to anticipate societal trends and needs and therefore develop more effective long-term plans (OECD, 2019[43]). Access to accurate and reliable data is essential for improving evidence-based decision making. The OECD Recommendation on the Governance of Infrastructure encourages countries to harness digital technologies, release open data and use data analytics to enhance infrastructure policy and decision making (OECD, 2021[14]). Data sharing across entities and sectors can promote transparency, helping to identify common challenges and opportunities across sectors, and promote collaboration by enabling different sectors to share knowledge and expertise. For example, in the Netherlands, the government collects water data and makes them publicly available for planning use by a range of actors (Box 2.8).

Box 2.8. Making water data available for infrastructure decision making in the Netherlands

Flooding events can cause damage and destruction to property and infrastructure. Flooding is becoming increasingly frequent with climate change and rising sea levels. As urban expansion continues, flooding in these areas can become more frequent due to insufficient drainage. This requires action to lessen the risk of urban flooding for infrastructure. Flood management systems can track patterns to identify areas likely to be flooded, looking at the probability that flooding will occur.

Governments can use sensors (GPS, water level, radar for thermal images) to collect data on water levels, resources, quality and water-related hazards. The data collected are transmitted to a central system and then analysed to enable flood prevention and better water resource management. This enables local authorities to identify mitigation solutions (e.g., dams and water management systems) or alternative areas where the risk of flooding is lower. A water height and flood management system can enable local authorities to predict future flooding and avoid building major infrastructure in high-risk areas. Local authorities can use the flood patterns to identify the probability of flooding for each area and use this information to improve decision making when selecting suitable locations for future housing and other infrastructure.

Rijkswaterstaat, an executive agency of the Dutch Ministry of Infrastructure and Water Management, manages and develops the Netherlands' main road and waterway networks. Rijkswaterstaat monitors the water level, discharge rates, wave height and flow speed using automatic measuring equipment at more than 450 locations. The data collected are made publicly available and used by water boards, provinces, municipalities, the private sector and researchers. The Rijkswaterstaat also collaborates with the Ministry of Agriculture, Nature and Food Quality and the Ministry of Defence on the Marine Information and Data Centre (IHM). Launched in 2012, the IHM makes available all government data on the North Sea in a single location. Rather than storing the data in a central location, the IHM functions as a portal, generating references to locations where data can be accessed. The data remain stored and maintained in their original location, ensuring they are current and accurate.

Source: (Global Infrastructure Hub, 2020[44]; Rijkswaterstaat, n.d.[45]; Marine Information and Data Centre, n.d.[46])

In Czechia, there is limited data available to support project appraisal and prioritisation. In addition, when data are collected, the large number of stakeholders in infrastructure planning and delivery creates challenges for quality and consistency, with data managed differently across sectors. The Ministry of Regional Development provides tools to municipalities to use demographic and economic data to develop strategies and prioritise projects (e.g., to forecast needs), but these tools are not currently linked to data on infrastructure investment, and municipalities may not always have the capacity to take advantage of the data. Officials confirmed during this study that a lack of data was a challenge for infrastructure planning at the municipal level. For example, data on housing are limited or insufficient: the main source of information on housing is the census of houses and apartments, which is carried out every 10 years, and administrative data are not leveraged to provide more current information. Asset management, including the monitoring and evaluation of infrastructure, is the responsibility of the asset owner and data on the condition of infrastructure are not shared or collected centrally.

The 2022 Programme for Government recognises the importance of data and commits to expanding its use in infrastructure planning and monitoring. This includes a commitment to using data to set a recommended level of infrastructure services for municipalities (e.g., for education, medical and social care, public transport, high-speed internet) and linking requirements to funding. It also commits to ensuring that plans, the achievement of objectives and efficiency are evaluated in the preparation and implementation of infrastructure by transport investment organisations, such as the Railway Infrastructure

Administration and the Waterways Directorate, and evaluating their performance against European peers (Government of Czechia, 2022[6]).

The Ministry of Regional Development could work with other infrastructure stakeholders to improve data quality and expand data sharing for project appraisal and prioritisation (ITF, 2021[47]). This could involve working with relevant ministries, state funds, agencies, regions and municipalities to develop infrastructure data guidelines and standards. Developing common data formats that all sectors can use for collecting, storing and sharing infrastructure data, and data-sharing protocols defining how data are shared and who has access, would ensure a common approach and avoid conflicts over data ownership. The ministry could also develop and disseminate guidelines on data collection and management to help ensure data is accurate and complete.

Strengthening the skills required for data use will be important. Collecting, managing, and using data effectively requires skills and resources. The Ministry of Regional Development could invest in training and capacity building for data management and analysis to ensure stakeholders have the necessary skills to collect, store and use data effectively. This could include providing technical training and workshops, as well as access to data management tools and resources. For example, in the 2020 OECD Survey on the Governance of Infrastructure, Czechia indicated that it maintains a national unit price database for infrastructure. Making this type of database more accessible and facilitating its use by a broad range of stakeholders could improve project appraisal and prioritisation.

The Ministry of Regional Development could also consider establishing an accessible data-sharing platform or repository to streamline data sharing on infrastructure with stakeholders. In the housing sector, the ministry's proposed Housing Investment Support Centres and Housing Investments Advisory Hub will already play a role in collecting and disseminating data on housing needs and projects. Over time, the ministry could consider playing this role for other sectors, improving access and increasing co-ordination and collaboration. However, developing an integrated data platform that crosses sectors raises various technical, organisational and regulatory challenges and would require significant investment of resources and strong commitment from stakeholders to ensure the benefits could be realised (World Bank, 2020[48]).

Standardise ex-post evaluations of infrastructure investments for evidence-based decision making

Ex-post evaluations can provide valuable insights and evidence to inform decision making. Alongside assessing how successful a project has been in achieving its stated aims, ex-post evaluations can also identify any unforeseen externalities, which are particularly important for informing future projects. In France, for example, some large projects put in place external bodies to track long-term environmental and economic impacts (Box 2.9). The accuracy of future appraisals can be improved by comparing ex-post outcomes with the expected outcomes identified in the appraisal of completed projects. Elements of the appraisal that may benefit from this approach include assumptions, projections and modelling methodologies. A stronger understanding of the uncertainty inherent in project appraisal can contribute to better scenario analysis, while information on the nature and extent of systemic bias (e.g., optimism bias) can help to correct these biases in future appraisals. Finally, by systematically assessing actual outcomes against initial claims, ex-post assessment can increase accountability (ITF, 2021[47]).

Box 2.9. Ex-post evaluations of transport projects in France

In France, ex-post evaluation of large transport projects has been mandatory since 1982. The aims are to: (a) inform the public about project outcomes, especially the extent and causes of any differences between outcomes and initial estimates; (b) account for the use of public funds by evaluating the effectiveness of investments; and (c) provide feedback to the project appraisal process.

The ex-post evaluation process is largely done independently of the entity responsible for the initial project appraisal. In some cases, independence is achieved by allocating responsibility to different parts of the same entity. For example, the Audit and Risks Department within SNCF Réseau (the network manager) performs evaluations of rail projects. In all cases, however, evaluations are supplemented by an independent opinion from L'inspection générale de l'environnement et du développement durable (General Inspectorate for the Environment and Sustainable Development).

Some projects adopt a permanent observatory model. Permanent observatories are external bodies that track projects over time, gathering data on projected costs, timelines and actual results. Contracts for the two most recent high-speed rail projects required the private operators to establish and finance permanent observatories to measure their environmental and economic effects.

Source: (ITF, 2022[49])

The Ministry of Regional Development could work with other infrastructure stakeholders to standardise and expand the use of ex-post evaluations to ascertain whether expected benefits were achieved and whether projects were cost-effective. This could include developing standardised, data-based approaches for conducting ex-post evaluations and ensuring evaluation results are available across sectors for planning and to inform operational decision making. This is already being done in some sectors: in the 2020 OECD Survey on the Governance of Infrastructure, Czechia indicated that the project appraisal process in the transport, energy and water sectors included ex-post analysis of similar projects. Similarly, Czechia's Evaluation Library[7], hosted by the National Coordination Authority, catalogues evaluation and monitoring information for projects and programmes financed by EU funds. Standardising these approaches and expanding them across sectors and funding sources could improve decision making and transparency and allow for comparison and learning across sectors.

Czechia could also expand existing commitments to evaluate the performance of transport sector investments and benchmark them against European peers to progressively include other priority sectors over time. This could provide greater insights into the effectiveness and efficiency of past investments, improve future decision making, and help to identify areas of success and areas for improvement. It could also include establishing a system for the ongoing monitoring of asset performance during the operational phase of the infrastructure lifecycle, potentially including introducing obligations for entities responsible for infrastructure to publicly report on its condition and use (OECD, 2020[11]).

Continuing to monitor and collect data on infrastructure performance after a project has been implemented can provide valuable inputs into decision making and allow for remedial action as required. The use of tools such as key performance indicators to oversee the performance of infrastructure service delivery can help to monitor and benchmark the performance of infrastructure in the delivery phase (OECD, 2017[1]). The effective monitoring of asset performance depends on ensuring the systematic collection, storage, and management of relevant data over the entire infrastructure lifecycle. Similarly, better data can support decision making for resilience: information about past risks and potential threats as well as systematic data collection on the resilience levels of infrastructure assets are key to understanding a system's continued capacity to withstand shocks. For example, Switzerland uses a comprehensive database (ProtectMe) to monitor the aging process and vulnerabilities of existing protective infrastructure, including information on the status of maintenance and protection capacity (OECD, 2021[14]).

Summary of key recommendations

Given the challenges of implementing a full suite of reforms, Czech authorities could consider sequencing the recommendations made above. By grouping recommendations according to the time horizon needed to implement them effectively (short term, and medium to long term), Czech authorities could allocate resources to reforms in a way which would provide incremental benefits. A potential sequencing is included below.

Short-term reforms

1. **Improve the quality and sharing of data.** Evidence-informed decision making on infrastructure investment can be supported by data ranging from the condition of existing assets, the use of infrastructure (e.g., traffic and ridership data), and demographic trends and distributions. Sharing data across entities and sectors can provide access to a broader evidence base, helping to identify common challenges and opportunities.

- The Ministry of Regional Development could work with relevant ministries, state funds, regions, and municipalities to develop infrastructure data guidelines and standards to improve data consistency and accuracy.
- The ministry could also invest in capacity building for relevant ministries, state funds, regions, and municipalities for data management and analysis to ensure they have the necessary skills to collect, store and use data effectively.

Medium to long-term reforms

2. **Introduce consistent and transparent appraisal of project costs and benefits across sectors.** A standard, transparent approach to project appraisal could support consistent prioritisation and the efficient use of resources across sectors. Project appraisal should consider Czechia's overarching economic, social and environmental objectives, but be flexible enough to account for differences across sectors in terms of needs, timelines, stakeholders and decision-making processes.

- Develop guidelines and methodologies for project appraisal through a joint approach with the Ministry of Regional Development and other infrastructure stakeholders, to ensure sectoral differences are reflected in a standardised approach.
- Increase the transparency and accountability of infrastructure investments by publishing project appraisals to enable review by external stakeholders. Consider expanding the independent review of project appraisals, for example by co-operating with external experts or enhancing the current role of the Ministry of Finance in project reviews.

3. **Standardise and expand the use of ex-post evaluations of infrastructure investments.** Ex-post evaluations are an important accountability mechanism, determining whether expected benefits were achieved. They can also inform future decision making. A common methodology and guidelines for ex-post evaluations across sectors and undertaking them systematically would improve future investment decisions and enhance accountability.

- Develop a standardised cross-sectoral methodology based on existing approaches for evaluating projects in the transport sector and projects financed by EU funds.
- Expand on existing commitments to evaluate the performance of transport sector investments and benchmark them against European peers to progressively include other priority sectors over time.

2.3 Investing in infrastructure delivery capacity

Even with strong strategic planning and robust project appraisal processes in place, poor delivery can limit the benefits of infrastructure investment (OECD, 2020[35]). How infrastructure is delivered impacts value for money, risk and affordability. Choosing high-value projects in a well-integrated strategic framework is of limited use if those projects are not delivered efficiently and effectively. Effective infrastructure procurement processes can also generate broader economic, environmental, and social returns and be used strategically to incentivise innovation, including in the transition to low-carbon infrastructure and the adoption of digital technologies (OECD, 2017[1]).

Inefficient infrastructure procurement can increase tendering costs, delay project implementation, reduce competition and inhibit innovation. While the infrastructure procurement process should deliver projects in a way that maximises value, procurement strategies are frequently based on the habits and capacity of contracting authorities rather than on strategic choices (OECD, 2021[14]). Smaller contracting authorities in particular may lack the resources, expertise, and experience required. Capacity building, shared services, collaboration, simplified procedures and a supportive regulatory framework can all help to overcome these challenges. Tailoring procedures to the needs and capabilities of small contracting authorities and providing clear guidance and standards to support compliance are other useful actions.

The capacity of the public procurement workforce is critical for efficient delivery and achieving value for money (OECD, 2023[50]). Effective procurement requires expertise in a range of areas, including project management, legal and regulatory frameworks, and technical knowledge of the services and works being procured. Given the complexity of infrastructure procurement, a lack of expertise or inadequate resources can lead to poor decisions, delays and cost overruns. Infrastructure procurement can be time-consuming and challenging for contracting authorities, leading to delays and inefficiencies. For this reason, the OECD's Recommendation on the Governance of Infrastructure advises adherents to ensure that the procurement workforce has the capacity to deliver value for money by providing tools to improve procurement skills and competencies (OECD, 2020[15]). Denmark's National Building Fund provides an example of how a central institution can improve infrastructure investment by smaller bodies through financial and technical support (see Box 2.10.).

Box 2.10. Denmark's National Building Fund

Almost 1 million people, approximately 17% of Denmark's population, live in the social and affordable housing sector, composed of around 600 000 housing units. The National Building Fund, created in 1967, is a key pillar of Denmark's social and affordable housing model. An independent institution outside the state budget, the Building Fund is financed by a share of tenants' rents (amounting to 2.8% annually of the total acquisition cost of the property), in addition to housing associations' contributions to mortgage loans (approximately 2% of the property acquisition cost). The fund finances the expansion of new social and affordable housing and the renovation of existing properties. This includes improvements to inside and outdoor areas, modernisation to improve access for elderly and disabled people, and energy improvements. Support from the fund is obtained through applications submitted by the housing organisations and allocated using objective criteria.

The fund's experience illustrates how the construction industry is central to the objective of renovating social housing: by mobilising the private sector through public procurement, the National Building Fund is able to implement a EUR 4 billion green renovation programme.

Along with financial support, the fund provides the sector with expert knowledge, data, and IT tools. It produces statistics, key figures and analysis of the social housing sector. Moreover, the fund holds various types of master data for the social housing sector. Based on the data it collects and maintains, the fund has developed various IT tools, such as an accounting database and a so-called Twin Tool that makes it easier to benchmark specific housing organisations against their peers.

Source: (Madsen, 2021[51]) (OECD, 2020[52])

Czechia's context and institutional structure intensify common public infrastructure procurement challenges. The infrastructure governance system is fragmented, with different entities responsible for infrastructure decision making, funding, and implementation, leading to co-ordination challenges. Many entities do not have long-standing experience undertaking infrastructure investment or the resources to invest in building capacity. Small municipalities can find it difficult and expensive to prepare tenders and administer contracts in accordance with the national public procurement framework. Despite a focus on green, social and innovation procurement at the policy level (the consideration of environmental, social and innovative criteria is mandatory for all tenders), the capacity of contracting authorities to carry out complex procurements is often limited. The overall administrative burden of public procurement and the need to comply with complex requirements is also seen as a significant barrier to accessing EU funds. The government has made efforts to increase market capacity through initiatives such as webinars for potential suppliers, but interest has been limited. The recent inflation (Chapter 1) has exacerbated these market capacity challenges, leading suppliers to revisit contracts due to rising input costs and, in some cases, abandoning projects. Czech authorities also face challenges from contracting authorities' weak capacity and skills to develop procurement strategies and prepare tender documents. The focus of public authorities, including at the national level, is primarily on complying with procurement legislation and regulations, rather than the strategic use of procurement to deliver outcomes and value for money.

Choosing the wrong procurement strategy can lead to cost overruns, delays, or quality issues. The choice of procurement strategy involves trade-offs between the capabilities to be retained in-house and those sourced from the market, whether projects should be procured through a single or several contracts (e.g. bundling lifecycle phases), and the bidder selection process (OECD, 2021[53]). Czechia has limited experience with the use of public-private partnerships (PPPs) and other non-traditional delivery models for major infrastructure projects. PPPs and other non-traditional models are complex to design, negotiate and implement. Expanding their use will require carefully evaluating available delivery models, including consideration of value for money and the optimal allocation of financial, legal and delivery risk.

By improving delivery capacity, the Ministry of Regional Development could help to ensure that Czechia is able to maximise value for money from its large planned infrastructure investments. The following sections propose steps to improve infrastructure delivery capacity in Czechia by increasing support for project preparation, using tools like framework agreements, developing public sector procurement capacity and developing a consistent, evidence-informed approach to decisions on infrastructure delivery models. While measuring the impacts of better infrastructure delivery is challenging, one study found that improving infrastructure delivery could save 15% of total infrastructure expenditure through measures such as streamlining project delivery, increasing investment in early-stage project planning and design, and taking a more strategic approach to procurement (Dobbs et al., 2013[34]). Though simplified, this figure provides a general sense of the scale of the opportunity.

Increase support for project preparation

The Ministry of Regional Development could work with other stakeholders to build capacity and increase support for project preparation. While some institutions, such as the Ministry of Transport, have sophisticated project preparation processes in place, others are less advanced. Smaller entities in particular face challenges with project preparation. For example, the costs of project design and land acquisition are not eligible for inclusion under most granting programmes, meaning that municipalities often lack the resources to put forward projects for consideration. Municipalities also find it expensive and technically challenging to contract the professional services (e.g., environmental impact assessments, technical feasibility studies) required to apply for infrastructure investment financing. These challenges in project preparation have a particularly large impact in the housing sector, as it is municipalities that are primarily responsible for the delivery of affordable housing projects. In the case of the State Investment Support Fund, municipal projects generally need to have obtained planning permission and building permits and gone through the procurement process before a grant or loan agreement is finalised. The grant or loan is only disbursed as construction work is carried out, which can create financing challenges. This approach, however, is not universal in Czechia: the State Environmental Fund has issued special calls for project preparation to provide support for large project development (including the development of feasibility and cost-benefit analysis).

To improve project quality and incentivise early planning and preparation, ministries and state funds could consider including project preparation in eligible costs when developing grant programmes. Preparation costs have been estimated to range from approximately 3-5% of total project costs (Global Infrastructure Hub, 2019[54]), but investing in project preparation can have significant downstream benefits. Smaller municipalities in particular could benefit from support with project design and preparation. Ministries and agencies could consider the increased use of two-round calls, with the first-round funding project preparation and design or reimburse preparation costs after construction approval.

The Ministry of Regional Development could also take steps to provide direct access to expertise, specialised support and advice on project preparation. Public sector organisations such as small municipalities could be provided with expertise or direct technical assistance in areas such as, for example, financial modelling and business case development. Specialised training could be offered in technical, economic, environmental and social analysis to support investment appraisals, as well as increased access to and training in data analytics tools. Support could also focus on preparing projects to align with EU objectives and requirements, such as the application of the 'Do No Significant Harm' principle. For example, the Ministry of Regional Development's proposed Housing Investments Advisory Hub could play a role in developing methodologies, formulating best practices, guidelines and frameworks for the effective preparation of affordable housing projects. These could include areas such as site selection, financial structuring, and stakeholder engagement. The Housing Investment Support Centres could work with municipalities to support the application of these methodologies at the local level. Box 2.11 provides examples from Ireland of initiatives and institutions working to provide both direct support and build the capacity of contracting authorities.

Box 2.11. Building project delivery skills in Ireland

The Office of Government Procurement's Commercial Skills Academy

Ireland's Office of Government Procurement (OGP), part of the Department of Public Expenditure, National Development Plan Delivery and Reform, was established in 2013 with the goal of maximising value for money and operational efficiency through the central management of public procurement. One of the OGP's roles is co-ordination and capacity building in the public procurement system.

The OGP established the Commercial Skills Academy in 2019. Its objective is to provide public servants with an understanding of key issues, commercial skills, and best practice approaches for effective project delivery throughout the entire lifecycle of a public investment project. The Commercial Skills Academy is centrally funded by the Irish government and delivered at no cost to participants. The academy is currently focused on Ireland's Capital Works Management Framework, which consists of a suite of best practice guidance, standard contracts and mandatory generic template documents that must be used by contracting authorities on projects which are more than 50% publicly funded. It also contains template prequalification questionnaires, instructions to tenderers, forms of tender and contracts.

The Commercial Skills Academy's offerings include:

- A six-day training programme in using the Capital Works Management Framework, focused on decision making rather than process. Most participants are construction qualified e.g. (engineers, architects) employees of organisations such as local authorities and the Department of Public Works, but eligibility is generally wide and also includes housing authorities, who are not strictly public sector employees.
- Online self-directed training providing an introduction to procurement legislation and rules, Ireland's Public Spending Code and the Capital Works Management Framework.
- Specialist masterclasses on key topics for the delivery of infrastructure projects such as dispute resolution and contract management. Training is delivered by practitioners from the public and private sector.
- Three-day training courses aimed at senior decision makers overseeing organisations delivering public-funded projects, and covering project governance and oversight, risk and cost management.
- Conference-style presentations on a specific theme such as green public procurement or building information modelling, with presenters from public and private industry.

Training sessions are also recorded and available online. The OGP also facilitates regional roundtables and networks to provide opportunities for networking and co-ordination among contracting authorities. As it begins to expand beyond the structured Capital Works Management Framework to other areas of procurement, the academy is placing a greater focus on understanding the existing competencies and proficiencies of the workforce.

The Housing Agency

Ireland's Housing Agency was established in 2012 as a centre of expertise to support housing policy development, and to collaborate with partners to implement effective housing programmes. The Housing Agency is a non-commercial state agency under the Department of Housing, Local Government and Heritage and is governed by a board appointed by the minister. Its operations are funded primarily through a grant from the department.

The Agency's Procurement Unit was created in 2016 and supports local authorities and approved housing bodies in Ireland with social housing construction, regeneration, infill, upgrade, and procurement projects. It has specific expertise, knowledge, and experience in the planning, design, and construction of public housing and has worked with partners on a range of housing projects, supporting the delivery of over 3 300 homes in 2021.

The agency offers technical assistance and support for all stages and sizes of public housing projects. This can include general design and procurement advice, preparing tender documents and managing the tender process for procuring consultants and works contractors in accordance with Irish and EU procurement regulations. It also provides support for project management and design, and contract administration. For example, it has established a framework agreement managed by Ireland's Office for Government Procurement for architect led-design teams.

Source: (The Housing Agency, 2022[55]; The Housing Agency, 2022[56])

Increase the use of framework agreements, particularly for procuring professional services

Framework agreements are umbrella agreements for the future supply of goods, services or works. They establish the terms governing contracts to be awarded by one or more contracting authorities during a given period, including maximum price, minimum technical specifications and, where appropriate, quantities (OECD, 2014[57]). For frequently purchased goods, services and works, a framework agreement can reduce administrative burdens for contracting authorities and suppliers alike, by allowing simplified ordering processes once the agreement is in place. If structured to allow second stage competition, where multiple suppliers under a framework agreement compete on price, they can also generate additional cost savings (OECD, 2016[58]). Framework agreements can also help address competition challenges: it can be difficult for small contracting authorities to attract bids from suppliers with the necessary expertise and experience on their own.

The Ministry of Regional Development could encourage the expanded use of procurement tools such as framework agreements. It could identify initial areas of focus for framework agreements by aligning the government's priorities, such as housing and the green transition, with the priorities of small contracting authorities, such as challenges with project preparation and planning. It could also work with other national bodies to provide smaller contracting authorities, such as municipalities, with access to frameworks developed by larger contracting authorities.

Framework agreements for the development of public housing projects could provide a useful test case. The proposed Housing Investment Support Centres could play a role in facilitating the development and management of framework agreements to enable municipalities to more easily access services for developing affordable housing projects. The Support Centres could work closely with municipalities to identify their specific requirements and establish framework agreements outlining the terms and procedures for municipalities to access a pool of pre-qualified service providers. By centralising the procurement process, the Support Centres would be able to streamline the selection and contracting of services, reducing the administrative burden for municipalities and ensuring consistency in quality and pricing.

Attention should be given to the design of framework agreements to avoid regional disparities which could hamper infrastructure investment objectives. As a result of the need to standardise, framework agreements run the risk of neglecting the needs of specific contracting authorities. This diversity of needs can be addressed by dividing frameworks into lots. In the case of Czechia, it would be important to ensure frameworks are accessible to contracting authorities across the country and that successful suppliers are not concentrated in specific urban areas. This could be accomplished by dividing frameworks into regional lots. Very small contracting authorities, such as some municipalities, might also struggle to attract bids due to the low value of their needs. This could be addressed by creating a low-value lot to award contracts below a certain threshold. To ensure that lots are awarded to different suppliers, contracting authorities can also limit the number of lots for which economic operators can bid or which a single economic operator can be awarded. These approaches, however, must be balanced against the risk that some lots may not receive bids or that economies of scale will be diminished (SIGMA, 2016[59]; OECD, 2014[57]).

Developing framework agreements requires an understanding of contracting authorities' requirements, as well as the capabilities and capacity of the market. Framework agreements also require follow-up to ensure that they allow for the successful matching of needs with market capabilities. Supporting contracting authorities and suppliers while initiating framework agreements helps to create a structured environment. Support can include information events, guidance for contracting authorities and suppliers on how to use the framework, help-desk services, and training to both contracting authorities and suppliers. For example, Finland has developed templates to be used by contracting authorities during the call-off stage to ensure that key procurement principles, such as fairness and transparency, are included (OECD, 2017[60]).

Develop the procurement capacity of the public sector

Infrastructure procurement involves complex legal, financial, technical and operational considerations that require specialised knowledge and skills. If public sector officials lack this procurement expertise, they may struggle to deliver infrastructure investments effectively. In Czechia, public procurement is seen as a significant barrier to accessing and efficiently using EU funds, hindering absorption and making it challenging to complete projects within programme time limits.

The large number of contracting authorities in Czechia makes it challenging to build the professionalisation of the procurement workforce. There are over 1 800 active contracting authorities at the central, regional and local level responsible for their own public procurement, without central co-ordination. While large contracting authorities often have a specialised purchasing department, regional and local authorities often lack full-time public procurement professionals (European Commission, 2020[61]). These smaller contracting authorities often need to hire consultants to undertake procurements, increasing project costs and administrative overhead.

The Ministry of Regional Development could provide infrastructure-specific support to increase the professionalism of the procurement workforce. The ministry is responsible for public procurement legislation and regulation in Czechia and has been active in professionalising public procurement through the development of training. This has included capacity building seminars and specialised training in specific areas (e.g., professional seminars for hospitals focused on the procurement of medicines and medical supplies). The ministry also co-operates with professional organisations and other relevant institutions to develop methodological guidance on public procurement. Other national institutions also provide support. The Ministry of the Environment publishes methodological guidance for green public procurement and the Ministry of Labour and Social Affairs has published reports highlighting good practice on the use of social procurement in Europe and Czechia (Ministry of Labour and Social Affairs, 2017[62]; Ministry of Labour and Social Affairs, 2019[63]; Ministry of the Environment, n.d.[64]). The Office for the Protection of Competition has also offered seminars and training on public procurement, including an educational programme for small communities focused on multi-criteria evaluation, prepared jointly with the Union of Towns and Municipalities of Czechia (European Commission, 2020[61]).

More capacity is also needed in the use of strategic procurement by contracting authorities. It is important for contracting authorities to consider non-financial criteria in order to achieve strategic policy goals, particularly those related to the green transition. However, strategic procurement can be more complex, requiring specific technical and legal expertise. Small contracting authorities may struggle to ensure compliance and are often risk averse, while sometimes lacking a clear understanding of the potential benefits. A 2020 report prepared by the Union of Towns and Municipalities highlighted the following barriers to the use of strategic procurement in Czechia (Union of Towns and Municipalities of Czechia, 2020[65]):

- Administrative complexity: Strategic procurement requires a higher level of experience and knowledge and there is no generic guidance or model forms that can be followed. It also requires decisions about when and how to apply different aspects of strategic procurement.
- Lack of market capacity and interest: Contracting authorities are already faced with a market environment characterised by low interest from potential suppliers. There is a concern that additional requirements will further discourage suppliers from bidding for public contracts. They are also concerned that suppliers will not be able to meet additional performance requirements related to strategic procurement.
- Higher prices and lower quality: Contracting authorities are concerned that the requirements of strategic procurement will result in higher prices. In the area of social procurement, they are reluctant to require the involvement of disadvantaged people in the labour market due to quality concerns.
- Challenges with managing supplier performance: Contract management and evaluating supplier compliance is more complex for strategic procurement. For example, contracting authorities found it more technically complex or administratively burdensome to verify whether suppliers were meeting environmental and social requirements.
- Challenges with compliance and control bodies: Contracting authorities are concerned that using strategic procurement imposes additional risks of non-compliance with legal and regulatory requirements. They reported that control bodies were generally not aware or supportive of strategic procurement. Contracting authorities tend to be particularly cautious in the case of procurements financed by EU funds.

In the 2020 OECD Survey on the Governance of Infrastructure, all surveyed countries reported employing a combination of financial and qualitative criteria to select proposals (Figure 2.6). However, less than half use lifecycle costs for awarding contracts (13 out of 30 OECD countries or 43%; 7 out of 16 EU countries or 44%). While Czechia did not respond to this question in the 2020 OECD Survey, officials interviewed for this project noted an increasing emphasis on sustainable procurement, with a focus on green, social and innovation factors. However, capacity challenges make more complex procurements challenging for many contracting authorities. Officials indicated that tender selection is almost always made on the basis of price rather than best value, as the use of non-financial criteria requires more capacity and expertise from contracting authorities. Recognising this challenge, the Policy Statement of the Government commits to expanding methodological support for public procurement to make it easier for buyers to consider non-financial criteria (Government of Czechia, 2022[6]). There may also be areas of good practice which could form the basis for knowledge sharing: Czech officials identified the rail sector as a good practice example of the use of best value in procurement.

Figure 2.6. Nearly all OECD countries combine financial and qualitative criteria to select proposals

Mechanisms used by OECD countries to help identify proposals offering the best value for money, 2020

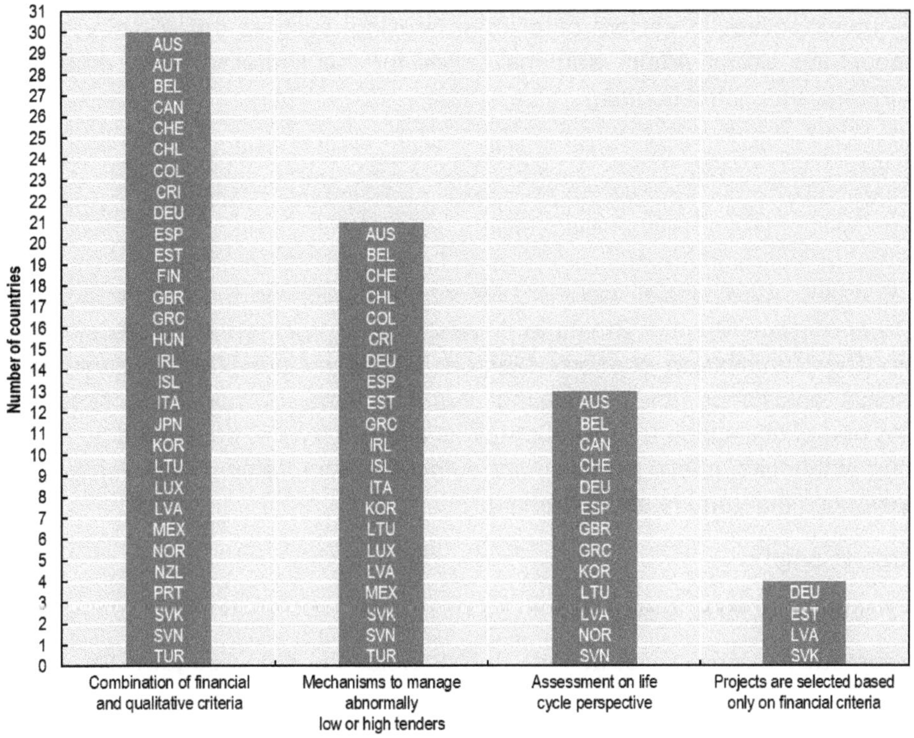

Note: Data for Belgium are based on the survey responses from Flanders only.
Source: OECD (2020), Survey on the Governance of Infrastructure.

Procurement capacity can be built through the use of methodological assistance tools (e.g., guidelines, manuals, standardised templates, a help desk, direct support and advice to implementing actual procurement procedures), and practical training (on-the-job training, mentoring, and job swapping). Examples include:

- Providing examples and guides to encourage innovation and the adoption of good practices in the construction industry. For example, a Danish Housing Authority initiative is working to provide easily accessible examples of cheap, sustainable construction for builders, consultants, project supervisors, contractors and manufacturers of building materials (Ministry of the Interior and Housing, 2021[66]). Encouraging and facilitating the use of modular construction is also anticipated to have benefits including reducing costs, accelerating build times, and providing greater cost certainty (McKinsey & Company, 2019[67]; Global Infrastructure Hub, 2020[68]).
- Developing templates and standardised contracts and tender documents to simplify the procurement process and reduce administrative burdens for contracting authorities and the private sector (as in Ireland's Capital Works Management Framework, outlined in Box 2.11.
- Encouraging and supporting the use of innovative tools such as building information modelling (BIM). By providing a comprehensive and integrated approach to project design, construction and management, the use of BIM can help to improve collaboration between stakeholders throughout the infrastructure lifecycle.
- Tools such as ProcurComp[EU], the European public procurement competency framework, may also be useful in identifying areas of strengths and weaknesses (Box 2.12).

There may be a role for the Ministry of Regional Development's proposed Housing Investments Advisory Hub and expert centres to develop good practices in procurement related to housing, and for regional centres to disseminate and promote methodologies. The hub and national centres could also work to ensure alignment and co-ordination across national institutions providing methodological support for procurement by municipalities in sectors other than housing, such as the Ministry of the Environment, Ministry of Labour and Social Affairs and the Office for the Protection of Competition, as well as engagement with relevant control bodies.

Box 2.12. ProcurComp^{EU}: The European competency framework for public procurement professionals

In 2017, the European Commission issued a Recommendation on the professionalisation of public procurement to encourage Member States to develop public procurement professionalisation policies and initiatives. The Commission supports Member States by providing guidance to practitioners, training, technical assistance and facilitating the exchange of good practices and innovative approaches. As part of this support, ProcurComp^{EU} is a voluntary tool developed by the Commission to help contracting authorities, public procurement authorities and training organisations to identify and address competences that require strengthening.

Overview of ProcurComp^{EU}

ProcurComp^{EU} consists of three elements:

- **A competency matrix** which defines 30 competences (knowledge, skills and attitudes) that public procurement professionals should demonstrate in order to carry out public procurement procedures that bring value for money. The competences are grouped in two main categories: procurement-specific competences and soft competences.
- **A self-assessment tool** which public procurement professionals and organisations can use to assess their levels of proficiency and organisational maturity in the different competences identified in the competency matrix.
- **A training curriculum** which outlines the content of training for developing the competences in the competency matrix. The training curriculum describes the standard training content and learning outcomes for 30 training modules.

ProcurComp^{EU} implementation case study: Slovenia

The Slovenian Public Procurement Directorate's (PPD) main tasks are public procurement policy design and implementation, developing e-procurement tools and services, and providing assistance to contracting authorities and economic operators that carry out or participate in public procurement procedures. The PPD implemented ProcurComp^{EU} as part of its professionalisation action plan. The PPD developed a Slovenian-specific competency framework (including competency matrix and job profiles), self-assessment tool and training curriculum adapted from ProcurComp^{EU}. These tools form part of the training programme, called the Public Procurement Academy. The PPD takes a gradual approach to the implementation of the training curriculum: it will first be voluntary, before potentially becoming mandatory, and could possibly lead to a certification. This approach will allow for the adjustment and refinement of the training curriculum content or implementation process to ensure it responds to the expectations and needs of stakeholders.

Source: (OECD, 2023[50]; European Commission, 2020[66]; European Commission, 2020[67])

Develop a consistent, evidence-based approach to deciding infrastructure delivery models

Public-private partnerships (PPPs) have become a prominent method for delivering public infrastructure globally. They can deliver value for money when the right institutional capacities and processes are in place. However, there should be no institutional, procedural or accounting bias either in favour for or against PPPs. Instead, long-term planning and project appraisal should guide project choice independently from decisions on how those assets are delivered (OECD, 2017[1]). The OECD Recommendation on the Governance of Infrastructure advises adherents to carefully evaluate available delivery modes against previously defined criteria based on projects' characteristics, optimal risks allocation and the use of value for money analytical tools (OECD, 2020[15]). Given the range of choices, countries should determine their approach to procurement based on a careful evaluation of the national, sectoral and project-specific context, rather than applying one delivery strategy to all projects by default.

There is a renewed interest in the use of PPPs in Czechia following a period when their use was not generally considered at a national level. This was largely due to negative experiences with PPPs in the 1990s and 2000s, which led to political sensitivity and discouraged the use of these alternative financing and delivery modes. A PPP Unit previously existed in the Ministry of Finance, and was responsible for preparing tender documentation, undertaking feasibility studies and providing guidance and advice, but it has become inactive. There is currently one highway project being delivered as a PPP at the national level: the D4 Highway PPP project consists of the construction of approximately 32 km of new highway, and the operation and maintenance of approximately 16 km of existing highway for a period of 28 years under a design-build-finance-operate-maintain model (including approximately four years of construction). A subsequent highway project, the D35, is also being prepared for PPP delivery.

The Policy Statement of the Government commits to evaluating the PPP delivery of the D4 motorway and to considering the use PPPs in other transport infrastructure projects (Government of Czechia, 2022[6]). While there is currently no formal system at the national level for deciding on the most appropriate delivery model, new national guidelines for the development of affordable housing through PPPs are currently being drafted. A legislative amendment is also underway which would enable the issuance of bonds to finance transport infrastructure and to implement PPPs across all transport modes (State Fund for Transport Infrastructure, 2022[68]).

The Ministry of Regional Development could work with the Ministry of Finance to establish a standard framework for making decisions on infrastructure delivery models. This could include using specific methodologies for assessing value for money, including creating an analytical tool for comparative assessment of service delivery options. Factors to be considered could include projects' scale and duration, the scope for innovation and design integration, and the assessment of relevant risk transfers and financial design (OECD, 2020[35]). This type of analysis should consider aspects such as the comparative costs of financing, construction, maintenance and operations over the whole lifetime of the project; whether project risks can be clearly defined and measured; the level of market competition and capacity; the extent to which the project outputs can be clearly and completely defined ex-ante; whether the project is of sufficient size to justify PPP transaction costs; and the potential for whole-of-life benefits and innovation from combining different phases in one contract (OECD, 2012[69]). This could allow the advantages and weaknesses of PPPs to be compared to traditional delivery and other forms of private capital involvement in infrastructure projects in an evidence-informed and consistent way.

To help ensure that decisions are informed by evidence and to build public trust, delivery model selection could be made more transparent. This could include publishing information about PPP projects and the value-for-money analysis and involving relevant stakeholders, such as civil society organisations, in the decision-making process. Analysis should be scaled to the complexity and size of the project. It could be conducted by the entity responsible for the project and reviewed by a body with the necessary expertise, such as the Ministry of Finance. In the 2020 OECD Survey on the Governance of Infrastructure, Czechia indicated that formal bodies such as parliamentary committees and audit institutions were involved in overseeing infrastructure delivery, but civil society organisations and the wider public were not. The OECD's Principles for the Public Governance of Public-Private Partnerships suggest that active involvement by non-government organisations can create transparency for problematic issues that might otherwise be overlooked and become serious problems if not addressed at an early stage (OECD, 2012[69]).

A strong decision-making framework could help ensure the PPP model is applied where there is evidence for increased value for money. Economic efficiency and value for money throughout the lifecycle of the asset should be central to decisions on how to mobilise private investment to deliver infrastructure. PPPs are therefore only one of several alternatives or tools for infrastructure financing, and their applicability depends on individual cases. While they offer advantages such as access to private sector financing and expertise, they can be complex and require careful oversight. Given their long-term nature, particular care should be given to assessing value for money and aligning the objectives of the public sector with the profit objectives of the private partner (OECD, 2012[69]).

The 2020 OECD Survey on the Governance of Infrastructure asked countries whether the decision to procure an asset was made before the choice of delivery mode (Figure 2.7). Most surveyed countries indicated that they always (11 out of 31 OECD countries or 36%; 8 out of 16 EU countries or 50%) or more than 50% of the time (11 OECD countries or 36%; 3 EU countries or 19%) decide on the procurement of an asset before choosing the mode of delivery. Only 23% of OECD countries (7 out of 31) reported choosing the delivery model before deciding to procure the project more than 50% of the time.

Figure 2.7. Most OECD countries usually decide to procure an asset before choosing the delivery mode

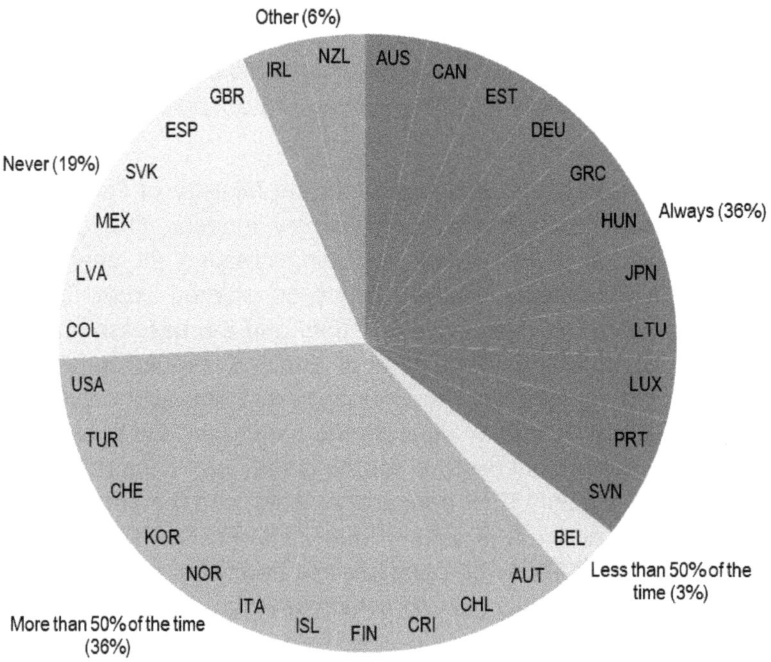

Note: Data for Belgium are based on the survey responses from Flanders only.
Source: 2020 OECD Survey on the Governance of Infrastructure.

Czechia could leverage the capacity being developed in the Ministry for Transport and State Fund for Transport Infrastructure through the implementation of projects like the D4 motorway to inform the future development and delivery of PPPs across government. This would allow the government as a whole to learn and improve the quality of future projects, help reduce risks, and deliver infrastructure more effectively. It could also help build institutional capacity across sectors and increase public confidence in the PPP model by showing that government is learning from past experiences and seeking to improve the PPP process. Developing governance guidelines for the management of PPP contracts, including defining the roles and responsibilities of different stakeholders, establishing dispute resolution mechanisms and undertaking ongoing monitoring and evaluation, would all be valuable.

Czechia could consider reintroducing a specialised PPP Unit rather than having skills and approaches developed and concentrated in specific sectors such as transport and housing. Given the complexity of PPPs and their infrequent use, it can be advantageous to pool critical skills in a PPP Unit that is made available to the relevant ministries and agencies (OECD, 2012[69]). The unit could serve as a resource for ministries, agencies and subnational governments, providing guidance and support on PPP project development and implementation. Its role could also include collecting potential projects to build a PPP pipeline and encouraging collaboration and information sharing between stakeholders involved in PPP projects.

Summary of key recommendations

Given the challenges of implementing a full suite of reforms, Czech authorities could consider sequencing the recommendations made above. By grouping recommendations according to the time horizon needed to implement them effectively (short term, and medium to long term), Czech authorities could allocate resources to reforms in a way which would provide incremental benefits. A potential sequencing is included below.

Short-term reforms

1. **Improve investment efficiency by increasing the use of framework agreements.** For frequently purchased services and works, a framework agreement can secure the required expertise, generate savings and reduce administrative burdens for contracting authorities and suppliers.

- The Ministry of Regional Development could develop and manage framework agreements for infrastructure services to enable smaller contracting authorities to efficiently access planning and project development services.
- Use framework agreements for services related to public housing projects as a useful test case. The Ministry of Regional Development's proposed Housing Investment Support Centres could play a role in facilitating the development and management of framework agreements by working closely with municipalities to identify their specific challenges and needs in this sector.
- Give careful attention to the design of framework agreements to avoid regional disparities which would hamper infrastructure investment objectives.

2. **Develop a consistent, evidence-informed approach to decisions on infrastructure delivery models.** There should be no institutional, procedural or accounting bias either in favour of or against PPPs. Long-term planning and project appraisal should guide project choice independently of decisions on how those assets are delivered. Given the range of choices, the approach to procurement should be based on a careful evaluation of the national, sectoral and project-specific context.

- The Ministry of Regional Development and the Ministry of Finance could establish a standard framework or analytical tool for decisions on infrastructure delivery models, including the comparative evidence-based assessment of delivery model options.
- Consider reintroducing a PPP Unit as a resource for ministries, agencies and subnational governments. Given the complexity of PPPs and their infrequent use, it can be advantageous to pool the skills and experience in a PPP Unit so that they can be made available to entities requiring such expertise.

Medium to long-term reforms

3. **Increase funding and direct support for project preparation to improve infrastructure delivery.** Smaller entities face challenges in project preparation, which is a particular issue for the housing sector as many municipalities lack long-term experience in undertaking investment or the resources to invest in capacity. This could be addressed by providing funding for project preparation activities and providing direct support in priority sectors such as housing.

- Ministries and state funds could include project preparation in eligible costs when developing grant programmes. Without the resources for project preparation, small municipalities can struggle to bring forward eligible projects.
- The Ministry of Regional Development could provide direct access to expertise, support, and advice on housing project preparation through its proposed Housing Investment Support Centres, given the importance of the sector in Czechia.

4. **Develop the procurement capacity of the public sector to improve value for money in project delivery.** Infrastructure procurement requires sophisticated legal, financial, technical and operational expertise. The large number of contracting authorities in Czechia makes it challenging to develop this expertise to deliver infrastructure projects effectively.

- The Ministry of Regional Development could provide infrastructure-specific support to increase the professionalisation of the procurement workforce, with a focus on increasing the use of non-financial criteria, including environmental criteria.
- The Ministry of Regional Development's proposed Housing Investments Advisory Hub and Housing Investment Support Centres would provide an opportunity to develop and directly apply good practices in the procurement of public housing. These capacity building activities could later be expanded to other sectors.

Notes

1 It is chaired by the Prime Minister and includes the ministers of the large infrastructure ministries.

2 https://portal.cenia.cz/eiasea/view/eia100_cr?lang=en

3 https://portal.cenia.cz/eiasea/view/SEA100_koncepce

4 https://dotaceeu.cz/cs/statistiky-a-analyzy/mapa-projektu

5 https://www.projektovezamery.cz/

6 Figures exclude countries that reported conducting assessments on an ad hoc basis.

7 https://dotaceeu.cz/cs/fondy-eu/narodni-organ-pro-koordinaci/evaluace/knihovna-evaluaci

References

Demmou, L. and G. Franco (2020), "Do sound infrastructure governance and regulation affect productivity growth? New insights from firm level data", *OECD Economics Department Working Papers*, No. 1609, OECD Publishing, Paris, https://doi.org/10.1787/410535403555. [4]

Department of Public Expenditure, NDP Delivery and Reform (2023), *Circular 06/2023: Update of the Public Spending Code Capital Spending Requirements*, https://assets.gov.ie/251585/daa5c0b1-4165-4a49-8668-d3137ac6e124.pdf. [37]

Department of Public Expenditure, NDP Delivery and Reform (2021), *National Development Plan 2021-2030*, https://assets.gov.ie/200358/a36dd274-736c-4d04-8879-b158e8b95029.pdf. [28]

Department of Treasury and Finance Victoria (2021), *Victorian Infrastructure Plan 2021*, https://www.dtf.vic.gov.au/sites/default/files/document/Victorian%20Infrastructure%20Plan%202021.pdf. [18]

Dobbs, R. et al. (2013), *Infrastructure productivity: How to save $1 trillion a year*, https://www.mckinsey.com/capabilities/operations/our-insights/infrastructure-productivity. [34]

European Commission (2021), *Analysis of the recovery and resilience plan of Czechia*, https://eur-lex.europa.eu/legal-content/EN/TXT/PDF/?uri=CELEX:52021SC0211. [7]

European Commission (2020), *ProcurCompEU Implementation in Slovenia*, https://commission.europa.eu/system/files/2021-04/procurcompeu-slovenia-en_1.pdf. [67]

European Commission (2020), *ProcurCompEU: European Competency Framework for Public Procurement Professionals*, https://commission.europa.eu/system/files/2020-12/procurcompeu-ecf_for_pp_en.pdf. [66]

European Commission (2020), *ProcurCompEU: Study on professionalisation of public procurement in the EU and selected third countries*, https://commission.europa.eu/system/files/2020-12/procurcompeu-study_prof_pp_en.pdf. [61]

European Commission (n.d.), *Open Data Portal for the European Structural Investment Funds*, https://cohesiondata.ec.europa.eu/2014-2020_cohesion_overview (accessed on 1 June 2023). [2]

Global Infrastructure Hub (2020), *Water Height and Flood Management System*, https://www.gihub.org/infrastructure-technology-use-cases/case-studies/water-height-and-flood-management-system/ (accessed on 5 April 2023). [44]

Global Infrastructure Hub (2019), *Leading Practices in Governmental Processes Facilitating Infrastructure Project Preparation*, https://cdn.gihub.org/umbraco/media/2344/gih_project-preparation_full-document_final_art_web.pdf. [54]

Government of Czechia (2022), *Policy Statement of the Government of Czechia*, https://www.vlada.cz/assets/jednani-vlady/policy-statement/Policy-Statement-of-the-Government.pdf. [6]

Government of Czechia (2019), *National Investment Plan of Czechia 2020-2050*, http://www.vlada.cz/assets/media-centrum/aktualne/Narodni-investicni-plan-CR-2020_2050.pdf. [8]

Government of Czechia (2017), *Strategic Framework Czechia 2030*, https://www.vlada.cz/assets/ppov/udrzitelny-rozvoj/projekt-OPZ/Strategic_Framework_CZ2030.pdf. [9]

Huerta Melchor, O. and J. Gars (2020), "Planning mobility in a fragmented metropolitan area: The case of Prague and its suburbs", *OECD Regional Development Papers*, No. 08, OECD Publishing, Paris, https://doi.org/10.1787/4cdf2d31-en. [20]

Infrastructure and Projects Authority (2021), *Assurance Review Toolkit*, https://www.gov.uk/government/collections/infrastructure-and-projects-authority-assurance-review-toolkit (accessed on 17 April 2023). [40]

Infrastructure and Projects Authority (2020), *About the IPA*, https://assets.publishing.service.gov.uk/government/uploads/system/uploads/attachment_data/file/973834/About_the_IPA_2020_12.03.21.pdf. [41]

Infrastructure Victoria (2021), *Victoria's Infrastructure Strategy 2021-2051*, https://www.infrastructurevictoria.com.au/wp-content/uploads/2021/08/1.-Victorias-infrastructure-strategy-2021-2051-Vol-1.pdf. [16]

ITF (2022), *Broadening Transport Appraisal: Summary and Conclusions*, ITF Roundtable Reports, No. 188, OECD Publishing, Paris, https://doi.org/10.1787/a0e2e0a6-en. [49]

ITF (2021), *Developing Strategic Approaches to Infrastructure Planning*, ITF Research Reports, OECD Publishing, Paris, https://doi.org/10.1787/d8d6651c-en. [47]

Kim, J., J. Fallov and S. Groom (2020), *Public Investment Management Reference Guide*, Washington, DC: World Bank, https://doi.org/10.1596/978-1-4648-1529-4. [42]

Madsen, B. (2021), *The Covid-19 legacy: More Resilient Procurement Strategies?*, https://www.oecd.org/gov/public-procurement/infrastructure-and-public-procurement-webinar-series-2021.htm. [51]

Marine Information and Data Centre (n.d.), *Marine Information and Data Centre*, https://www.informatiehuismarien.nl/uk/about-us/ (accessed on 5 April 2023). [46]

Ministry of Industry and Trade (2020), *The National Energy and Climate Plan of Czechia*, https://www.mpo.cz/en/energy/strategic-and-conceptual-documents/the-national-energy-and-climate-plan-of-the-czech-republic--252018/. [31]

Ministry of Industry and Trade (2015), *State Energy Policy of Czechia*, https://www.mpo.cz/assets/en/energy/state-energy-policy/2017/11/State-Energy-Policy-_2015__EN.pdf. [32]

Ministry of Labour and Social Affairs (2019), *Responsible Public Procurement: European Practice*, https://sovz.cz/wp-content/uploads/2019/10/responsible-public-procurement-european-practice.pdf. [63]

Ministry of Labour and Social Affairs (2017), *Socially Responsible Public Procurement in Czechia: Selection of Best Practice Case Studies*, https://sovz.cz/wp-content/uploads/2017/08/sovz_case_studies_en_komplet.pdf. [62]

Ministry of Regional Development (2021), *Housing Concept of Czechia 2021+*, https://mmr.gov.cz/getmedia/30528174-7e61-421e-a058-5f39aa4f09c9/KB-2021-_komplet-web(C)_max.pdf.aspx?ext=.pdf. [29]

Ministry of Regional Development (2019), *Regional Development Strategy of Czechia 2021+*, Ministry of Regional Development, https://mmr.cz/getmedia/a9985cb6-b672-4a97-a92c-c4c68bea2925/EN-III_ma_SRR-prac_doplneni-schemat-a-map_kontrola.pdf.aspx?ext=.pdf. [10]

Ministry of Regional Development (n.d.), *Strategy Database: Portal of Strategic Documents in Czechia*, https://www.databaze-strategie.cz/cz/info (accessed on 10 July 2023). [22]

Ministry of the Environment (n.d.), *Lean public administration*, https://www.mzp.cz/cz/setrna_verejna_sprava (accessed on 5 May 2023). [64]

Ministry of Transport (2021), *Transport Policy of Czechia for the period 2021-2027, with an outlook until 2050*, https://www.mdcr.cz/getattachment/Dokumenty/Strategie/Dopravni-politika-a-MFDI/Dopravni-politika-CR-pro-obdobi-2014-2020-s-vyhled/Dopravni_Politika_CR_ENG.pdf.aspx. [30]

Ministry of Transport (2018), *Departmental Guideline for the Evaluation of Economic Effectiveness of Transport Construction Projects*, https://www.sfdi.cz/soubory/obrazky-clanky/metodiky/2017_03_departmental-methodology-full.pdf. [33]

OECD (2023), "Delivering environmentally sustainable and climate-resilient infrastructure", in *Government at a Glance 2023*, OECD Publishing, Paris, https://doi.org/10.1787/2387658e-en. [19]

OECD (2023), *OECD Public Governance Reviews: Czech Republic: Towards a More Modern and Effective Public Administration*, OECD Public Governance Reviews, OECD Publishing, Paris, https://doi.org/10.1787/41fd9e5c-en. [5]

OECD (2023), "Professionalising the public procurement workforce: A review of current initiatives and challenges", *OECD Public Governance Policy Papers*, No. 26, OECD Publishing, Paris, https://doi.org/10.1787/e2eda150-en. [50]

OECD (2023), *Public Investment in Bulgaria: Planning and Delivering Infrastructure*, OECD Public Governance Reviews, OECD Publishing, Paris, https://doi.org/10.1787/b73ef3b4-en. [13]

OECD (2023), "Stakeholder participation in infrastructure decision making", in *Government at a Glance 2023*, OECD Publishing, Paris, https://doi.org/10.1787/59c7c2b2-en. [24]

OECD (2023), "Strengthening environmental considerations in public investment in Ireland: Assessment and recommendations", *OECD Public Governance Policy Papers*, No. 35, OECD Publishing, Paris, https://doi.org/10.1787/83b97aca-en. [38]

OECD (2022), *Survey on the Governance of Infrastructure - Part I: Ensure transparent, systematic and effective stakeholder participation*. [26]

OECD (2021), *OECD Implementation Handbook for Quality Infrastructure Investment: Supporting a Sustainable Recovery from the COVID-19 Crisis*, OECD Publishing, https://www.oecd.org/finance/oecd-implementation-handbook-for-quality-infrastructure-investment.htm. [14]

OECD (2021), “Procurement strategy in major infrastructure projects: Piloting a new approach in Norway”, *OECD Public Governance Policy Papers*, No. 06, OECD Publishing, Paris, https://doi.org/10.1787/38996343-en. [53]

OECD (2020), “Infrastructure Governance Review of Argentina”, *OECD Journal on Budgeting*, https://doi.org/10.1787/f2574b7b-en. [39]

OECD (2020), *OECD Compendium of Policy Good Practices for Quality Infrastructure Investment*, OECD Publishing, http://, www.oecd.org/finance/oecd-compendium-of-policy-good-practices-forquality-infrastructure-investment.htm. [35]

OECD (2020), *Policy Actions for Affordable Housing in Latvia*, https://issuu.com/oecd.publishing/docs/latvia_housing_report_web-1. [52]

OECD (2020), *Recommendation of the Council on the Governance of Infrastructure*, https://legalinstruments.oecd.org/en/instruments/OECD-LEGAL-0460. [15]

OECD (2020), *Supporting Better Decision-Making in Transport Infrastructure in Spain : Infrastructure Governance Review*, OECD Publishing, Paris, https://doi.org/10.1787/310e365e-en. [11]

OECD (2020), *Survey on the Governance of Infrastructure*, https://qdd.oecd.org/subject.aspx?Subject=GOV_INFRA. [23]

OECD (2019), *The Path to Becoming a Data-Driven Public Sector*, OECD Digital Government Studies, OECD Publishing, Paris, https://doi.org/10.1787/059814a7-en. [43]

OECD (2017), *Getting Infrastructure Right: A framework for better governance*, OECD Publishing, https://doi.org/10.1787/9789264272453-en. [1]

OECD (2017), *Recommendation of the Council on Open Government*, https://legalinstruments.oecd.org/en/instruments/OECD-LEGAL-0438. [25]

OECD (2017), “Strategic practices for the effective use of framework agreements in Chile”, in *Public Procurement in Chile: Policy Options for Efficient and Inclusive Framework Agreements*, OECD Publishing, Paris, https://doi.org/10.1787/9789264275188-6-en. [60]

OECD (2017), *The Governance of Land Use in the Czech Republic: The Case of Prague*, OECD Regional Development Studies, OECD Publishing, Paris, https://doi.org/10.1787/9789264281936-en. [12]

OECD (2016), *The Korean Public Procurement Service: Innovating for Effectiveness*, OECD Public Governance Reviews, OECD Publishing, Paris, https://doi.org/10.1787/9789264249431-en. [58]

OECD (2014), *Manual for Framework Agreements*, https://www.oecd.org/gov/ethics/manual-framework-agreements.pdf. [57]

OECD (2012), *Recommendation of the Council on Principles for Public Governance of Public-Private Partnerships*, https://legalinstruments.oecd.org/en/instruments/OECD-LEGAL-0392. [69]

OECD (n.d.), *Ireland: National Development Plan 2021-2030*, https://infrastructure-toolkit.oecd.org/wp-content/uploads/Ireland_NDP.pdf. [27]

Office of Projects Victoria (n.d.), *Victorian Major Projects Pipeline*, http://www.opv.vic.gov.au/Pipeline (accessed on 17 April 2023). [17]

Rijkswaterstaat (n.d.), *Rijkswaterstaat Publication Platform*, https://open.rws.nl/ (accessed on 5 April 2023). [45]

Ruiz Rivadeneira, A. and P. Mcmaster (2023), "Mapping institutional arrangements for infrastructure governance in OECD countries", *OECD Working Papers on Public Governance*, No. 62, OECD Publishing, Paris, https://doi.org/10.1787/31825d0d-en. [21]

Schwartz, G. et al. (eds.) (2020), *Well Spent*, International Monetary Fund, Washington, D.C., https://doi.org/10.5089/9781513511818.071. [3]

SIGMA (2016), *Division of Contracts into Lots*, OECD Publishing, https://www.sigmaweb.org/publications/public-procurement-policy-brief-36-200117.pdf. [59]

State Fund for Transport Infrastructure (2022), *Budget of the State Fund for Transport Infrastructure for 2023 and the medium-term outlook for 2024 and 2025*, https://www.sfdi.cz/soubory/obrazky-clanky/rozpocet/2023_rozpocet_text-rozpoctu.pdf. [68]

The Housing Agency (2022), *Annual Report 2021*, https://www.housingagency.ie/sites/default/files/2023-01/The%20Housing%20Agency%20-%202021%20Annual%20Report%20English.pdf. [56]

The Housing Agency (2022), *Strategic Plan 2022-2024*, https://www.housingagency.ie/sites/default/files/2022-01/Housing%20Agency%20Strategic%20Plan%202022-2024%20online.pdf. [55]

Union of Towns and Municipalities of Czechia (2020), *Examples of Good Practice in Voluntary Associations of Municipalities*. [65]

World Bank (2021), *Infrastructure Governance Assessment Framework*, https://thedocs.worldbank.org/en/doc/96550c14d62154355b6edc367d4d7f33-0080012021/infrastructure-governance-assessment-framework-december-2020. [36]

World Bank (2020), *Infratech Value Drivers*, World Bank, https://openknowledge.worldbank.org/entities/publication/675dc4d5-56fb-535d-9c32-d6d2b17e0dd0. [48]

3 Improving subnational infrastructure investment

This chapter analyses the challenges in the Czechia infrastructure governance system at the subnational level and makes recommendations to address them. After providing an overview of the main features and challenges of subnational infrastructure in Czechia, it focuses on ways to implement a place-based approach to infrastructure planning and to build strong and fruitful partnerships across governments. It also looks at the importance of strengthening inter-municipal co-operation and increasing subnational administrative capacity to improve the quality and efficiency of infrastructure investment. Finally, the chapter examines how to increase the funding and financing capacity of Czech subnational governments to meet infrastructure investment needs.

Summary of recommendations

Given the challenges of implementing a full suite of reforms simultaneously, Czech authorities could consider sequencing concrete actions under broader recommendations. By grouping actions according to the time horizon (short term, and medium to long term) needed to implement them effectively, Czech authorities could allocate resources to reforms in a way which would provide incremental benefits. However, it should be noted that the concrete actions listed below, irrespective of their time horizon, are complementary and interconnected.

Table 3.1. Summary of recommendations and concrete actions to support their effective implementation

	Short term	Medium to long term
Subnational level recommendation 1: Implement a place-based approach to infrastructure planning among levels of government		
Concrete actions to support the implementation of recommendation 1	**1.1. Foster effective co-ordination across sectors and levels of government to enable place-based infrastructure planning.** There are several venues that Czechia can explore. Regardless of the platform, it is crucial to involve both decision-makers (e.g., ministers) and technical infrastructure planners in the dialogue. **1.2. Support regions to achieve more integrated and forward-looking infrastructure planning.** Regions play a critical role in place-based infrastructure planning, both in co-ordinating sectoral infrastructure in the regions and co-ordinating local infrastructure planning beyond administrative jurisdictions – this significant role should be further recognised in the multi-level infrastructure planning system.	**1.3. Promote high-quality joint municipal infrastructure planning, especially at the scale of functional areas (e.g., micro-regions) to maximise local investment outcomes.** Czechia could provide financial and non-financial incentives as well as targeted capacity building activities in this regard.
Subnational level recommendation 2: Establish strong and fruitful partnerships across levels of government		
Concrete actions to support the implementation of recommendation 2	**2.1. Establish an overarching co-ordination platform in which national and subnational actors could align the planning, prioritisation, and implementation of infrastructure investment projects.** A co-ordination platform needs to bring	**2.2. Develop formal contractual agreements across levels of government to align objectives for efficient and resilient infrastructure investments and make national and subnational governments real partners.** Contracts may help

	Short term	Medium to long term
	together at a minimum representatives from the Ministry of Regional Development, Ministry of Transport, Ministry of the Environment and the Ministry of Finance as well as the different association of municipalities, including representatives from Prague and the 13 regions.	Czechia identify common targets, set clear and transparent objectives, share information, and make credible engagements. 2.3. **Strengthen stakeholder engagement at all levels of government to better assess investment needs, the environmental and social sustainability** as well as the social acceptability of infrastructure projects, among other benefits.
Subnational level recommendation 3: Reinforce inter-municipal co-operation		
Concrete actions to support the implementation of recommendation 3	3.1. **Reinforce co-operation across Czech municipalities throughout the investment cycle to enhance the quality and effectiveness of infrastructure.** To address high administrative fragmentation at the local level, it is crucial to reach a relevant scale and the adequate capacities to invest in infrastructure.	3.2. **Target and encourage inter-municipal co-operation for infrastructure investments at the functional scale.** In urban and rural areas, investments are best planned when seen from the perspective of functional areas with networked villages, towns and more dispersed areas as economic relations and flows of goods and people do not stop at the administrative border.
Subnational level recommendation 4: Enhance subnational administrative capacities for quality infrastructure investment		
Concrete actions to support the implementation of recommendation 4	4.1. **Diagnose capacity gaps in all type of regions and municipalities.** In order to properly target assistance and capacity building at the subnational level, it is crucial to have a clear picture of which capacities are missing and where. 4.2. **Strengthen national and regional support and assistance to plan, prepare and implement infrastructure investments at the local level.** The national and regional levels – which often have higher capacities than small municipalities – together with the associations of municipalities, play a key role in supporting, advising and providing municipalities with specific knowledge and skills. 4.3. **Embed a cross-sectoral and multi-level perspective into capacity-building activities.** One the most important barriers for	

	Short term	Medium to long term
	quality place-based infrastructure is the siloed approach to infrastructure at all levels of government. **4.4. Provide special resources and tools for regions and municipalities to better prepare and procure infrastructure projects.** One of the major bottlenecks for quality infrastructure at the subnational levels is at the preparation phase. **4.5. Leverage the role of national and regional governments and the associations of municipalities to build capacities at the local level.** In line with the current efforts to better prepare local staff workforce, it is important to provide co-ordinated capacity building activities to create institutional capacities within municipal administrations to better plan, prepare and deliver infrastructure projects.	
Subnational level recommendation 5: Reinforce funding and financing sources for subnational infrastructure investment		
Concrete actions to support the implementation of recommendation 4	**5.1. Address funding gaps to support quality subnational infrastructure by regions and municipalities.** There are different complementary avenues for this.	**5.2. Adopt innovative financing instruments to boost subnational infrastructure investment.** Mobilising finance is essential to help subnational governments meet the high up-front costs of infrastructure investment and to spread those costs across the future beneficiaries of an investment.

Introduction

Regions and local governments play a key role in making our societies more resilient and sustainable. It is they who are confronted with, and have to manage, the health, economic, and environmental challenges that often arise locally or have an impact on local populations and communities. COVID-19 and the energy crisis, for example, have shown that much of the infrastructure affected falls under the responsibility of subnational government, including health care (hospitals, primary care health centres, etc.), social services, education (primary and secondary schools, higher education), public transport, roads, social housing, utility networks (water, waste, energy, etc.), and ICT infrastructure (OECD, 2021[1]). Across all OECD countries, subnational governments define and execute key infrastructure investments in strategic sectors such as energy, transport, water and telecommunication infrastructure, and also in access to quality health and education services (OECD, 2022[2]). In OECD countries on average, subnational governments are responsible for 57% of total public investment; in Czechia the share is 46%.

At the same time, it is now more urgent than ever to invest strategically in place-based infrastructure to bridge territorial disparities and tackle the big challenges of climate change, demographic trends, and digitalisation, among others. Megatrends and shocks create different public investment needs, challenges and opportunities across regions. This is also true for Czechia, where regional differences are stark: in 2021, the population density ranged from 66.9 inhabitants/km^2 in South Bohemia to 2 752.8 inhabitants/km^2 in the Prague region (OECD, 2022[3]). The regional GDP per capita for Prague was 3.6 times higher than in Karlovy Vary region, and twice as high as the average regional GDP per capita (OECD, 2022[4]). Disparities are also evident in infrastructure provision. Some regions are not sufficiently connected to the backbone transport infrastructure (road and rail) (e.g., the Karlovy Vary, South Bohemian and Liberec regions). Some regions are under-served by public transport, and in others there is generally poor access to public and commercial services (e.g., highspeed internet access) (Ministry of Regional Development, 2019[5]).

Investment therefore needs to be place-based and tailored to the needs and realities of different localities and regions. However, designing and implementing place-based infrastructure investment in Czechia is particularly challenging, as regions and municipalities need to deliver while navigating a complex administrative structure. As described in Chapter 1, the Czech multi-level governance system is complex, with challenges including the large number of small municipalities; the different types of municipalities with different responsibilities; the absence of mechanisms to co-ordinate investment across levels of government; and siloed approaches to investment. Other critical issues are linked to the capacities of regional and local governments to plan and deliver infrastructure. This all puts pressure on the efficiency of the public administration and the capacity of regions and municipalities to deliver quality infrastructure.

Adequate multi-level governance mechanisms that allow for place-based infrastructure will be crucial for Czechia to maximise the returns on infrastructure investment, invest in a smarter way and put resilience and environmental objectives at the core of infrastructure investment across all levels of government. Such mechanisms need to ensure proper co-ordination, both vertically within levels of government and horizontally across sectors and jurisdictions. The OECD Recommendation on Effective Public Investment Across Levels of Government – an OECD legal instrument with 40 adherents – provides guidance on all the challenges outlined above (Box 3.1).

Box 3.1. The OECD Recommendation on Effective Public Investment across Levels of Government

In 2014, the OECD Recommendation on Effective Public Investment Across Levels of Government was endorsed by the OECD Regional Development Policy Committee (RDPC) and adopted by the OECD Council. The recommendation aims to help countries assess the strengths and weaknesses of their public investment governance capacity for regional development across all levels of government. It serves as a guide to setting priorities for improving the co-ordination mechanisms and capacities of subnational governments in the management of public investment.

The recommendation sets out 12 principles grouped into 3 pillars of policy recommendations that represent 3 systematic challenges to efficiently managing public investment at both the national and subnational levels. These 12 principles cannot be seen in isolation: they offer a whole-of-government approach that addresses the roles of different levels of government in the design and implementation of a critical and shared responsibility. All the principles are complementary and there is no hierarchy among them. They are also intended to be used in conjunction with other OECD policy guidance and tools.

Figure 3.1. Effective multi-level public investment governance rests on three pillars and 12 principles

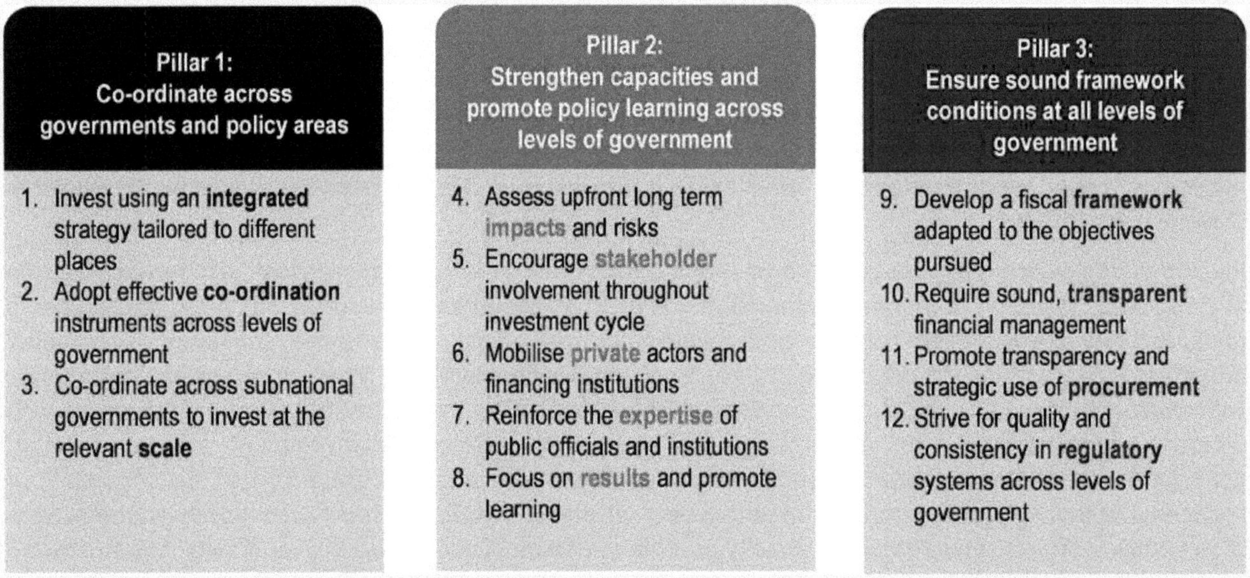

Source: OECD (2019), *Effective Public Investment across Levels of Government: Implementing the OECD Principles*, OECD, Paris, https://www.oecd.org/effective-public-investment-toolkit/OECD_Public_Investment_Implementation_Brochure_2019.pdf

Fine tuning multi-level governance and adopting a place-based approach to infrastructure is particularly urgent for making the most of EU funds for investment. Over 2014-2020, Cohesion Policy funding accounted for 40% of total public investment in Czechia. Over 2021-2027, Czechia will invest EUR 26 billion under the Cohesion Policy (for details, see Chapter 1). Nearly a quarter of these funds will be used to support integrated regional development, especially regional connectivity, urban and regional infrastructure, local education infrastructure, etc. The new Just Transition Mechanism (EUR 2 billion) will also have a strong territorial dimension, targeting the Karlovy Vary, Moravian-Silesian and Ústí regions (European Commission, 2023[6]; Ministry of Regional Development, 2023[7]; Ministry of Environment, 2023[8]). Much of the implementation of the Czech Recovery and Resilience Plan (RRP), supported by

EUR 7 billion in grants, rests in the hands of Czech regions, cities and towns. With physical infrastructure and green transition being at the core of the plan's 26 components, the main building block of the Czech RRP is investment geared towards cross-cutting policy issues, such as energy efficiency through residential and public building renovation (EUR1.4 billion); sustainable mobility through improving railway infrastructure, and promoting electric charging stations and cycle pathways (EUR 1.1 billion); as well as the circular economy through upgrading recycling infrastructure (EUR 141 million) (European Commission, n.d.[9]) (European Commission, 2021[10]). The recovery plan is a unique opportunity for regions and municipalities to adopt a place-based approach to infrastructure while investing in quality infrastructure, addressing long-term priorities for sustainability and resilience, and achieving more balanced development across the country.

This chapter begins with an overview of subnational infrastructure investment in Czechia, including an assessment of territorial inequalities and the various needs and challenges facing the Czech regions, including administrative fragmentation (section 3.2). Section 3.3 focuses on implementing a place-based approach to infrastructure planning, in particular on how to improve strategic place-based infrastructure planning across levels of government to ensure that infrastructure responds to local needs and is planned at the right scale. After providing some insights into how to improve the way in which national and subnational levels co-ordinate on infrastructure issues (section 3.4), the chapter focuses on how to strengthen inter-municipal co-operation for investment, recognising that this is one of the most prominent challenges for subnational infrastructure (section 3.5). Finally, the chapter focuses on administrative and fiscal capacities of regions and municipalities – and ways to strengthen them to ensure quality infrastructure (section 3.6 and 3.7).

3.1 An overview of subnational infrastructure investment in Czechia

Regions and municipalities play a central role in public infrastructure

Subnational governments in Czechia are key providers of economic and social infrastructure. They have broad responsibilities for economic infrastructure (transport, energy/electricity, water and sanitation, telecommunication, waste) and social infrastructure (health, aged care, education, community, social housing, social protection, and emergency services), which in many cases are shared with the national government. Regions and municipalities differ in their areas of responsibility. Municipalities are responsible for primary schools and nurseries; social services, including housing and water infrastructure; local roads and health centres and small hospitals, among others. Regions are responsible for hospitals, secondary schools and second-class roads. A detailed breakdown of the infrastructure roles and responsibilities between municipalities and regions is shown in Table 1.1 in Chapter 1. In 2021, subnational government investment, including regions and municipalities, represented 43.7% of total public investment, below the OECD average for unitary countries, which was 48% (Figure 3.2).

Figure 3.2. Subnational public investment as a percentage of total public investment, 2021

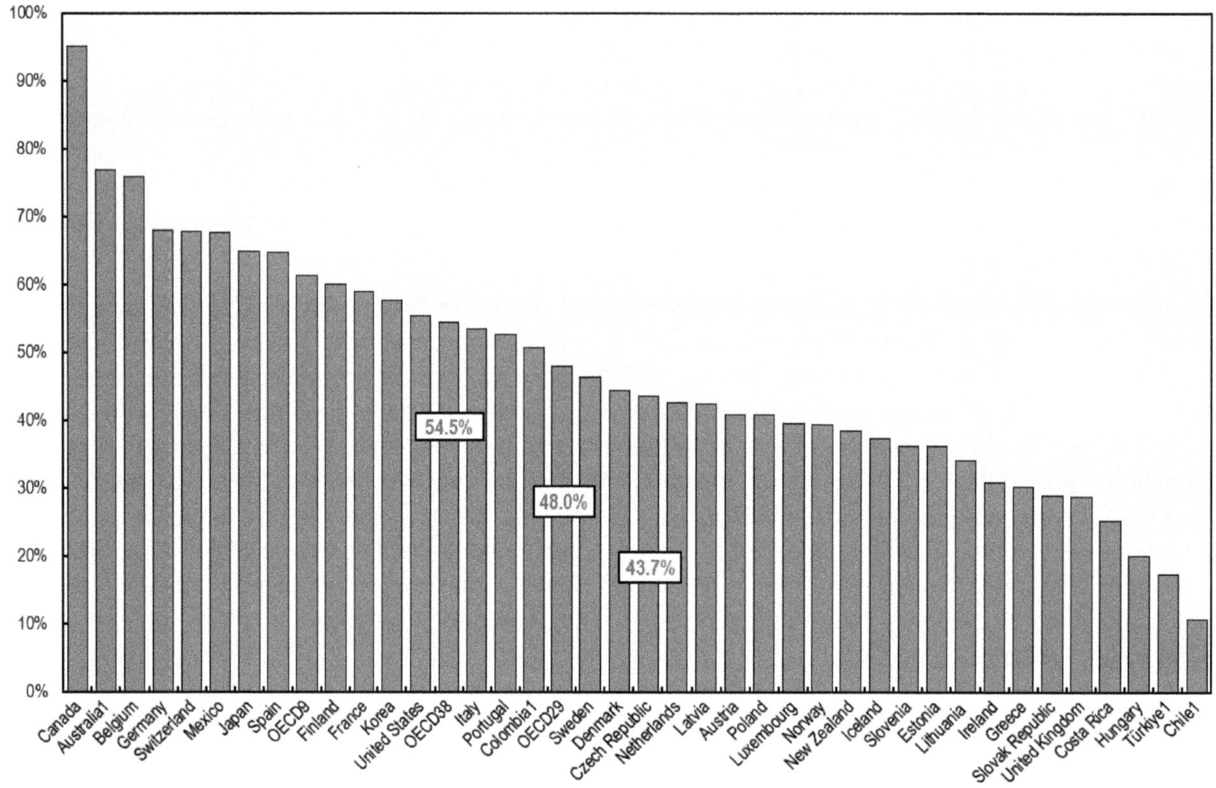

Note: OECD38: weighted average for all OECD countries; OECD29: weighted average for unitary countries ; OECD9: weighted average for federal countries [1] Data from IMF Government Finance Statistics: https://data.imf.org/.

Source: (OECD, 2023[11]), *Subnational Governments in OECD Countries: Key data.* https://www.oecd.org/regional/multi-level-governance/NUANCIER%202023-3.pdf

Capital expenditure at the regional level started to increase slightly after the de facto establishment of autonomous regions in 2000, although municipalities remain the principal investors. Between 2010 and 2020, regional capital expenditure per capita grew from CZK 2 404 to CZK 4 152 – a 72.6% increase (Figure 3.3). The same trend can be seen at the municipal level – over the last 10 years, municipal public investment has grown by 50%. The municipal level remains the primary subnational government investor, accounting for 64.3% of subnational government investment in 2020, while regions only account for 35.7%. In contrast, while the City of Prague – which has a unique dual status as both a region and a municipality – remains the most important investor in the country, public investment in the city has decreased by almost 36% over the last 10 years. It is also worth noting that municipal investment per capita in small municipalities (below 500 inhabitants) is very low, representing less than half of investment per capita in medium-sized municipalities (5 000-10 000 inhabitants). The low levels of investment in small municipalities compared to medium or large cities is largely due to a lack of skills and administrative capacity to deal with complex investment projects (OECD/UCLG, 2022[12]).

Figure 3.3. Evolution of regional and municipal capital expenditure in Czechia, 2010-2020

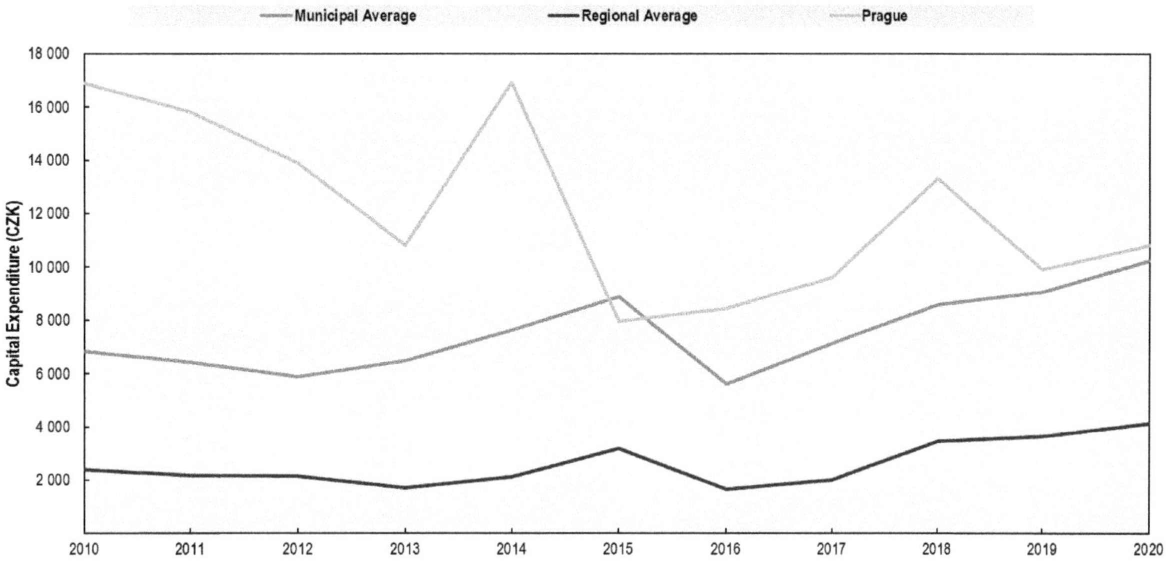

Source: Ministry of Finance Monitor data portal, https://monitor.statnipokladna.cz/; Czech statistical office.

Quality and effective infrastructure investment is needed to address important regional disparities

Czechia faces important territorial inequalities that have increased over the last 20 years. Regional income inequality, as measured by the Theil index at the small region level (TL3 level), has increased overall since 2000 (Figure 3.4). This tendency also holds true for 15 out of 27 OECD countries with available data. Regional inequality has plateaued at relatively high levels after decreasing slightly from its peak in the aftermath of the 2008 global financial crisis. Importantly, regional inequalities in Czechia have increased faster than GDP per capita growth. One of the explanatory factors behind the increasing regional inequality is regional productivity (OECD, 2023[13]).. As can be seen in (Figure 3.4), Czechia experienced an increase in the Theil index of GDP per capita over 2000-2020. Inequality reached its maximum in 2008. It means than over the last 20 years, while labour productivity has increased overall, it grew much more in high-productivity regions than in low-productivity regions. The Top 20%/Mean ratio was 0.054 higher in 2020 compared to 2000, indicating increased polarisation. The Bottom 20%/Mean ratio was 0.036 lower in the same period, indicating bottom divergence. (OECD, 2023[14]).

Figure 3.4. Trends in GDP per capital inequality indicators, TL3 OECD regions, 2000-2020

GDP per capita growth/regional inequality trajectories based on GDP per capita at the TL3 level, 2000-2020. Indexed to 2000 (2000=1)

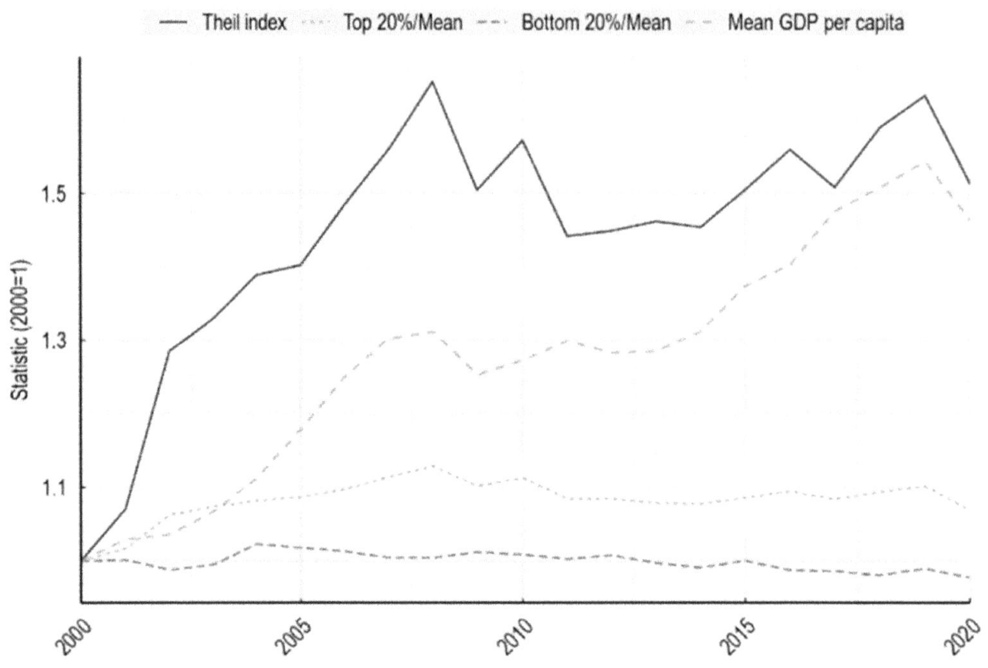

Note: Top/bottom calculated as population equivalent (top/bottom regions with at least 20% of the population). The interpretation of top/bottom 20% GDP per capita is that 20% of the population in the country holds 20% of the value. Top 20%/Mean calculated as mean GDP per capita in top 20% regions over mean TL3 GDP per capita in a given year. Bottom 20%/Mean calculated as mean TL3 GDP per capita in bottom 20% regions over mean TL3 GDP per capita in a given year. To improve data consistency, input series are aggregated when TL3 regions are part of the same FUA. To improve time series, TL3 missing values have been estimated based on the evolution at higher geographic level. The figures are normalized, with values in the year 2000 set to 1.
Source: (OECD, 2023[13]), *OECD Regional Outlook 2023: The Longstanding Geography of Inequalities*. https://doi.org/10.1787/92cd40a0-en

The capacity of regions and municipalities to invest also differs across the country. Regional public investment varies strongly – from less than CZK 2 000 per capita in the Zlín Region to almost CZK 6 400 per capita in the Hradec Králové Region. The City of Prague is an outlier, with over CZK 10 000 in capital expenditure per capita (Figure 3.5), despite having decreased. Regional investment per capita is only above the country average in four other regions: Pilsen, Vysočina, Pardubice and Hradec Králové (Figure 3.6). In practical terms this variation means that the availability, accessibility and quality of existing infrastructure – including transport, energy, education and health infrastructure – also varies across regions.

Figure 3.5. Capital expenditure varies significantly across Czech regions

Regional capital expenditure per capita, 2020

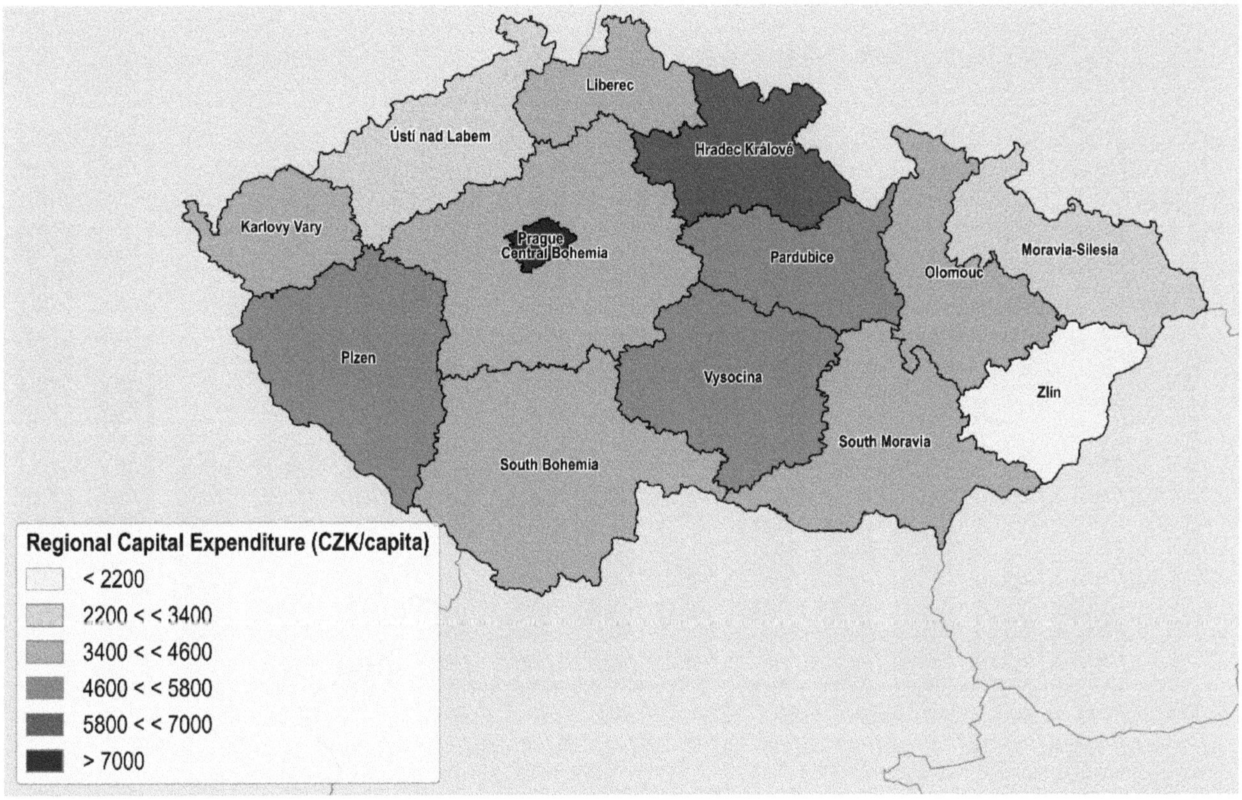

Source: Czech statistical office.

Figure 3.6. In most regions, per-capita capital expenditure is below average

Regional capital expenditure per capita, 2020

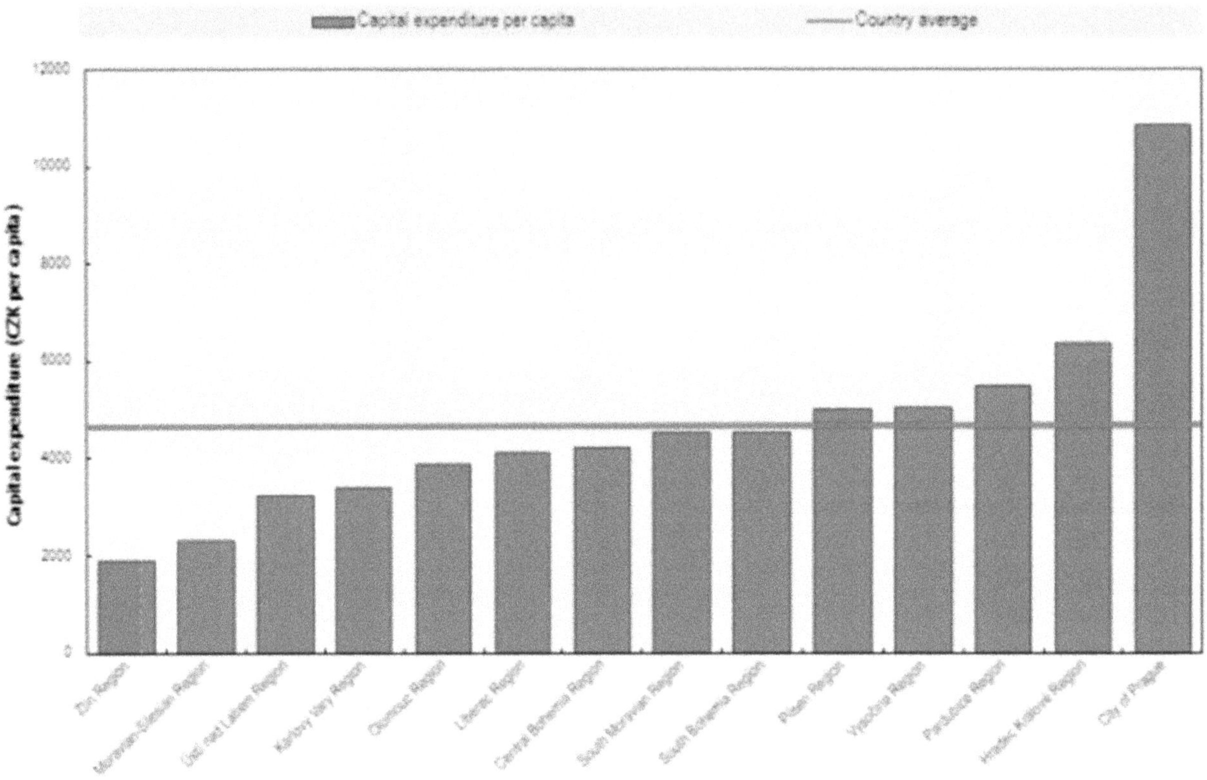

Source: Czech statistical office.

The efforts needed to address the twin transition, attain EU targets and achieve the objectives of the Czech Recovery and Resilience Plan also vary across Czechia's regions. While in the majority of large regions per capita greenhouse gas emissions are below the OECD average of 11.5 tCO2e, the Central Bohemian Region, Moravia-Silesia and Northwest all have per capita emissions that are above the OECD average (OECD, 2021[15]). The Moravia-Silesia and Northwest Bohemia regions also lag behind the rest of the country in terms of productivity, unemployment rate, educational outcomes, share of people at risk of poverty and life expectancy (European Commission, 2021[10]). These regions, along with Prague, Central Bohemian and the Northeast Region, also rely largely on coal. As highlighted by the EC, the situation in the Northwest Region is particularly challenging as living standards have diverged from the rest of the country over the last two decades (European Commission, 2021[10]).

This means that not only are there significant disparities in existing infrastructure quality, but also that Czech regions will have different transition pathways with different future infrastructure needs and investment capacity. If Czechia aims to reduce total GHG emissions by 14% by 2030 compared to 2005 (Government of Czech Republic, 2019[16]), targeted and place-based infrastructure investments by regions and municipalities will be needed. As recognised by the RRP, regional and local governments need to invest in renewable energy, local energy community networks as well as in a modern and attractive public transport network. This includes, for example, investing in active mobility infrastructure such as bike lanes and a clear strategy to further develop zero/low emission vehicles (European Commission, 2021[10]). It is thus crucial to design and implement place-based and regionally-balanced infrastructure investments that not only ensure the alignment between subnational, national and global objectives, but that also address climate, digital and resilience objectives.

Administrative fragmentation is a key challenge

Czechia is one of the most fragmented OECD countries, both at the local and regional levels. It has one of the highest number of municipalities of all OECD countries, and the smallest (Box 3.2). As we saw in Chapter 1 (Section 1.1), in 2020, the average municipal size in Czechia was 1 710 inhabitants, well below the OECD average of 10 250 and the EU average of 5 960 (Figure 1.2, Chapter 1). In 2023, 96% of municipalities had fewer than 5 000 inhabitants and 89% had fewer than 2 000 inhabitants. The average municipal area is also the lowest in the OECD: on average, Czech municipalities have an average area of 13 km^2, compared to 234 km^2 across the OECD. Regions are also small by international standards. Only 3 of the 14 regions are large enough to qualify as NUTS 2[1] regions for EU regional funding purposes (Prague, Central Bohemian and Moravian-Silesian regions). The remaining 11 regions are NUTS 3 regions which, for statistical purposes, are grouped to form 5 additional NUTS 2 regions (OECD, 2020[17]) (OECD, 2023[18]). The average size of Czech regions is 2.5 times smaller than the average size of the EU28 NUTS 2 regions in terms of inhabitants, and 4 times smaller in terms of area (Ministry of the Interior of the Czech Republic, 2018[19]).

The high number of small municipalities represents one of the greatest challenges to infrastructure investment. It undermines the capacity of Czech regions and local governments to design and implement quality and efficient infrastructure investments at the right scale. Large municipalities, particularly those that have more delegated competences and more staff, can tap into a more diverse range of professional skills. Meanwhile small municipalities face severe difficulties in attracting, hiring or retaining adequate skills for public investment. In the housing sector, for example, one of the reasons for the low level of investment in new social housing is that a large share (71%) of all municipally-owned land belongs to municipalities that have less than 1 000 inhabitants (OECD, 2021[20]). Such small municipalities might not have the capacity needed to provide affordable housing on their land. When municipalities do intend to develop social housing, they are faced with several obstacles, the most important being the shortage of funds (both from their own financial resources and from the state) (OECD, 2021[20]). In such a context, inter-municipal co-operation is largely the only option for running quality investment projects.

Box 3.2. Czechia's highly fragmented territorial organisation

Czechia's administrative fragmentation is partly due to a law passed in the early 1990s that enabled municipalities to split. In the 1990s, and contrary to many OECD countries where mergers have been the rule, municipal fragmentation in Czechia increased sharply – from 4 100 municipalities in 1990 to 6 230 in 1994. In 2000, the rising fragmentation ended with the 2000 Act on Municipalities, which introduced a requirement of having at least 1 000 inhabitants to create a new municipality and includes an option for voluntary municipal mergers. However, it did not offer any concrete incentive for municipalities to do so. To minimise the effects of municipal fragmentation, the 2000 Act on Municipalities also promotes inter-municipal co-operation through public contracts for performing certain functions, and voluntary municipal associations.

Source: (OECD, 2023[18])

3.2 Implementing a place-based approach to infrastructure planning

Czechia has substantial potential to integrate a place-based approach to infrastructure planning across all levels of government but needs to overcome its deeply rooted sectoral silos and limited territorial dimension in infrastructure planning. Czechia already has a place-based Regional Development Strategy (Ministry of Regional Development, 2019[21]), well-developed inter-governmental dialogue platforms, and a mature multi-level spatial planning system, all solid foundations for place-based infrastructure planning. Even so, infrastructure planning is still predominately led by individual sectors, without effective co-ordination or being anchored to the regional development strategy. This results in weak strategic prioritisation of infrastructure across all levels of government, and ineffective investment. Overcoming these obstacles will require long-term institutional reforms to drive changes in the country's infrastructure planning system and culture.

Another obstacle to place-based infrastructure planning is Czechia's high territorial fragmentation, as outlined above. This hinders the achievement of economies of scale and undermines capacity in local infrastructure planning, resulting in significant gaps in planning quality (e.g., a weak evidence base, lack of prioritisation, etc.). While some supra-local investment planning does take place – such as Sustainable Urban Development Strategies and Community-led Local Development (CLLD) strategies and plans – joint municipal infrastructure planning based on socio-economic linkages across jurisdictions is far from being common practice in Czechia. The question is how to consolidate existing knowledge and systems to build institutional capacity for place-based infrastructure planning.

Align place-based infrastructure planning across government levels

Czechia has three pillars that together guide infrastructure planning at all levels (Table 3.2): regional development policy, spatial development policy, and sectoral policies (transport, waste, water management, etc.). Each pillar includes several planning documents at the national, regional, supra-local and local levels. The spatial planning system is the only legally hierarchical system among levels of government – higher level documents contain binding decisions that must be considered in lower-level documents -, underpinned by a widespread network of planning offices (ESPON, 2021[22]).

Table 3.2. Three policy pillars guide multi-level infrastructure planning system in Czechia

	Regional development policy	Spatial development policy	Sectoral policies
Relevant law/regulation	Act on Regional Development Support	Act on Spatial Planning and Building Rules ("Building Act")	Sectoral planning regulations (e.g., transport, water, etc.)
National	Regional Development Strategy 21+; Rural Development Concept; Smart Cities Concept	Spatial Development Policy	Sectoral strategic documents (e.g. Transport Policy 2021-27 with an outlook to 2050; National River Basin Management Plans, etc.)
Regional	Development Strategy of the Region; Regional Action Plan	Territorial Development Principles	Sectoral strategic documents
Supra-local	Sustainable Urban Development Strategy (SUD); Community-led Local Development (CLLD) Strategy; Integrated Territorial Development Plans		
Local	Local development strategy/programme/plan	Local Territorial Plan; Regulatory Plan	Sectoral plans (mostly in cities)

Source: Authors, based on (Ministry of Regional Development, 2022[23]; Ministry of Regional Development, 2021[24]).

Within regional development policy, Czechia, like many other OECD countries, has developed or strengthened multiple mechanisms to better co-ordinate investment strategies for regional development (Figure 3.7). These include an integrated national investment strategy with a territorial dimension, permanent and ad hoc inter-ministerial committees for territorial development issues, and territorial proofing requirements, as fostered by the OECD Recommendation on Effective Public Investment across Levels of Government (OECD, 2014[25]). The Regional Development Strategy 21+, for example, serves as an integrated national strategy to guide public investment in regions and municipalities (Box 3.3). The National Standing Conference and the 13 Regional Standing Conferences are regular dialogue platforms for national and subnational actors to exchange on investment needs and priorities in the territories (Ministry of Regional Development, 2023[26]).

Figure 3.7. Czechia has several mechanisms to co-ordinate regional investment strategies

Question: "*At the national/federal level, has your country developed or strengthened any of these mechanisms as a means to better co-ordinate public investments strategies for regional development?*"

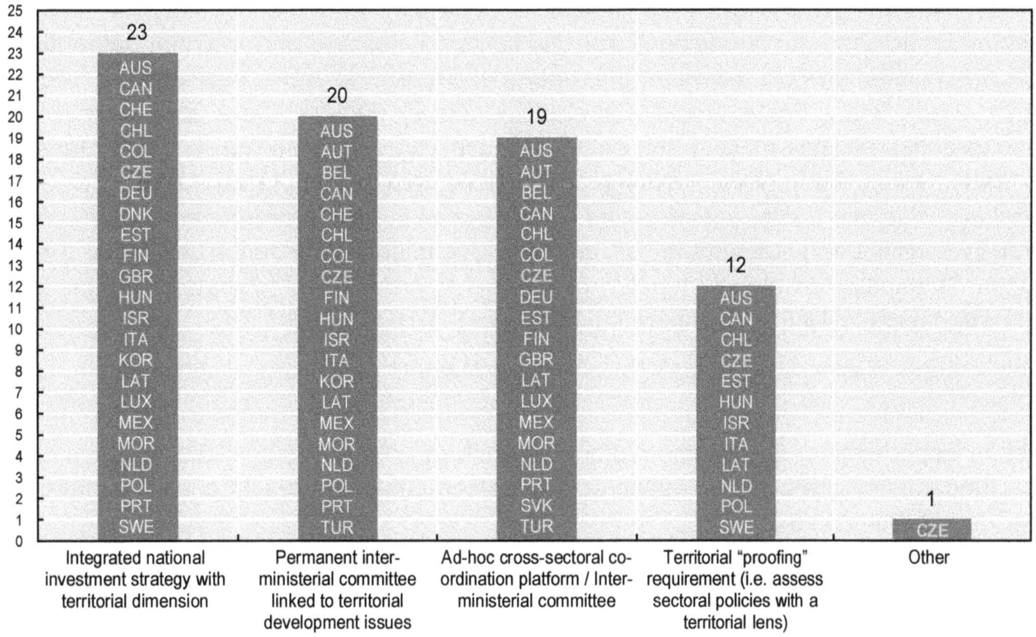

Note: Results from the 2018 monitoring survey of the OECD Recommendation on Effective Public Investment across levels of Government. N=27

Source: (OECD, 2019[27]), *Effective Multi-level Public Investment: OECD principles in action*. https://www.oecd.org/effective-public-investment-toolkit/Full_report_Effective_Public_Investment.pdf.

Box 3.3. Czechia has regional and spatial development policies

The Regional Development Strategy 21+ (RDS 21+) defines five different types of territories in Czechia based on their potential and specific needs: metropolis, agglomeration, regional centre, structurally affected region, and economically and socially vulnerable area. Through these, it seeks to offer tailored support for the development of the country's regions. For example, for metropolises it prioritises a more integrated public transport system, enhanced urban mobility, and affordable housing, while for agglomerations priorities include accessibility to education infrastructure and affordable housing, especially for vulnerable groups and those outside segregated and excluded localities. The RDS 21+ also includes a thematic focus on national subsidy schemes and other long-term instruments that will help address regional disparities. It also aims to mainstream the territorial dimension in sectoral policies.

The Spatial Development Policy of Czechia (4th edition) sets national priorities for sustainable development as a framework for regional and local spatial planning. It defines development areas, development axes and specific areas where balance between environment quality, social cohesion and the economy is distorted. It also assigns specific tasks for national and regional authorities, as well area-specific requirements to consider the territorial impact of large infrastructure projects (new motorways, roads, etc.). For example, for each motorway section, there are explicit criteria and conditions to guide decision making and planning, such as connecting with existing roads to certain cities to better serve the region, ensuring connections with bordering countries, giving priority to transport flows in certain areas, or minimising the impact on the environment, and so on. In Czechia, it is binding to consider requirements in all planning documents and during the issuing of planning permissions. The spatial development policy also has a mandate to co-ordinate any plans for changes in transport and technical infrastructure in the territory.

Source: (Ministry of Regional Development, 2019[5]; Ministry of Regional Development, 2021[24])

Despite these opportunities, the fragmentation and lack of co-ordination in the infrastructure planning system are fundamental obstacles to implementing a place-based approach to infrastructure investment. This challenge is multifaceted:

1. **Lack of systematic co-ordination across sectoral infrastructure planning.** While some sectoral infrastructure planners consult other relevant planning sectors to ensure policy synergies and alignment, this depends on the practices of individual line ministries. Overall, the Czech public administration system operates under a well rooted siloed approach (OECD, 2023[18]). There is a low awareness among infrastructure planners about the wider context of their investment decisions and the possible externalities for other fields. Most officials representing different institutions and levels tend to take a 'zero-sum game' approach to interactions with others, instead of seeking for 'win-win' solutions. This tendency to go beyond one's own institutional remit hinders active co-ordination (ESPON, 2021[22]), including the much-needed dialogue among different planners and stakeholders on the strategic objectives of infrastructure investment, the pursuit of criteria to prioritise and select them, and the seizing of potential complementarities across infrastructure sectors.
2. **Infrastructure planning that is not anchored to regional development priorities and objectives even when it has strong territorial impact.** According to stakeholders, the Ministry of Regional Development provides comments, feedback and methodological advice to sectoral infrastructure planners on the territorial dimension of sectoral infrastructure investment. There are ad hoc cases where infrastructure planners in line ministries consult with the Ministry of Regional Development, typically when considering the territorial aspect is a funding requirement (e.g., for

EU funds), but this does not happen systematically. There is no incentive, mandate, or any effective mechanism to make sure that the infrastructure planning process or prioritisation criteria properly take into account regional development policies. The RDS 21+ also identifies the lack of clear definitions or methodology to support infrastructure planners in addressing the territorial dimension in planning.

3. **A spatial planning process that does not proactively co-ordinate infrastructure investments, and is not connected with regional policy.** Spatial planning in Czechia is heavily influenced by sectoral policy, which appears to address the impact of sectoral infrastructure investment plans rather than co-ordinate them. This applies to all levels – for example, it is not unheard for sectoral departments in local authorities to simply request to transfer a decided infrastructure investment project to the Local Territorial Plan. Additionally, regional and spatial policy in Czechia operate at the national, regional and local levels in parallel, without many links or much cross-influence. For example, spatial plans are not updated in synchronisation with regional development strategies and programmes (ESPON, 2021[22]). Therefore, the strategic and development perspective of infrastructure investment (e.g., advancing regional development goals) is often not considered in spatial planning.
4. **Lack of systematic, effective and regular dialogue between national infrastructure planners and subnational governments**. The approach to consulting and engaging with subnational actors may vary across line ministries and is often passive and one-way (e.g., asking for written comments). For example, line ministries may ask for written comments from the Unions of Municipalities and Towns, Associations of Regions and other subnational government associations in infrastructure planning. They also occasionally consult subnational governments on planning matters, including through participating in the National Standing Conferences. Given the fragmented and sector-driven system, subnational government representatives indicated that they do not always have the capacity or time to provide detailed and constructive inputs to all the infrastructure planning documents. Subnational stakeholders also identified, in some cases, the lack of clarity and frequent changes in national policies, which hinders their implementation of national infrastructure investment, and/or subnational infrastructure planning.

There is a need for a dialogue platform spanning sector and subnational governments to regularly exchange infrastructure investment needs at all levels and to reach consensus on priorities and key principles in place-based infrastructure planning. There are several venues that Czechia could explore. First, Czechia has been planning to develop a Regional Policy Committee for inter-ministerial co-ordination. This committee has the potential to serve as a platform for ensuring synergies across sectors in infrastructure planning and prioritising infrastructure investment in order to advance regional development goals. Second, as highlighted in Chapter 2, Czechia could make greater use of the Council on Public Investment. The council's agenda and mandate could include a focus on strengthening the place-based approach to infrastructure planning. Third, the National and Regional Standing Conferences could be a venue for the Ministry of Regional Development to co-ordinate periodically with line ministries, regions and municipalities through dedicated discussions on strategic infrastructure planning. Inter-ministerial co-ordination models developed in Sweden and Italy could also offer inspiration to Czechia (Box 3.4). The Italian example in particular offers concrete measures for building inter-ministerial partnerships and engaging effectively with subnational governments.

Box 3.4. Examples of cross-sectoral fora for co-ordinating place-based investment

Sweden's Forum for Sustainable Regional Development

In Sweden, it is the job of regional development policymakers to convince other ministries that they should put on their "territorial lenses" when planning and designing sector policies. The Forum for Sustainable Regional Development 2022-2030 is one important co-ordination platform. It is positioned as part of the implementation of the National Strategy for Sustainable Regional Development throughout Sweden 2021-2030. The forum is chaired by the Secretary of State for Regional Development. It is divided into two groups: one promotes dialogue between national and regional politicians, and the other fosters dialogue between national and regional civil servants (at director level). Sweden has also created policy labs; for example, to explore concrete policy approaches to rural development. In addition, Sweden relies on involving state agencies – including public servants/operational staff and decision makers – in regional matters. This is because these agencies support the implementation of regional development policy by different sectors while taking into account regional specificities that influence the achievement of sectoral aims.

Italy's inter-ministerial committee to co-ordinate infrastructure in deprived areas

Italy has 20 regions and 7 904 municipalities, and an average municipal size of 7 535 inhabitants. Over half of municipalities are located in "inner areas". These areas far from large and medium-sized urban centres have experienced demographic decline and land abandonment, their essential infrastructure and services – education, health, and mobility – are relatively low quality and opportunities for economic activities and jobs are limited. To counteract marginalisation and demographic decline within these inner areas and unlock their development potential, Italy developed the National Strategy for Inner Areas for the 2014-20 programming period. Within the framework of this strategy, the national government defined a set of integrated projects and their expected outcomes through an inter-ministerial committee created to align objectives, adapt sectoral policies to territorial specific needs and match different sources of financing.

Partnership among various line ministries is key to the design and implementation of this place-based strategy. Its implementation is financed by allocations from multiple operational programmes, as well as national funds and other public/private funds. An ad hoc Technical Committee was created to govern the strategy, co-ordinated by the Cohesion Policy Department at the Presidency of the Council of Ministers and consisting of representatives from the ministries of education, health, agriculture, transport, etc. The Technical Committee, together with subnational government representatives (regions and autonomous provinces), was responsible for selecting inner areas to be funded under the strategy. Seventy-two inner areas were selected, covering over 1 000 municipalities. The main criteria for selection included their distance from infrastructure and services, demographic trends, as well as local authorities' capacity to implement projects. There were two selections phases:

1. Desk research, which assessed the various proposals submitted by the reference regions (quantitative assessment). The assessment included demography, availability and accessibility to various infrastructure and services (e.g., digital, health, schools, among others).
2. Field missions, which were essentially focus group discussions for each submitted inner area (qualitative assessment). They were organised by the Technical Committee in collaboration with regional and local territories. These focus groups followed a standard methodology covering four sessions – local development, healthcare, education, and transport. Each session typically included one expert from the relevant ministry, as well as regional and local

actors such as education and health facility managers, infrastructure users, businesses, local associations, etc.

The selected inner areas then prepare their individual investment strategies, which will be submitted to the Department of Cohesion Policy for approval. Once approved, a Framework Programme Agreement will be signed by the relevant national, regional and local authorities to secure the implementation of the inner area strategy. The agreement includes detailed financial commitments from different parties, as well as objectives and expected outcomes, etc.

Source: (OECD/UCLG, 2022[28])

Support regions to adopt more strategic and forward-looking infrastructure planning

Infrastructure planning in Czechia tends to focus on individual investments rather than be driven by a strategic and long-term vision, which increases its vulnerability. During the OECD interviews for this report, stakeholders highlighted two weaknesses of infrastructure planning at both national and subnational level:

1. Strategic plans are not used effectively to prioritise and select infrastructure investment projects, or to guide design and implementation. Instead, they are used to draw on funds for investment projects.
4. Infrastructure planning is not forward-looking or driven by any long-term vision. For example, infrastructure planners only start to think about embedding resilience measures into infrastructure investments when there are floods or other climate-related crises.

This piecemeal approach and lack of resilience planning often increases costs, including recovering the costs and renovating or upgrading existing infrastructure; these could have been avoided if a forward-looking perspective had been incorporated into infrastructure planning. Czechia has already seen a notable increase in the number of days of heavy rainfall, while droughts have also become more frequent and longer in duration (International Energy Agency, 2022[29]). For example, the Southwest region of the country has a relatively high share of population exposed to floods (OECD, 2022[30]). Building resilience into infrastructure requires a more strategic and stronger territorial dimension as well as technical expertise in projection and foresight. Equally critical is understanding the territorial dimension and engaging regional and local stakeholders in infrastructure planning to gain buy-in to the vision and the need to build more resilient and future-proof infrastructure.

Czech regions have relatively well-developed systems, and experience, in strategic planning, including for infrastructure investment (e.g., education, regional transport, etc.). The 14 regions are responsible for creating the development strategies (or programmes) for their regions and ensuring implementation. These strategies are expected to identify the regions' development objectives and priorities and co-ordinate sectoral policies and investment. Regions are also responsible for defining the Territorial Development Principles which regulate and co-ordinate infrastructure of regional importance and guide local land-use and spatial planning. Regions also develop sectoral strategies (Table 3.2). In particular, as an instrument to implement the RDS 21+, Regional Standing Conferences develop and approve Regional Action Plans (RAPs). The aim of RAPs is to enhance the integrated and efficient use of EU funds, and they cover topics such as regional transport, secondary education, health care and social services infrastructure, among others. They support the allocation of Integrated Regional Operational Programmes funds at the regional level based on assessment of regional needs (e.g., the total length of Class II roads in the region, numbers of students at secondary schools, etc.)

However, sectoral fragmentation in infrastructure planning trickles down to the regional level, hindering the effectiveness of integrated and long-term regional infrastructure planning. On average, Czech regions have to cope with 25 strategic documents, excluding implementation plans and supporting documents (Ministry of Regional Development, 2022[23]). The extent to which these strategies guide and influence infrastructure investment in the region vary. For example, development plans for water supply and sewage, floods, roads and connectivity, and transport services are of significant importance for infrastructure. Yet these sectoral infrastructure plans have different timelines, are updated separately, and there is no mechanism to co-ordinate across sectors in order to capture investment synergies. Although each region has a regional development strategy and the Territorial Development Principles which serve as the umbrella framework, it is not yet common practice to use them to reconcile and co-ordinate sectoral interest or prioritise infrastructure investment for the region. In addition, the 14 regional development strategies often have a time horizon of three to seven years. Only two regions have a strategy in place with a horizon of more than ten years (and one of them is from 2009-2020, which has not been updated) (Ministry of Regional Development, 2022[23]). Consequently, the regional development strategic documents appear to accommodate and react to sectoral infrastructure investments, rather than defining the vision and guiding infrastructure decisions.

Stakeholders also noted that in some cases the lack of clarity and frequent change of national polices and guidance create difficulties for effective and sustainable regional infrastructure planning. The information provided by line ministries to regions is not always clear and sometimes open to interpretation. In some cases, the high staff turnover in line ministries leads to inconsistency in policy messages. Regions are often required to adapt to the changes without sufficient discussion or preparation. Political changes at both the national and regional level also introduce instability into infrastructure investment. Strategic planning is rarely used to guide and prioritise infrastructure investment; instead infrastructure programmes and projects driven by political priorities and agenda prevail.

Local infrastructure strategies are used as a pipeline to draw on funding, but are not always realistic. Some stakeholders stated that strategic infrastructure planning is not yet valued in many local public administrations in Czechia. Strategic documents are prepared as an inventory of pipeline projects and as a reference to support funding applications. While this is logical, local infrastructure planning is unlikely to be based on robust need assessment or stakeholder inputs. For example, some local development strategies include initiatives such as fairs and parks, which may be too ambitious considering the localities' assets, population, or resources. Others emphasise fashionable industries (e.g., cycling tourism, high-tech fields, etc.), without reflecting on the background, needs or assets of the given place. In some other cases, strategies are linked to the election cycle and serve as short-term political programmes. Strategic planning is viewed as a formal "tick-the-box" exercise rather than a meaningful process to better pursue and advance local development objectives. Another outstanding challenge is stakeholder engagement in infrastructure investment prioritisation. Active local participation and leadership are needed to secure ownership of strategies and their smooth implementation.

Along with increasing co-operation, there is a need for continuous capacity building on strategic infrastructure planning for local authorities. The Ministry of Regional Development has been providing substantial methodological support to municipalities in planning. There are several options that Czechia could consider in building local infrastructure planning capacity in a more targeted and effective fashion:

- Strengthen the focus on organisational arrangements to support more effective stakeholder engagement in local infrastructure planning. Given that strategic capacity is context-based and evolves over time, institutionalisation is particularly important for new organisational arrangements like networking platforms, joint working groups, new bodies created for strategy implementation, etc. The Centre for Advisory Support targeting Areas of Strategic Intervention could be one example, as their advisory support has a specific focus on partnerships and engagement (Box 3.16).
- Promote peer learning and knowledge sharing – not only among municipalities, but also targeting LAGs or micro-regions. For small municipalities in particular, there is potential for the national government to support train-the-trainer programmes. Local consulting companies, universities, and other stakeholders that work closely with municipalities in infrastructure planning could be engaged

in these networks of knowledge sharing. The "Small Towns in Germany" could be an inspiration, mobilising several formats and activities to promote exchange (Box 3.16).

- Deliver capacity building programmes that are better targeted to different types of territories and municipalities. The high number and diversity of Czech municipalities mean there is no one-size-fits-all solution to building local infrastructure planning capacity. Instead of providing templates and standardised training, the government could consider carrying out surveys and focus group consultations with representatives of municipalities and micro-regions/LAGs to identify their capacity needs in infrastructure planning specifically, and use the results to design capacity building programmes that address the most common challenges. An OECD project with the Bulgarian and Greek national Manging Authorities to build beneficiary capacity could be an example to follow. In Bulgaria, an online survey was conducted to understand the main capacity gaps of beneficiaries and their preferred forms of support from the national level, with a special focus on the planning and use of ITIs. The survey received over 280 responses and resulted in an action plan for beneficiary support. In Greece, a similar survey was carried out to help identify the topics and modules that were most pertinent for beneficiary needs so as to design a series of knowledge-sharing workshops. The survey received over 310 responses from beneficiaries and the first knowledge-sharing workshop attracted nearly 100 participants.
- Encourage cooperation between regions would also lead to more territorially-oriented infrastructure development. Planning infrastructure across regions would help better pursuing place-based infrastructure investment while also making sure that big infrastructure projects reach relevant scale, specially when it comes to transport and connectivity. There are several countries that are moving in this direction. Chile, for example, has defined "macro-regions" that join four or five administrative regions to plan infrastructure for a territory with similar characteristics, acknowledging that the potential of infrastructure investment can be more fully exploited if territorial synergies exist. These macro regions might share a common identity, productive structures, and geographic and development challenges.

Czechia would benefit from more direct and regular dialogue between regions and national infrastructure planners – not only to understand needs, but also to reach consensus on infrastructure prioritisation and provide clearer guidance and direction to regions on planning and prioritising investment. While regions should be responsible for their own development goals and priorities, a clear understanding of national policies and frameworks can help them generate plans that align with national agendas. There are many ways to construct and facilitate this dialogue. For example, the Ministry of Regional Development can facilitate thematic meetings between regions and national infrastructure planners from line ministries to discuss regional infrastructure priorities. Ireland offers an advanced example of a well-developed multi-level infrastructure planning system under the National Planning Framework which supports cross-sectoral regional planning (Box 3.5). Regional roundtables like those in the United Kingdom offer another way of engaging with regions, which might be closer to Czechia's institutional context (e.g., Regional Standing Conference). The key strength of the UK's initiative is its focus on long-term strategic planning and strengthening regional and local infrastructure planning (Box 3.5). In the long term, such dialogue could potentially lead to a set of principles co-designed by national infrastructure planners and subnational governments to help plan and prioritise infrastructure investment. This is the case for the Infrastructure Decision-Making Principles in Australia, which are used for both national and subnational governments.

Box 3.5. Enable strategic regional planning

Ireland's National Development Plan 2021-2030 (NDP) and National Planning Framework 2040 together serve as the investment plan for the country. They provide the structure for the Regional Spatial and Economic Strategies (RSES) prepared by the regional assemblies. These RSESs inform decisions related to regional public infrastructure investment aligned with the NDP, and guide local city and county planning, economic policy and investment. The RSESs take a cross-sector approach that combines a spatial strategy, an economic strategy and a climate strategy. Each strategy is prepared within a regional co-ordination framework to gather input from local authorities and other relevant stakeholders, including the Department of Housing, Planning and Local Government, the Department of Public Expenditure National Development Plan Delivery and Reform

In the **United Kingdom**, the National Infrastructure Commission is responsible for long-term strategic infrastructure planning through the 30-year National Infrastructure Assessment. Fact-finding tours to regions ("regional roundtables") are carried out to collect evidence and insights for the latest interim Assessment report. The commission discusses various investment issues with regional and local stakeholders, with a focus on fostering resilience through investment in some regions, including enhancing flood mitigation measures and preparing for future weather extremes. The importance of adapting regional and local strategies to a changing context, such as the COVID-19 pandemic, is also highlighted. The commission recently launched a partnership programme for cities and city regions across the country to share knowledge and expertise and to help local leaders develop long-term strategies that link transport, housing, and job opportunities.

Source: (OECD, 2020[31]). (National Infrastructure Commission, 2022[32]; 2022[33]).

Among local authorities, especially small ones, building strategic capacity for infrastructure planning is a considerable challenge given their already stretched human resources and financial resource constraints. In OECD and EU countries, worrying gaps in local strategic capacity include a lack of focus in identifying development needs and problems, insufficient justification of objectives and their intervention logic and the need for better thematic integration. This need for better focus and thematic integration applies particularly to countries such as Czechia, which have less experience in integrated approaches, high Cohesion Policy budgets, or where the introduction of territorial tools has prompted policy experimentation.

With support, regions could play a more active role in co-ordinating local infrastructure planning, in particular to capture socio-economic linkages within functional areas. The role of regions in co-ordinating local infrastructure planning is currently very limited. Within spatial planning for example, even with the legally hierarchical system, regions can only intervene in local planning when it comes to infrastructure of regional importance. Territorial Development Principles must not infringe upon the planning powers of self-governed municipalities. This condition limits the regions' influence over, for example, cross-municipal co-ordination, especially for bigger infrastructure projects or projects that need to target populations across multiple municipalities (ESPON, 2021[22]). Additionally, Territorial Development Principles and regional infrastructure planning overall do not typically look at functional areas and are often not sufficient to support economic, social or environment links across municipalities, especially between urban centres and surrounding municipalities.

Improve data for more strategic infrastructure planning

Abundant territorial data could be better used to support regional infrastructure planning and to co-ordinate local planning. According to a recent study, spatial planning authorities collect and regularly update data on territory, but the data models vary among regions. Other public authorities also collect geographical data on, for example, the environment, health, and transport services. Data are thus often fragmented, incompatible and sometimes unshared, in particular with spatial planners (ESPON, 2021[22]). In addition, stakeholders indicate that national planning authorities usually only collect data for municipalities with extended power, yet regions are well positioned to collect and analyse more granular and local-level data. More importantly, there is a need to strengthen regions' capacity in using integrated data to forecast infrastructure needs. Such information can not only be used to reconcile sectoral interests and to prioritise infrastructure in the region, but also to showcase the socio-economic linkages across local administrative units within the region. The Milano-Bologna "regional imaginary" project could provide food for thought for Czechia (Box 3.6). The national government could consider creating a task force to support regions in enhancing infrastructure planning by developing integrated datasets and providing technical support, mobilising existing resources and platforms such as the regional information services.[2]

Stakeholders identified local-level data gaps as one of the barriers to high-quality local infrastructure planning and prioritisation. Indicators and data are critical for municipalities to understand local needs and development trends, set objectives and prioritise, and select and monitor infrastructure investment. However, many municipalities, especially the small ones, do not have the capacity and expertise to identify the indicators, or collect and analyse the data needed to set objectives and priorities for infrastructure planning. Higher levels of government (national and/or regional) need to address these local data gaps. This can be achieved by developing municipal level data, providing manuals and catalogues on the various databases and sources, as well as offering training to local planners in using data for infrastructure planning.

Box 3.6. A metropolitan-regional "imaginary" to support infrastructure planning in the Milano-Bologna urban region

Italy's Milano-Bologna urban region, as a functional area, has a relatively complex territory composition: it encompasses the two metropolitan cities of Milan and Bologna, as well as the provinces of Piacenza and Pavia. There is no common governance framework that is sufficient to co-ordinate infrastructure investment to tackle the scope of the various socio-economic challenges within this urban region. A common narrative in strategic planning for infrastructure and other investments is also lacking.

ESPON, an EU funded programme that delivers quality expertise to public authorities responsible for designing territorial policies, carried out in 2002-2021 a project to support this urban region to develop a common narrative, or "imaginary". This included an overview and mapping of all existing co-operation initiatives and functional complementarities within the urban region. A case study on selected infrastructure (e.g., connectivity) was carried out, providing an overview of the main challenges and opportunities. Based on this, a step-by-step strategy to implement the relevant spatial integration scenario was produced, following the priorities identified and including the use of relevant tools. A visual platform was generated that maps "needs-based spatial imaginaries". The map compiles data such as population density, numbers of households served by high-speed internet connection, level of peripherality, housing dispersion, number of shares in public utilities per municipality, among others. This project visualises the socio-economic linkages, and most importantly, the investment needs within the urban region across municipal jurisdictions.

Source: (ESPON, 2021[34]; ESPON, 2021[35])

Summary of key recommendations

Given the challenges of implementing a full suite of reforms, Czech authorities could consider sequencing the recommendations made above. By grouping recommendations according to the time horizon needed to implement them effectively (short term, and medium to long term), Czech authorities could allocate resources to reforms in a way which would provide incremental benefits. A potential sequencing is included below.

Short-term reforms

1. **Foster effective co-ordination across sectors and among different levels of government to enable place-based infrastructure planning.** There are several possible co-ordination venues that Czechia can explore, as indicated below. Regardless of the platform, it is crucial to involve both decision makers (e.g., ministers) and technical infrastructure planners in the dialogue.

- Operationalise the Regional Policy Committee proposed by the Ministry of Regional Development, with a focus on ensuring synergies across sectors in infrastructure planning and prioritising infrastructure investment to advance regional development goals.
- Explore further the use of the Council on Public Investment to strengthen the place-based approach to infrastructure planning.
- Engage periodically with infrastructure planners in line ministries to co-ordinate with regions and municipalities through the National and Regional Standing Conferences.

2. **Support regions to achieve more strategic and forward-looking infrastructure planning.** Regions play a critical role in place-based infrastructure planning, both in co-ordinating sectoral infrastructure in the regions and co-ordinating local infrastructure planning beyond administrative jurisdictions – this significant role should be further recognised in the multi-level infrastructure planning system. The national government can also provide technical support to fully materialise the potential of regions in infrastructure planning.

- Launch a series of thematic meetings or workshops involving regions and infrastructure planners in line ministries to discuss regional infrastructure priorities. The Ministry of Regional Development could facilitate the discussion between regional representatives and national infrastructure planners. Discussions could be based on the framework provided in RDS 21+ (the five types of territories and their infrastructure needs and priorities in each region) and the Spatial Development Policy (concrete measures in infrastructure planning to address the needs and issues in specific areas).
- Develop a common set of principles or a framework to help both national and subnational governments to plan and prioritise infrastructure investment. These should be co-designed by infrastructure planners at all levels and supported by regular regional-national dialogue.
- Create a task force to help regions build an integrated database of infrastructure needs, especially to capture infrastructure needs that cross local administrative units. The Ministry of Regional Development has various economic, social, environmental data structured around administrative units (regions, districts, municipalities) across the country. Building on this, Czechia could consider convening a task force made up of the Ministry of Regional Development, Czech Statistical Office, regional representatives, academia, line ministries (as advisors or on an ad hoc basis), etc. to help regions build similar database to capture, visualise, and analyse infrastructure needs in their region, especially highlighting the linkages/common needs beyond administrative jurisdictions.

Medium to long-term reforms

1. **Promote high-quality joint municipal infrastructure planning, especially at the scale of functional areas (e.g., micro-regions) to maximise local investment outcomes.** Czechia could provide financial and non-financial incentives as well as targeted capacity building activities to support this.

- Provide financial and non-financial incentives to encourage municipalities within a functional area to jointly plan infrastructure investments. For example, the national government could make joint municipal infrastructure planning based on functional areas a condition to unlock additional funding in some national funding schemes, or as one of the criteria in project selection/prioritisation for national funding.

- Map and identify data gaps at the local and micro-regional level and enhance the availability of infrastructure-related data for joint planning. This action could be undertaken in tandem with the action on creating an integrated database on infrastructure needs for regions.
- Start a pilot action to provide hands-on support to a group of municipalities to develop an infrastructure investment strategy, with a special focus on fostering data-sharing, agreement and partnership-building between large urban cities and small municipalities in the process (for example, agglomerations that plan to use ITIs). The lessons learned from the pilot should be then disseminated to other municipalities.
- Develop a continuous information campaign and capacity-building programmes to support municipalities to carry out joint infrastructure planning. These can include workshops and seminars that involve experts and local authorities from other countries to share experiences.
- Explore the possibility of creating an institutional structure at the functional area level (for example, micro-region councils or committees comprising local authority representatives and other non-public local stakeholders) responsible for infrastructure planning, in order to move away from standalone local plans for each municipality.

3.3 Establishing strong, fruitful partnerships across government

Aligning and co-ordinating actions across levels of government is essential for quality and inclusive public infrastructure investment. In all countries, not just Czechia, national and subnational governments share responsibilities on infrastructure investment. This means that co-ordination is essential to align investment objectives, address local needs and achieve long-term policy objectives. Aligned policy objectives favour investments that address the multi-dimensional challenges of climate change, urbanisation, and demographic pressures, among others. Co-ordination is also necessary to identify investment opportunities and bottlenecks, minimise the risk of investments working at cross-purposes, ensure adequate resources and capacity to undertake investments, and create trust among actors at different levels of government. As highlighted by the OECD Recommendation on Effective Public Investment Across Levels of Government (Box 3.1), the impact of public investment depends to a significant extent on how governments manage this shared competency across levels of government (OECD, 2021[1]).

At the same time, co-ordinated action when setting priorities and implementing investments is essential to harness the comparative advantages of both national and subnational governments. Subnational authorities tend to have an advantage in determining local needs, identifying which and where actions work best, and their greater accountability may contribute to a more efficient management of the investment process (OECD, 2022[36]). National governments, arguably, are better placed to take into account economy-wide spillovers and returns to scale. They also tend to have adequate technical capabilities for accurate cost benefit analysis, which are often missing at the local level (OECD, 2022[36]).

Build on important steps to improve co-ordination across levels of government

Co-ordinating investment priorities across levels of government is particularly challenging in Czechia, due to the absence of a legal or institutional framework and the high degree of territorial fragmentation. The COVID-19 pandemic underlined the difficulties that the country faces when it comes to co-ordination between national and subnational policymakers. A study of local government strategies during the COVID-19 crisis, for example, revealed that a complicated and bureaucratic administrative setting did not allow key decision makers at the national and local levels to quickly share information and take informed decisions to devise the optimal response in a short period of time (Plaček, Špaček and Ochrana, 2020[37]). When it comes to specific investment projects or service delivery, there is no legal framework or dedicated mechanism for different levels of government to co-ordinate or co-operate (OECD, 2023[18]). In some cases

– especially for EU-funded investments – all levels of government co-ordinate investment projects when it is required to obtain funding. At the same time, it is extremely difficult to effectively co-ordinate the more than 6 000 municipalities that are responsible for infrastructure investment. An institutional setting that facilitates dialogue between national, regional and local representatives is thus of outmost importance.

Czechia has gradually strengthened co-ordination between national and subnational levels for a range of purposes through various mechanisms or initiatives that co-ordinate priorities among these levels:

- The national and regional standing conferences gather subnational stakeholders to prepare action plans that form the basis of the calls for tender for EU financed investment. Regional standing conferences generally discuss the substance of calls for EU funding programmes, aligning their timetables and communicating regional proposals for investment to the national level through the National Standing Conference. The regional standing conferences also prepare documents for managing authorities upon request, co-ordinate activities within their territory and prepare the annual report on the implementation of the regional action plan. There are also various working groups under the conferences for specific subjects. Various stakeholders highlight that since their creation, these conferences have been successful in co-ordinating EU-funded investment.
- The Ministry of Regional Development has also been active in ensuring proper co-ordination. For example, it actively collected inputs from and co-ordinates with regions for the design and implementation of the Regional Development Strategy 21+. While this process has been effective in ensuring that national policies reflect the development needs of regions and municipalities, it is not designed to co-ordinate infrastructure investment.
- The planned Government Committee on Regional Policy is another initiative that could further strengthen co-operation between the national and subnational levels. As specified in more detail below, for this committee to accomplish its objectives, investment policy should be at the core of its mandate.

However, there is still much room to improve how national and subnational governments work together towards the same objectives. Other than the mechanisms mentioned above, most initiatives or platforms in Czechia are either siloed or focus only partially on investment projects. And while the standing conferences offer potential for co-ordinating investments financed through EU funding programmes, their focus is not on co-ordinating overall investment priorities across all sectors (OECD, 2023[18]). For infrastructure investment sometimes it is the regulatory process itself that requires some sort of co-ordination to happen. For example, the construction of a regional-level road requires each municipal government to issue a permit for the section located in their municipality.

To address these issues, OECD countries have resorted to a range of tools to strengthen the coherence of infrastructure investment among levels of government (Box 3.7). These include co-financing arrangements, contracts, formal consultation processes, national agencies or representatives working with subnational areas, and regular inter-governmental dialogue. A 2018 OECD survey shows that the vast majority of countries surveyed (24 out of 27 countries) have at least one of these mechanisms in place to co-ordinate across levels of government, especially co-financing arrangements and/or regional development strategies/programmes (OECD, 2019[123]). If well-designed, by limiting the potential for excessive procedures and red tape, these tools can help to better clarify responsibilities across levels of government, and thereby facilitate the effective implementation of investment (OECD, 2021[1])

Box 3.7. Mechanisms to ensure inter-governmental co-ordination in OECD countries

In the **Netherlands,** the Multi-Year Plan for Infrastructure, Spatial Planning and Transport (MIRT) is an investment programme set up by the Ministry of Infrastructure and Water Management, with the aim of improving investment coherence for several areas: spatial planning, economic development, mobility, and liveability. The MIRT is organised into "regional agendas" where co-operation among national, provincial, and municipal governments and third-sector actors can take place. Any Dutch Ministry and subnational public entities can participate in this programme. Each submitted project will pass through an MIRT Consultation Committee guided by those regional agendas and be finalised in a collective agreement.

In 2019, **Korea** introduced the balanced national development project, which includes a Regional Development Investment Agreement (RDIA) to enhance co-ordination and co-operation across levels of government and promote large-scale projects in the regions. These agreements help local governments – including municipalities and metropolitan authorities – establish multi-year regional development plans with corresponding financial support. RDIAs are based on four principles:

1. The "principle of co-operation" stipulates that all parties maintain a co-operative relationship.
5. The "principle of autonomy" guarantees local governments maximum autonomy to choose projects.
6. The "principle of strategy" ensures all parties agree that the project is strategic.
7. The "principle of specificity" means that the size, cost, duration, and method of financing are all specified.

These projects are jointly promoted and funded by all levels of government for specific regions. The ratio of co-funding by local governments varies depending on their financial situation. Additionally, the Balanced Committee – which includes representatives from ministries, the consultation body of the Local Autonomy Act, and a central administrative agency — and the Ministry of Land, Infrastructure and Transport may operate a support team if requested by the relevant ministries and local governments. Research on institutional improvement may also be provided.

Source: (OECD, 2022[38])

Mobilise a range of tools for collaboration and co-operation

The recent OECD Public Governance Review of Czechia highlighted the lack of an overarching cross-sectoral and multi-level platform to facilitate and institutionalise dialogue among levels of governments (OECD, 2023[18]). Such a platform would allow national and subnational actors to align the planning, prioritisation, and implementation of infrastructure investment projects. There are several options for Czechia to either create or reactivate a body to oversee and co-ordinate infrastructure investment across the country, whilst ensuring it contributes to regional development priorities. In all cases, a co-ordination platform needs to bring together, at a minimum, representatives from the Ministry of Regional Development, Ministry of Transport, Ministry of the Environment and the Ministry of Finance, as well as the different association of municipalities, including representatives from Prague and the 13 regions (see Chapter 2).

Since their establishment, the OECD advised expanding the role and scope of the national and regional standing conferences for EU-funded projects to all significant investment projects, cutting across ministries and levels of government (OECD, 2016[39]). Czechia could leverage the experience of the conference members to make sure infrastructure investments are co-ordinated among ministries and levels of government at both national and regional levels. In particular, it would be important to give a prominent role to the regional standing conferences – through a dedicated working group in each of the conferences – to further discuss and decide on infrastructure investments within their territory as they have easier and more direct interaction with municipalities. If this alternative is pursued, it will be crucial to clearly define the regional conferences' role, responsibilities and decision-making capacity so they can contribute effectively to national and subnational regional development objectives.

There is an opportunity to give the Government Committee on Regional Policy a leading role in co-ordinating infrastructure investment and linking it with regional development priorities. As infrastructure investment is the backbone of regional development policy, if this committee seeks to enforce the implementation of the regional development policy across the country, it might be the right body to co-ordinate all sectoral investments across levels of government and take advantage of the political momentum of regional development policy. For this to work, however, not only should the MRD sit on the Committee, but also relevant sectors that have an impact on regional development and infrastructure as mentioned above.

Formal contractual agreements across levels of government may also help align objectives for efficient and resilient infrastructure investments. OECD countries are increasingly resorting to contractual arrangements to strengthen partnerships among levels of government. Contracts may have a range of benefits, including promoting dialogue and learning amongst the different actors involved. They are effective instruments for identifying common targets, setting clear and transparent objectives, sharing information and making credible engagements. While serving different objectives, contracts might help to ensure that national policies and regional and local priorities align and "synergetically" contribute to national development targets (OECD, 2017[40]). Contracts can be adapted to the needs of different regions and city types. The key point is to specify the regional development priorities to be addressed by contracts and the infrastructure projects included in them, which can be supported by a careful assessment of the needs and opportunities in each place.

In the United Kingdom, the Netherlands and France, for example, city deals and other contracts between levels of governments have been implemented to support development and sustainability objectives. France, for example, which has similar challenges to Czechia in terms of local administrative fragmentation, has a strong history of contractual arrangements dating back to the 1980s. Recently, France has adopted so-called recovery and ecological transition contracts (*contrats de relance et de transition écologique*, CRTE) for inter-municipal co-operation bodies for the 2020-2026 period to territorialise the objectives of the ecological transition (Box 3.8). In Czechia this type of arrangement may help in aligning green objectives while also building capacities and encouraging infrastructure investments at the relevant scale.

Box 3.8. OECD examples of the use of contracts to align government levels

Chile's Programming Contracts (*Convenios de programación* - CP) are formal binding agreements between one or more regional governments and one or more national ministries, specifying measures and procedures to be undertaken in investment projects of common interest over a specified period of time. The steps for creating a CP are: 1) identification of projects; 2) signing of a protocol of purpose that initiates negotiations between the parties while defining the objectives and areas of intervention and the resources that each institution will contribute; 3) deciding on investments that will be included in the agreement, that have a technical recommendation from the National Public Investment System (SNI); 4) drafting the programming contract and negotiation (technical); and 5) presenting the agreement to the regional council for approval and signature. After the approval and execution of the agreement, a monitoring and evaluation stage follows during which a technical team with representatives from all parties involved is supposed to monitor its execution. Projects are carried out using the resources of both line ministries and regional governments. These agreements can also include other public or private national, regional or local institutions. The participants in a CP do not receive additional or complementary resources; they must re-allocate existing funds to invest in the project established in the CP, and the Budget Directorate (of the Ministry of Finance) has to approve the CPs before their implementation. These agreements offer a useful legal framework for co-ordinating regional and national priorities and responsibilities. They have been mostly used for shared planning and financing of large infrastructure projects.

France has a long history of contractual arrangements linked to the decentralisation of specific tasks to regions, departments and, to some extent, municipalities. State-region contracts, launched in 1984, initially aimed at building regional capacity through a long process of negotiation between subnational governments and the central government's deconcentrated bodies. These contracts established the objectives, implementation and funding modalities for specific tasks. They can also have implications for financial transfers from the central level to subnational levels. France is now in its sixth generation of state-region contracts, and through this process, regions have developed extended capacities and responsibilities for economic development, employment and vocational training, including larger budgets and the involvement of new actors (e.g. academics, civil society). In 2020, France introduced Recovery and Ecological Transition Contracts for inter-municipal co-operation bodies (*Contrat de relance et de transition écologique - CRTE*). These contracts last until 2026 and provide a framework for the territorialisation and co-ordination of a range of public policies that, as a whole, contribute to the challenges of territorial cohesion and the ecological transition. The priorities of the contract are defined locally and agreed upon with the state. Inter-municipal cooperation bodies can access funding for the projects covered by the contracts from a variety of sources, including the Local Investment Support Grant (DSIL), EU funds, state government ministries involved in the contract, and the private sector.

Since 2013, **Iceland** has used successive five-year contracts between its regions and the national government to ensure the financing and implementation of regional-level plans. For example, the Northwest Region has signed three consecutive contracts with the Ministry of Transport and local authorities and the Ministry of Education and Culture to support implementation of its regional plan, which emphasises regional development, innovation, culture, environmental issues, education and population. These contracts ensure funding against clear and measurable success indicators established by the region. The Northwest Region's experience is that this approach has helped increase central government's trust in the region. Trust has also increased on the part of the region, as has its capacity. Over time, the region has had to abide by fewer rules, has seen its allowance for administrative costs increase, and constraints removed on the distribution of funding between priority projects and competitive funds. In addition, more autonomy has been granted to the region in appointing representatives to Competitive Fund Distribution Committees. There is also the option now for other ministries to be part of the contract.

Since 2010, the **United Kingdom** has developed a comprehensive policy on devolution and local economic growth. Government interventions to support economic growth are being pursued at different scales (cities, functional urban areas, regions, pan-regions) to ensure all parts of the country benefit from sustainable economic growth. "Devolution deals" build on previous "city deals" to cover city regions, as well as local authorities in both urban and rural areas, to improve policy co-ordination between cities and their regions. Devolution deals mostly involve the devolution of powers and governance changes (an elected city region mayor). They are agreements (contracts of usually ten years or more) signed between the government and "combined authorities" at the city-region level and are bottom-up proposals focused on leveraging investment for locally determined priorities. In England, key devolved policy areas include consolidated transport budgets, single place-based funding pots, long-term investment funds to support jobs and growth, greater local control of unemployment programmes and piloting of business rates (property tax) retention.

Source: (OECD, 2017[41]) (OECD, 2022[42]) (OECD, 2017[40])

To pursue the contractual path, Czechia could pilot some contracts between national ministries, regions, and municipalities for specific infrastructure investments that pursue the objectives of the Regional

Development Strategy 21+ and the National Investment Plan 2020-2050, while encouraging co-operation across municipalities. Such an approach could be used to ensure collaboration at the micro-regional level in areas that are not covered by Integrated Territorial Investment (ITI) instruments and CLLD. Pilot contracts could target the housing sector – a top priority for the current administration – to ensure that housing policy not only involves the Ministry of Regional Development, but also the Ministry of Transport, the Ministry of Environment, the Ministry of Education and the Ministry of Health, together with regions and municipalities that are in charge of ensuring the basic infrastructure and services in their communities. Indeed, improving housing affordability in Czechia implies a concerted effort from a range of sectors and levels of government to ensure not only that people's ability to rent or buy housing is improved, but also that households are able to afford to live in their accommodation. Cheaper housing far away from a city centre may lead to a long commute with high fuel costs, increasing the overall cost of housing and decreasing well-being (OECD, 2021[20]). The advantage of a pilot action is that the national government can provide hands-on support and identify lessons learnt from the process, which can then be scaled up to other sectors or municipalities.

Engage with the private sector and civil society

A range of stakeholders, including the private sector, NGOs and citizens, can have a great influence on many aspects of an infrastructure project. This is highlighted in the OECD Recommendation on Effective Public Investment across Levels of Government. Large infrastructure projects are often highly politicised and susceptible of being undermined by a lack of consensus. Stakeholder consultation is of key importance to build consensus and ensure transparency around how the project meets the needs of directly affected citizens and society at large. Engaging stakeholders from the early stages of the investment cycle, and later, during feedback and evaluation, can enhance the quality of investment from an environmental, economic, and social perspective. It also helps build support for investment choices, while also preventing the risk of capture by specific interest groups (OECD, 2014[25]). Well-managed participation may also help to limit corruption, capture, and mismanagement, in particular for big and complex infrastructure projects. Information on public investment plans, expenditure and results should be exposed to some level of public scrutiny to promote transparency, accountability and trust. Consultation processes should be inclusive, open and transparent, and promote transparency and integrity (OECD, 2022[38]). In this sense, early stakeholder engagement can be a two-way virtuous circle enabling better policy and investment outputs and outcomes in the long term (OECD, 2019[43]).

OECD countries are increasingly adopting mechanisms to involve stakeholders from the early stages of the investment process. This is particularly true when it comes to private sector involvement. The 2018 monitoring survey reveals that more than half of surveyed countries have established mechanisms to engage private sector representatives – often Chambers of Commerce – in identifying priorities for public investment. At the local level – especially in cities – stakeholder engagement for project prioritisation seems to be gaining ground. Proof of this is an increase in participatory budgeting at the local level that get citizens involved in a municipality's budgetary allocation and its investment priorities. Stakeholder advisory groups, citizen assemblies, open houses, workshops with residents and surveys are some of the main channels for obtaining citizen feedback on investment projects or urban (re)development projects. This type of participatory practice may contribute to improving information flows between government and citizens. It also enhances accountability as it stimulates frequent citizen checks on policy makers and politicians (OECD, 2019[27]).

While there are some good practices in Czech regions and municipalities to involve stakeholders in decision-making processes, there are still major shortcomings. The recent OECD Public Governance Review of Czechia (OECD, 2023[18]) pointed to the lack of a participatory culture in the country, which translates into low engagement by stakeholders at the local level when it comes to planning. An analysis by the Ministry of the Interior identified that interest groups are often invited to provide comments and feedback at some stage in the planning or project design process, but their involvement tends to be reduced in later phases. There are also local governments that tend to assess development needs and set priorities without consulting local interest groups at all (Ministry of the Interior of the Czech Republic, 2020[44]) (OECD, 2023[18]). Indeed, stakeholder engagement can be costly for regions and municipalities as it requires funding and time – these processes can thus be perceived as an additional burden that subnational governments – especially small municipalities – may not be able to support (De Barbieri, 2018[45]). It is thus necessary to provide incentives, tools and technical assistance for subnational governments to engage stakeholders more actively in the infrastructure investment cycle.

Stakeholder participation could be improved by promoting a standardised approach across ministries, agencies and state funds that could be applied and targeted to regions and municipalities. Chapter 2 states that providing central guidance which is actionable and specific to infrastructure could ensure that participation practices are applied systematically, improving their effectiveness. Such guidance for subnational governments should be developed in partnership with the associations of regions and municipalities so that they address effectively the challenges they face to implement these processes – which might be different from the national-level challenges. For example, in accordance with the recommendations of the OECD Public Governance Review, this guidance could include a checklist with actionable practices to help municipalities organise stakeholder engagement activities, accompanied by concrete examples of those practices. The Ministry of Regional Development and the associations of regions and municipalities could take the lead in identifying good practice in stakeholder engagement at the local level so as to start creating an engagement culture at the subnational level. A study of stakeholder engagement in municipalities in the Slovak Republic identifies opportunities for creating a methodological framework for local governments to adopt fit-for-purpose tools for stakeholder engagement in local strategic planning (OECD, 2023[18]). A similar study in Czechia could be led by the Ministry of Regional Development and could explore the challenges and ways forward to tailor support to different municipalities in helping them to engage effectively with stakeholders.

Subnational governments also need to map out different groups of stakeholders in their jurisdiction (as suggested in Chapter 2 for the national level). The guidelines could also outline how to conduct this mapping, as well as including a simple "decision-making tree" to help regions and municipalities choose appropriate channels and instruments for engaging with stakeholders for different purposes (e.g. identifying needs, priorities and opportunities for investment; discussing specific infrastructure projects in the pipeline, etc.) (OECD, 2023[18]). In any case, it is important to consider that these guidelines will differ according to whether they are developed for big cities or regions, or small municipalities. Ideally, tools to support small rural municipalities should differ from those used by large cities, as they likely face different challenges and needs and have different capacities to engage stakeholders.

Regions and big cities can play a key role in integrating stakeholders' views in the investment cycle. Stakeholders targeted by the national and subnational levels are different. Given citizens' closer proximity to regions, together with greater capacity of regions than small municipalities, regions can ensure that the views of a range of stakeholders are considered effectively. In the Netherlands, for example, many urban regions have set up "Economic Boards", which consist of a triple-helix co-operation between subnational governments, knowledge institutes (e.g. universities), and the private sector to identify investment opportunities that can spur development in the regions (OECD, 2022[38]). At the regional level, the Czech regional standing conferences might take on such a role through a dedicated working group that discusses and decides infrastructure investments (see above).

Summary of key recommendations

Given the challenges of implementing a full suite of reforms, Czech authorities could consider sequencing the recommendations made above. By grouping recommendations according to the time horizon needed to implement them effectively (short term, and medium to long term), Czech authorities could allocate resources to reforms in a way which would provide incremental benefits. A potential sequencing is included below.

Short-term reforms

1. **Establish an overarching co-ordination platform to allow national and subnational actors to align the prioritisation, and implementation of infrastructure investment projects.** Whichever model is chosen, it will need to bring together, at a minimum, representatives from the Ministry of Regional Development, Ministry of Transport, Ministry of the Environment and the Ministry of Finance, as well as the various associations of municipalities, including representatives from Prague and the 13 regions. Some options include:

- Create a new body that gathers together all sectors contributing to regional development, as well as regional and local representatives, and led by the Ministry of Regional Development. It could include a working group focusing specifically on infrastructure investment based on the advisory group created by the Ministry of Regional Development to supervise this OECD review (see Chapter 2).
- Reactivate and expand the scope and representation of subnational governments in the Council for Public Investment.
- Expand the role and scope of the national and regional standing conferences for EU-funded projects to all significant investment projects cutting across ministries and levels of government. Clearly define the regional conferences' role and decision-making capacity while ensuring they can contribute effectively to national and subnational regional development objectives.
- Mandate the Government Committee on Regional Policy to co-ordinate infrastructure investment and link it with regional development priorities cutting across all relevant sectors and levels of government.

Medium to long-term reforms

2. **Develop formal contractual agreements across levels of government to align objectives for efficient and resilient infrastructure investment and create real partnerships between national and subnational governments**. Contracts may help Czechia identify common targets, set clear and transparent objectives, share information, and make credible engagements. Contracts need to be adapted to the needs of different regions and city types so that they help to ensure that national policies and regional and local priorities align and "synergetically" contribute to national development targets. A phased approach could be taken:

- Pilot some contracts for specific infrastructure investments that pursue the objectives of the Regional Development Strategy 21+ and the National Investment Plan 2020-2050. The housing sector could be targeted.
- Establish contracts with a group of municipalities at the micro-regional level to encourage inter-municipal co-operation in areas that are not covered by Integrated Territorial Investment (ITI) instrument and CLLD.

3. **Strengthen stakeholder engagement at all levels of government to better assess investment needs, environmental and social sustainability,** as well as the social acceptability of infrastructure projects. This engagement needs to happen from the very beginning of the infrastructure cycle, once an investment need or gap is identified. Czechia could adopt a series of complementary measures to improve stakeholder participation:

- Target guidance developed at the national level to regions and municipalities. Such guidance for subnational governments should be developed in partnership with the associations of regions and municipalities so that they address subnational challenges effectively.
- Ensure guidance is simple and clear to ensure subnational governments can make proper use of it. It could include:
    - A checklist with actionable practices to help municipalities organise stakeholder engagement activities, accompanied by concrete examples of good practices identified by the Ministry of Regional Development and the associations of regions and municipalities.
    - Guidance on how to map out different groups of stakeholders in regions and cities.
    - A simple "decision-making tree" to help regions and municipalities choose appropriate channels and instruments for engaging with stakeholders for different purposes (e.g. identifying needs, priorities and opportunities for investment, discussion on specific infrastructure projects in the pipeline, etc.)
- Integrate key stakeholders in the discussions held by regional permanent conferences or any other platform that promotes dialogue across levels of government at the regional level. The Czech regional standing conferences might take on this role through a dedicated working group that discusses and decides on infrastructure investments.

3.4 Reinforcing inter-municipal co-operation

As economic relations and flows of goods and people do not stop at an administrative border, investments are best planned at the scale of functional areas made up of networked villages, towns and more dispersed areas (OECD, 2020[46]). This is particularly true when it comes to an efficient green transition; authorities must consider land use and transport at a scale that considers central cities and suburbs together (Box 3.9). In Prague, for example, the lack of a functional approach to public transport planning meant there were no public transport options connecting the city and outlying areas, leading to increased car ownership and traffic (OECD, 2018[47]).

Municipal infrastructure planning in Czechia is characterised by territorial fragmentation. The majority of municipalities are too small to have sufficient human and financial capacity to carry out integrated and robust infrastructure planning. Additionally, individual municipal infrastructure planning without co-ordinating with neighbouring municipalities is likely to lose out on economies of scale in infrastructure investment, leading to low efficiency in the use of public resources. The national government could play a more active role in providing targeted incentives and tools to promote joint municipal infrastructure planning. At the same time, joint planning alone cannot address all the existing gaps in municipal infrastructure planning (e.g., weak data and evidence base, lack of clear and robust investment prioritisation criteria, etc.). In fact, joint municipal infrastructure planning requires new capacities – in joint data collection and compilation, in stakeholder engagement processes, and setting up the governance mechanisms for joint strategising, among others. Along with offering incentives for joint planning, the national government therefore needs to ensure effective capacity building to allow municipalities to leverage joint planning to close planning gaps.

Czechia is striving for a stronger focus on functional areas for infrastructure planning, which does not fit within one jurisdiction only. The catchment areas of education and health care services, for example, often cross local boundaries. Mobility flows also often go beyond the boundaries of local administrations in Czechia, given its many small municipalities. Inter-municipal co-operation can help to ensure that infrastructure investments occur at the scale of these "functional areas" and can promote efficiency by reaping the benefits of economies of scale and by enhancing policy synergies among jurisdictions. Inter-municipal co-operation may be particularly useful for small municipalities with insufficient public resources to deliver quality public goods to their citizens efficiently and to derive economies of scale through their own investment projects. Cross-jurisdiction co-ordination can be encouraged through financial and non-financial incentives and agreements between jurisdictions.

Inter-municipal co-operation in Czechia has been a longstanding concern. Given the high administrative fragmentation at the local level, several OECD analyses have already pointed to the need to strengthen inter-municipal co-operation across the country, especially at the functional scale. More flexibility and stronger incentives for such co-ordination from the national and regional levels are needed to ensure that municipalities have the right incentives in place and the knowledge to act.

Box 3.9. Inter-municipal co-operation for joint infrastructure projects

In the **Netherlands**, the Hague Metropolitan Area (MRDH) brings together 23 municipalities to work towards a sustainable region with clean, quiet and energy-efficient transport. The current package contains a total of 26 measures, and each is carried out by an average of seven municipalities. The communities take on between 3 and 25 measures aimed at reducing CO_2 emissions. The MRDH picks up 14 measures based on its core tasks and supplements them with 2 new measures. A number of measures are being taken on by a larger group of municipalities, such as creating Metropolitan cycle routes (20 municipalities) and the expansion of charging infrastructure (18 municipalities).

In **France**, inter-municipal co-operation bodies with own-source taxes (*établissements de co-operation intercommmunale à fiscalité propre* - EPCI) are playing an increasing role as local public investors as they are in charge, of water and waste management, transport, and infrastructure among others. While in 1993, their investment expenditure amounted to 8% of municipal investment, they now account for 25%. The 1 254 EPCI (grouping all 35 000 French municipalities) include 21 *métropoles* (including the three largest metropolitan areas, Paris, Lyon, and Aix-Marseille-Provence). EPCIs assume limited, specialised and exclusive powers transferred to them by member communes. They are governed by delegates of municipal councils and must be approved by the state to exist legally. To encourage municipalities to form an EPCI, the national government provides a basic grant plus an "inter-municipality grant" to preclude competition on tax rates among participating municipalities. EPCIs draw on budgetary contributions from member communes and/or their own tax revenues.

A law amended in 2020 in **Lithuania** reinforces the territorial concept of the functional area for implementing regional policy. This was preceded by a 2017 White Paper that defined the functional area, or functional region, as a system of economic development, worker migration, and urban-rural partnerships using common infrastructure, transport and service networks that go beyond administrative boundaries. Regional policymakers are now required to consider functional areas, as opposed simply to municipal administrative boundaries, when formulating regional development or multi-regional development plans.

Source: (OECD, 2021[48]) (OECD, forthcoming[49])

Make existing municipal co-operation more long term and stable

Czech municipalities are increasingly co-operating to overcome administrative fragmentation, but usually just for single-purpose projects. The increase in inter-municipal co-operation in Czechia is due to a vast legislative framework that enables formal and voluntary co-operation among neighbouring municipalities, in particular for autonomous competences. Voluntary associations of municipalities (VAMs) are the most basic and common form of inter-municipal co-operation (Box 3.10). As reported in various OECD studies, VAMs vary in nature, purpose and membership, but the majority are one-off single-purpose associations often related to infrastructure and public service delivery in transportation or sewerage (OECD, 2016[39]) (OECD, 2020[17]) (OECD, 2023[18]). VAMs often rely on external, temporary sources of financing, such as from the state budget or EU funds, rather than funding provided by member municipalities or their own revenues from service provision (OECD, 2020[17]). They also receive funds from their members, but mayors are reluctant to raise membership fees to ensure adequate and stable financing (OECD, 2020[17]) (OECD, 2023[18]). However, it is not common for VAMs to carry out joint infrastructure investment planning – i.e., developing cross-jurisdiction strategies either for sectoral or overall infrastructure investment.

Inter-municipal co-operation can occur through the use of contracts set up by small municipalities to delegate some services that they are required to provide, typically to a municipality with extended powers – the so-called municipalities with extended area of competence (ORP). The ORPs are obliged to have a zoning plan (unlike smaller municipalities) that typically covers the area of smaller municipalities surrounding them. They also typically co-ordinate all the municipalities and stakeholders within their competence area. There are 205 municipalities of this type in Czechia.

Co-operation across municipalities also happens through the Shared Service Centres (CSSs), a project implemented by the Union of Towns and Municipalities. CSSs are established to undertake public procurement, especially responsible procurement, which not only considers the most economically advantageous alternative, but also the impact on employment, social affairs and the environment. The Union of Towns and Municipalities has recently released a report containing good practice examples to encourage their implementation across the country. According to the association, CSSs' most important achievement is knowledge sharing.

Box 3.10. Czechia's Voluntary Associations of Municipalities

VAMs vary in nature, purpose and membership. They may be established as joint stock companies (which can invest in another body alongside private companies) or public bodies. They can have a single purpose (e.g. an investment project) or offer the ongoing provision of a service (e.g. waste removal). Funding can come from members, user charges or grants, or they can be established without funding.

The number of VAMs has been growing steadily since 1990, with significant growth around 2000 following the adoption of the Law on Municipalities (128/2000) that banned other forms of inter-municipal co-operation (Box 3.2). In 2022, there were 702 VAMs registered in the country, but some of them do not perform any activities.

A new draft amendment to the Law on Municipalities is under discussion. This amendment would create a new, larger form of VAM: the Community of Municipalities. A Community of Municipalities should ideally join together the majority of municipalities with "extended powers", or ORPs (Type III) from the same administrative district. The objective is to strengthen inter-municipal co-operation at the scale of a "micro-region", to ensure co-ordination of public services (e.g. social services), joint delivery of administrative activities and territorial strategic development, including strategic and spatial planning. According to the draft law, the status of Community of Municipalities can be acquired if the union groups at least 20 municipalities or at least three-fifths of all municipalities from the administrative district, if fewer than 30 municipalities belong to this administrative district. Member municipalities should together include at least 60% of the population of the administrative district. A municipality can be a member of only one Community of Municipalities. The draft law envisages only voluntary membership at this stage.

Source: (OECD, 2016[39]) (OECD, 2020[17]) (OECD, 2023[18])

Local Action Groups (LAGs), established to deliver rural development policies under the EU LEADER/Community Led Local Development Strategy (CLLD), are also a popular form of inter-municipal co-operation. LAGs cover a wide area and share of the population in Czechia, spanning over 90% of the country's territory and 94% of all municipalities (Saradín and Zapletalová, 2022 [17]). Some evidence suggest that LAGs have been increasingly adopted for "soft" projects on education, employment and environment, in contrast to the "hard" infrastructure projects which were the main focus of the first LAGs in the country (Saradín and Zapletalová, 2022 [17]). LAGs can access European Structural and Investment funds such as the ERDF, ESF, Cohesion Fund, EAFRD and EMFF. There are several examples of successful LAGs (Box 3.11) and in some cases this success seems to rest on their participatory approach – which has had a positive impact on democracy at the local level. In the 2014-2020 programming period, 178 CLLD strategies were funded. Urban municipalities can also develop Sustainable Urban Development Strategies for the use of the Integrated Territorial Investment (ITI) instrument. These groups, however, do not necessarily have a focus on joint infrastructure planning. The scope of the LAGs also remains unclear, including the extent to which they correspond to functional areas for investment.

While municipalities can be part of several VAMs, they can only belong to a single LAG. Often, LAGs and VAMs do not have the same partnering municipalities. This, coupled with the fact that VAMs work under the supervision of the Ministry of the Interior, carrying out only autonomous competences, while LAGs fall under the Ministry of Regional Development, undermine the synergies and coherence of both forms of co-operation.

Box 3.11. Local Action Groups in Czechia

Local Action Group of Mezilesí

The Local Action Group Mezilesí was founded in 2005 with the aim of supporting environmental, economic and social development of the Mezilesí region. It comprises five municipalities, as well as representatives from non-government organisations, business sectors and citizens. Mezilesí is a rural region and the members of the LAG are mostly small municipalities with around 500 citizens.

Besides implementing the CLLD, the LAG Mezilesí also supports municipalities in preparing projects financed by EU funds, focusing its efforts on sustainable development, energy efficiency, waste management and green energy. At the heart of the LAG is the municipality of Kněžice, which is Czechia's first village to be independent in heat and electricity through the Kněžice Bioenergy Centre. One of the key pillars of the LAG is in fact the experience of Kněžice; the LAG itself serves as a peer-learning forum.

The Bioenergy Centre has triggered an energy-saving attitude aimed at reducing greenhouse gas emissions in neighbouring towns. Mayors of the five municipalities signed the European Covenant of Mayors for the submission of a Sustainable Energy Action Plan (SEAP), with the view to cutting carbon dioxide emissions in their territory by more than 20% while attaining the same percentage of energy savings and renewable energy sources. The LAG's municipalities have also joined the project "Towards 100% RES rural communities".

Source: (European Development Agency, n.d.[50])

There is still substantial scope to strengthen inter-municipal co-operation further in Czechia, especially in sectors like spatial planning and housing, where it remains very limited. An OECD survey conducted in

2021 showed, for example, that only 30% of surveyed municipalities had a dedicated housing strategy and only 11% co-ordinated their housing policy with surrounding municipalities (OECD, 2021[20]). Moving from single purpose and one-off co-operative arrangements towards long-term and stable inter-municipal co-operation throughout the whole investment cycle is necessary to foster quality infrastructure in the entire country. Joint action for investments – especially for physical infrastructure – makes it possible to reach a relevant scale and enhance synergies among policies of neighbouring (or otherwise linked) subnational governments. Reaching an efficient scale and viability for infrastructure investment can make private involvement more attractive and may also allow municipalities or regions to have a better chance of receiving the aid from national/supra-national organisations.

Several OECD countries have taken this approach. In the United States, for example, the Pennsylvania Department of Transportation aggregated the construction and maintenance of a few hundred small bridges into a single PPP project under its old bridge rehabilitation programme. With the average cost of an individual bridge as low as approximately USD 2 million, these did not make for a viable single PPP project. In the UK, the Partnerships for Church of England Schools was created to bundle several small schools with a new built capital cost of around GBP 2 million into "geographically coherent" groups in order to facilitate the procurement of the private partner (OECD, 2019[51]).

Introduce concrete incentives for inter-municipal co-operation

Offering financial incentives could help to strengthen inter-municipal co-operation. Co-ordinating investments is difficult, even when actors recognise the need for it. It can be hampered by transaction costs, competitive pressures, resource constraints, differing priorities, and fears that the distribution of costs or benefits from co-operation will be one-sided (OECD, 2022[36]). This is probably why in the EU, fewer than 40% of municipalities co-ordinate with peers when planning infrastructure projects (European Investment Bank, 2021[52]). Some recent evidence from Czechia points in this direction, showing that large Czech municipalities do not consider inter-municipal co-operation to be cost-effective (Bakoš et al., 2021[53]). Establishing financial incentives for municipalities to co-operate from the planning phase onwards may help overcome these costs, especially when co-operative arrangements involve the participation of a large number of small municipalities (OECD, 2023[18]).

An OECD survey conducted in 2019 revealed that 16 out of 27 surveyed countries had put in place specific incentives to foster co-operation across municipalities (OECD, 2019[51]). Financial incentives might include special grants for municipalities that join in shared efforts, special tax regimes for associations of municipalities, additional funds for joint public investment proposals, or bonus grants for municipalities that generate savings through co-operation (OECD, 2019[54]). For instance, France offers special grants and a special tax regime in some cases; other countries, like Estonia and Norway, provide additional funds for joint public investments. Slovenia introduced a financial incentive in 2005 to encourage inter-municipal co-operation by reimbursing 50% of staff costs of joint management bodies – which led to a notable rise in the number of such entities. In Galicia, Spain, investment projects that involve several municipalities get priority for regional funds (Mizell and Allain-Dupré, 2013[55]; OECD, 2019[56]). Poland is also gradually moving in this direction by providing additional funding for municipalities in a functional area that prepare a joint strategic plan (OECD, 2021[57]). These incentives may also help overcome political costs linked to co-operation and the sustainability of an association or agreement that usually depends on the political will of the mayor or local administration (OECD, 2023[18]).

Box 3.12. Financial incentives for inter-municipal co-operation in OECD countries

In **France**, a highly fragmented country, law no. 92-125 of February 1992 promoted inter-municipal co-operation schemes as integrated territorial projects with own-source taxation powers (EPCI à fiscalité propre). EPCIs can take various forms, such as “communities of communes,” “communities of cities” or “agglomeration communities.” In 2014, the law NOTRe simplified this complex system by setting up a minimum threshold for inter-municipal cooperation (15 000 inhabitants instead of 5 000), resulting in a decrease in the number of IMC structures with own-source tax from 2 456 in 2013 to 1 255 in 2022. EPCIs assume limited, specialised and exclusive powers transferred to them by member communes. They are governed by delegates of municipal councils and must be approved by the state to exist legally. To encourage municipalities to form an EPCI, the national government provides a basic grant plus an “inter-municipality grant” to preclude competition on tax rates among participating municipalities. EPCIs draw on budgetary contributions from member communes and/or their own tax revenues. They are in charge of water and waste management, transport and infrastructure, among others.

In **Slovenia**, inter-municipal co-operation has risen in recent years, especially for projects that require a large number of users. In 2005, amendments to the Financing of Municipalities Act provided financial incentives for joint municipal administration by offering national co-financing arrangements: 50% of the joint management bodies’ staff costs are reimbursed by the national government in the next fiscal period. The result has been an increase in municipal participation in such entities, from 9 joint management bodies in 2005 to 42 today, covering 177 municipalities. Their most common tasks are inspection (waste management, roads, space, etc.), municipal warden service, infrastructure planning and internal audit.

The region of Galicia in **Spain** has many small municipalities with limited institutional capacity and spread out geographically, which increases the cost of providing public services. The regional government has taken steps to encourage economies of scale. It provides financial incentives for voluntary (“soft”) inter-municipal co-ordination arrangements. Investment projects that involve several municipalities get priority for regional funds. Such inter-municipal agreements tend to be popular in the water sector. Local co-operation is also being encouraged in the urban mobility plan for public transport, involving the seven largest cities in the region. The regional government has also imposed a “hard” co-ordination arrangement by creating the Metropolitan Area of Vigo, an association of 14 municipalities. Although the metropolitan area was defined by the regional government, it was based on a history of “light co-operation” among 12 municipalities (out of 14). Voluntary municipal mergers may be encouraged in the future.

Source: (OECD, 2020[58]; OECD, 2023[18])

Czechia could capitalise further on its existing structures by providing targeted incentives to promote joint infrastructure planning that looks beyond the focus on EU-funded investment to consider functional areas. For example, the national government could make joint municipal infrastructure planning based on functional areas a condition to unlock additional funding in some national funding schemes, or as one of the criteria in project selection/prioritisation for national funding. This is the approach taken by the Swiss agglomeration programme (Box 3.13). The idea is to encourage groups of municipalities to outline a clear vision and plan for infrastructure investment, with concrete criteria for selecting investment projects that could capture the functional linkages across municipalities and bring development benefits to the area. The national government could also provide technical support (e.g., experts, advisory services) for municipalities that would like to carry out joint infrastructure planning. At the same time, many municipalities do have a strong interest to plan and deliver infrastructure within their jurisdictions, but some potentially consider neighbouring municipalities as competitors for funding. This challenge is not unique to Czechia, but experience shows that with the right incentives and mechanisms, a co-operative culture could be fostered in the long-term. The national government has planned support to LAGs for investment planning and project preparation, including providing guidelines and methodological support. The LAGs and CLLD could be a good start and could be helped towards shifting the mind-set of municipalities, as in the example of the Brandenburg initiative in Germany (Box 3.13).

Box 3.13. Providing incentives for local strategic planning at the right scale

The Swiss federal agglomeration programmes

The Swiss federal agglomeration programmes, funded and administered through the Federal Road and Agglomeration Traffic Fund, provide competitive grants for public and individual transport infrastructure in agglomerations. The Federal Fund contributes 30-50% of the funding to the selected investment projects and higher quality projects can receive a higher share of grants.

The funding programme is designed to incentivise co-ordination and co-operation among local authorities. As a condition to access the grants, local authorities need to plan and implement projects in a co-ordinated way to address local needs. They need to harmonise their transport, urban development and land-use plans and develop their agglomeration programmes jointly across administrative units. Some local authorities have developed model projects precisely to build collaboration and create an agglomeration programme to access the fund. In 2015, the canton of Uri and eight municipalities in the Lower Reuss Valley jointly developed an agglomeration plan for the federal programme. The plan outlined the goals and strategies for the Lower Reuss Valley's future development with respect to housing, landscape and transport. Around 40 agglomerations across the country have participated in this programme.

"Strengthen our strengths" strategy in Brandenburg, Germany

The reunification of Germany required transforming the east German socialist planning economy and integrating it into the west German market-oriented capitalist one. The country struggled to achieve convergence in infrastructure development, competitiveness and employment levels, with the social security system serving as a key stabiliser. In 2004-2005, Brandenburg revisited its territorial development approach, and launched a strategy centred on the key strengths of 15 core regional growth areas, empowering them to "strengthen our strengths". It was implemented via an open access and "competitive" funding programme designed to encourage the active development of project proposals that built on an area's inherent growth potential. Under this strategy, Brandenburg's municipalities with over 25 000 inhabitants were invited to send proposals for growth that built on their unique assets and advantages. This "competition" encouraged towns to collaborate in putting forward proposals. The process for formulating the proposals was important as it required talking to various sectors in the public administration, businesses, education institutes and universities. This changed the mentality of regional and local officials from one of asking for direct support from the State Chancellery to one that actively explored what they needed and identifying potential areas for growth. In addition, in Brandenburg, as in many other countries and regions, there is risk that the investment scale becomes smaller and smaller without co-operation. To address this, the Chancellery focuses on projects in which local protagonists in the regions can co-operate for regional development, striking a balance between a bottom-up and top-down approach in investment.

Source: OECD (2020[31]);

Collaboration on infrastructure investment can also be encouraged by providing technical support to plan, design, prioritise, procure, implement and maintain infrastructure. Small municipalities in Czechia often lack this capacity. In this context, peer learning, pooling expertise and exchanging experiences becomes crucial. Some OECD countries have opted to encourage collaboration by providing consulting and technical assistance, promoting information sharing, or providing specific guidelines on how to manage such collaboration. Arrangements to solve capacity issues have been prevalent among the Nordic countries (Denmark, Finland, Norway and Sweden), but they have also been practised in Chile, France,

Italy and Spain, among others. Regions might play a key role by organising peer learning, offering technical support, and acting as political facilitators. As has been highlighted by the recent OECD Public Governance Review of Czechia (OECD, 2023[18]), the development of a clear toolbox or guidelines on how to jointly plan and implement infrastructure investments should accompany this process. Capacity-building processes might particularly focus on infrastructure strategic planning at the micro-regional level, either by peer learning or through external experts who can support municipalities, for example in assessing need, prioritising and procuring infrastructure projects. Section 3.6 below discusses subnational capacity building in more detail.

The OECD Public Governance Review also suggests that to strengthen inter-municipal co-operation, Czechia could identify a specific set of tasks that should be performed by a group of municipalities, mandating inter-municipal co-operation over a legally defined set of public services. This could be extended to strategic infrastructure investments that contribute, for example, to the implementation of the recovery and resilience plan, or to achieve the green and digital transition objectives. This would need to be accompanied by appropriate financing mechanisms to properly prepare and execute the investment in joint infrastructure.

The success of joint municipal infrastructure planning relies on the political buy-in from municipalities and local communities, especially to generate support for long-term reforms. Joint municipal infrastructure planning needs to be fostered through a bottom-up approach. Citizens, local communities, and municipalities need to understand the value of such co-operation, i.e. that it could help advance their local agenda while also supporting regional development and the country. One study pointed out that the infrastructure and spatial planning culture in Czechia at both national and subnational level strongly relies on experts in architecture and urban design, without sufficient attention to collective intelligence and bottom-up stakeholder inputs to address cross-cutting development issues such as climate change, sustainable development, social inclusion, etc. (Maier, 2020[59]; ESPON, 2021[22]).

Summary of key recommendations

Given the challenges of implementing a full suite of reforms, Czech authorities could consider sequencing the recommendations made above. By grouping recommendations according to the time horizon needed to implement them effectively (short term, and medium to long term), Czech authorities could allocate resources to reforms in a way which would provide incremental benefits. A potential sequencing is included below.

Short-term reforms

1. **Reinforce co-operation across Czech municipalities throughout the investment cycle**. To address high administrative fragmentation at the local level, Czechia needs to move from single purpose and one-off co-operative arrangements towards long-term and stable inter-municipal co-operation across sectors and throughout the whole investment cycle. The following complementary actions could be taken:
   - Introduce financial incentives for municipalities to co-operate from the planning phase onwards. Financial incentives could include special grants for municipalities that join efforts, special tax regimes for associations of municipalities, additional funds for joint public investment proposals, or bonus grants for municipalities that generate savings through co-operation.
   - Strengthen the administrative capacities of Voluntary Associations of Municipalities (VAMs). Provide systemic financial support so that VAMs have sufficient personnel and administrative capacities to implement investment activities. Encourage inter-municipal co-operation by providing consulting and technical assistance (e.g. on needs assessment, prioritising, and procuring

infrastructure projects), promoting information sharing, and developing specific guidelines on how to manage such collaboration.

- Identify key infrastructure investments that should be conducted by a group of municipalities, such as those that contribute to the implementation of the recovery and resilience plan, or to the green and digital transition. Financial incentives (e.g. specific transfers, funding or financing for joint infrastructure) could be directed towards these specific projects to ensure that the group of municipalities can properly prepare and execute them.

Medium to long-term reforms

1. **Target and encourage inter-municipal co-operation for infrastructure investments at the functional scale.** In urban and rural areas alike, investments are best planned at the scale of functional areas of networked villages, towns and more dispersed areas, as economic relations and flows of goods and people do not stop at the administrative border. For this to happen, it is crucial to develop data on functional areas to produce a more accurate picture of actual circumstances than administrative areas.

3.5 Enhancing subnational administrative capacity for quality infrastructure

Effective and quality infrastructure investment requires substantial institutional capacity. Smaller subnational governments often lack the broad range of skills needed to identify, plan, finance, construct and manage quality infrastructure. They can also face significant capacity challenges in public procurement and may rely on external support to undertake large or specialised investment projects (OECD, 2022[2]). This is not only the case in Czechia, but also across OECD countries. In 2015, 65% of the subnational governments surveyed in a joint OECD-Committee of the Regions survey reported that the capacity to design adequate infrastructure strategies is lacking in their city/region (OECD-CoR, 2015[60]). In 2020, a survey by the European Investment Bank showed that one-third of EU municipalities highlighted the lack of technical capacity as a major obstacle for infrastructure investment (European Investment Bank, 2021[52]). Alongside regulatory red tape, lack of technical capacity was also highlighted as holding back investment in green and climate change-related infrastructure (European Investment Bank, 2021[52]). Box 3.14 lists some of the priority areas for subnational government capacity building.

Box 3.14. Institutional capacities at the subnational level for quality infrastructure investment

Effective and quality subnational infrastructure investment requires substantial institutional capacity, including staff with appropriate skills and fit-for-purpose processes and systems.

Among other areas, subnational governments usually require greater capacity in:

- Strategic planning: to support the identification of long-term regional and local development priorities that guide infrastructure investments and other complementary policy actions (such as land use changes) in line with regional and local development strategies.
- Project planning and appraisal: to help ensure specific infrastructure investments are well defined, efficiently prioritised, provide value for money and contribute to regional and/or local development objectives. A useful tool can be online project preparation and monitoring platforms established by multilateral development banks to help national and subnational governments prepare quality infrastructure investment projects.
- Public financial management: to budget and manage life-cycle investment costs, align budget frameworks, monitor and account for financing flows, account for risks and contingent liabilities

and undertake auditing processes. For example, the World Bank and other partners have launched the City Creditworthiness Initiative to build the public finance management capacity of cities, aiming to enhance their creditworthiness.

- Public procurement: to clearly articulate and prioritise the objectives of procurement to private constructors and assess options against value-for-money criteria and other objectives.
- Monitoring and evaluation: to conduct regular and rigorous ex-post evaluation and use monitoring and evaluation information to enhance decision making.

Source: (OECD, 2022[38])

Prioritise capacity building at the regional and local levels

Czech subnational governments often lack the capacity to plan, prepare, procure and deliver infrastructure projects. This is one of the major infrastructure bottlenecks in Czechia. Several OECD reports, including the OECD Economic Survey 2020 (OECD, 2020[17]) and the OECD Public Governance Review (OECD, 2023[18]), have noted that strengthening municipal administrative capacity is a key priority for Czechia. This is particularly true when it comes to public investment – a task that requires a certain level of expertise. Small municipalities cannot always ensure sufficient and qualified staffing (Ministry of the Interior of the Czech Republic, 2018[61]), and it is also difficult for them to retain staff. In some cases, when an employee leaves who has gained experience in planning, prioritising or procuring they “take away” all their knowledge in managing investment projects. This trend is aggravated by population shrinking and ageing. This is in stark contrast with administrations in the big cities, which have a more stable structure and specialisation of tasks; even with a high turnover rate, they manage to build institutional knowledge and train new employees (OECD, 2023[18]).

The capacity gap is even more acute when it comes to future challenges like improving green and digital infrastructure in regions and municipalities. These challenges require innovative public procurement approaches such as green public procurement to ensure that contractors meet certain requirements (i.e. standards relating to energy efficiency, carbon emissions or water use). Green public procurement can help align purchasing decisions with wider subnational government objectives (OECD, 2022[38]). To achieve this, subnational governments require a mix of technical and specialist knowledge together with a broad range of professional competences.

Czechia has set capacity building as a key priority. The country has undertaken a series of initiatives that aim at bridging the capacity gap in regions and municipalities (Box 3.15). The Czech public administration’s reform agenda (Client-oriented Public Administration 2030), for example, sets an ambitious medium to long-term vision for the future and positions varied learning and development opportunities as a key part of building skills, particularly relating to analytical capability (OECD, 2023[18]). One of the objectives of this agenda is precisely to improve the knowledge and skills of local self-government officials, as well as elected representatives of self-governing units. However, as of today, training for the local public workforce – led by the Ministry of the Interior – is mostly focused on the administrative aspects of officials’ tasks.

In parallel to the training efforts led by the Ministry of the Interior, the Ministry of Regional Development has also taken a proactive role in supporting municipalities as part of the regional development policy. The ministry has created a web-based application that supports municipalities in designing their municipal development strategies and/or programmes, offering practical tools to develop them (e.g., statistical data, templates and samples of supporting documents and studies, e-learning courses, handbooks for municipalities, etc.). All municipal development strategies are published on the website to encourage peer-learning as a way of building strategic planning capacity among municipalities (OECD, 2023[18]). The MRD has also been active in professionalising public procurement. The Office for the Protection of Competition, for example, has offered seminars and training on public procurement, including an educational programme for small communities focused on multi-criteria evaluation with the Union of Towns and Municipalities of Czechia (European Commission, 2020[62]) (see Chapter 2).

As part of its implementation of the National Recovery Plan, Czechia is planning to put a strong emphasis on capacity building for investment. Under Component 4.1 (see Box 3.15), and through an amendment to its recovery plan, Czechia aims at preparing regional investors for the transition to a green and digital economy through training activities, methodological co-ordination and financial assistance for preparing projects to meet the objectives of a green or digital Europe, as well as to increase the efficiency of public investment, to strengthen investment readiness or absorption capacity and to increase the share of PPP projects in Czechia. Another key component of the National Recovery Plan is the creation of Regional Housing Investment Support Centres, which will bring expert support for municipal rental housing investment. These centres will disseminate investment know-how at both the regional and local levels through methodological support, linking municipalities with local experts, co-ordinating local housing policies and supporting the preparation of projects intended for support by national financial instruments.

Box 3.15. Building Czechia's subnational public workforce capacity

The role of the Ministry of the Interior

The Ministry of the Interior has formal responsibility for learning and development in local self-governments even though it is not the employer of local self-government officials. The ministry defines minimum standards for special training largely focused on the administrative aspects of officials' tasks. Senior officials are required to take mandatory training on management and human resource issues within two years of their appointment. Aside from some ad hoc initiatives, broader competences – 'soft skills' – are not currently a sustained focus of most learning content. The ministry also prepares the entry exam taken by all new subnational public employees, as set out in the forthcoming amendment to the Act on Officials of Territorial self-governing units. In the future, officials will have to pass a general entrance exam, as well as a separate exam ("special professional competence exam") to be taken within 18 months of taking up duty in order to exercise delegated powers.

A forthcoming amendment to the Act on Officials of Territorial Self-governing Units proposes changes to the training system to improve access to training by simplifying the accreditation system for training programmes, and through tighter quality controls by reducing the number of accredited training institutions.

The role of CzechInvest

Czech Invest is an Investment and Business Development Agency subordinated to the Ministry of Industry and Trade of Czechia that supports business and investment. The agency helps to attract foreign direct investment and develop domestic companies through its services and development programmes. CzechInvest also promotes Czechia abroad and acts as an intermediary between the EU and small and medium-sized enterprises in implementing Structural Funds in Czechia. As part of its activities, CzechInvest works through its 13 regional offices to detect investment needs in the regions, including developing industrial zones, brownfield sites or any project that offers opportunities for working with the private sector. To make the investment ecosystem work better, CzechInvest supports municipalities in project preparation and funding options.

Czechia's Recovery and Resilience Plan

Component 4.1 of the National Recovery and Resilience Plann developed by the Ministry of Regional Developmentn focuses on systemic support to the public administration to increase the readiness and efficiency of public investment in Czech regions in view of the EU's green and digital economy and housing affordability objectives. The main goal is to strengthen the capacity of public administrations to prepare and implement investment programmes financed by public funds, including EU funds.

As part of the component, Czechia has established a new national advisory centre and eight Regional Housing Investment Support Centres (RCs) under the State Fund for Investment Support. The RCs aim at supporting the implementation of housing investment in regions and municipalities by disseminating know-how and providing methodological and professional support. The Unit for Housing Investment Support within the RCs will be responsible for the management and methodological guidance of the RCs and will act as the secretariat of the Housing Investments Advisory Hub (HIAH) (see chapter 2).

Source: (OECD, 2023[18])

Across the OECD, national and subnational governments have implemented initiatives to build capabilities at the subnational level for planning, designing and delivering infrastructure investment projects (Box 3.16). According to the OECD monitoring survey, 17 out of 27 surveyed countries have developed a specific strategy to strengthen subnational capabilities to design and manage public investment strategies and/or projects (OECD, 2019[51]). Providing technical assistance is another common form of capacity building for subnational governments. Some countries also use digital platforms (e.g., e-learning) with the aim to narrow the capacity gaps across regions and localities and facilitate peer learning. Other mechanisms include incentives for subnational government to pool expertise for infrastructure planning and implementation (OECD, 2019[51]) and to build investment capacity, for example for PPPs (discussed below) and climate finance. National associations of municipalities are very effective as capacity-building and knowledge-sharing platforms, and for disseminating good practice and benchmarking local and international experiences.

For training to be successful and targeted to the actual needs of subnational governments, the Ministry of Regional Development should work together with regional governments and the associations of municipalities to identify needs, and define the scope, targeted audience and content of such training. Training can be targeted to a group of regions or municipalities facing similar challenges, or can be focused on specific issues such as technical, economic, environmental issues, or social analysis to support investment appraisal. Capacity building should take place regularly, in a structured manner, so that knowledge is retained at the institutional level in spite of the turnover of government officials.

Inter-municipal co-operation is also crucial to pool expertise across local governments and promote peer-learning. One of the greatest opportunities for gaining added value of inter-municipal co-operation schemes is for small or less prepared municipalities to learn from bigger or better prepared ones. In Czechia, the VAMs do not only help to reach the right scale for investment, they also offer economies of scale for sharing knowledge and skills for project preparation and management. Encouraging cities to partner with small municipalities will be crucial for this (see above). In this respect, the Shared Service Centres (CSS) might be a good practice to pursue (see Section 3.5). The Regional Centres – in co-ordination with associations of municipalities – could also act as hubs to gather good practice across municipalities and organise peer-learning exchange among local authorities to tackle specific and common issues within the region. The planned Regional Centres could also facilitate training, as in Poland, for example (Box 3.16).

Box 3.16. OECD country experiences in building subnational investment capacity

Chile's National Investment System offers specialised training courses for national and subnational officials in formulating and evaluating public investment projects. It has a dedicated module on field training and regional workshops for entities in charge of preparing investment initiatives (i.e., mainly municipalities and other public services at the local level). The objective is to develop the appropriate competencies of subnational civil servants in the design and preparation of investment projects, as well as in the methodologies of social evaluation. Training sessions take place in the municipalities and are organised by investment analysts from the Regional Office of the Ministry of Social Development in each region.

In **Germany**, the initiative "Small Towns in Germany" is a package of programmes and activities for small town development, aiming to strengthen their functionality. It targets over 2 100 towns across Germany, mostly in peripheral areas. In 2019, as part of this initiative, the Federal Ministry for Housing, Urban Development and Building launched a pilot called "Small Town Academy", which offers a purpose-built platform for networking, exchange of experiences and advanced training on urban development. A pilot phase (between 2019-2022) was used to define suitable content and formats, which led to the final launch of the platform in 2023. The planned activities include advice from experts who come to the municipality and forge creative strategies (mobile coaching teams), or tandems among mayors who exchange views on a common topic in urban development over the long term. These activities will generate model projects that test different urban planning and project management methods, and will lead to a collection of learning and exchange modules.

In **Poland**, to support the implementation of the National Strategy for Regional Development 2030 (NSRD 2030), the Ministry of Development Funds and Regional Policy launched a pilot project to create the Centre for Advisory Support (*Centrum Wsparcia Doradczego*, CWD), aiming to strengthen the institutional capacity of local authorities to participate in strategic development activities, including planning, designing and managing infrastructure projects in 894 Areas of Strategic Intervention (ASIs). The CWD aims at building capacity and strengthening the territorial approach to investment, i.e., helping build cross-jurisdiction partnerships with other ASI communes and with non-public socio-economic partners, such as civil society organisations, in order to tackle local development challenges and create competitive advantages.

In **Scotland** (UK), the Scottish Government has established the Scottish Futures Trust (SFT) as a centre of expertise to improve the efficiency and effectiveness of infrastructure investment in Scotland. The SFT has launched "Hub" programmes to improve the planning, procurement and delivery of smaller public infrastructure projects (primarily education and health). This programme was tailored to meet the specific needs of five designated hub territories across Scotland. It also provides an opportunity to share skills and experience across public entities at all levels (education and health boards, local authorities, etc.), enabling knowledge transfer and increasing public investment efficiency. In addition to this programme, the SFT also carries out independent expert reviews of various stages of local investment projects, using their expertise to support knowledge sharing among local authorities. It has also developed a step-by-step guide on place-based decision making for all levels of government to plan and deliver investment.

Source: (Malik-Kapler, 2021, Unpublished[63]; European Commission Joint Research Centre, 2022[64]) (European Commission Joint Research Centre, 2022[64]); https://www.kleinstadtakademie.de/.

Strengthen national and regional support for infrastructure investments at the local level

The national and regional levels need to actively support municipalities to overcome capacity challenges resulting from Czechia's fragmented local administration. Often support to help small municipalities prepare investment projects might be preferable to training, which might not be targeted to the specific and varied needs of municipalities, or not be truly beneficial as municipal employees do not have sufficient resources or time to participate, and high turnover rates mean the knowledge may be quickly lost.

In this sense, the two initiatives that Czechia is planning to establish as part of the National Recovery Plan - the National Advisory Centre and the Regional Housing Investment Support Centres - are fundamental, if well managed and co-ordinated. The National Advisory Centre aims at supporting regions and municipalities with project preparation, especially for projects that support the green and digital transitions. This centre will use standardised tools and methodologies for public investment, including PPPs, building information modelling (BIM) projects, and setting long-term standards. While this centre will not necessarily only provide support to housing investments, the plan is for at least the first call for projects to focus on this sector. In parallel, the Regional Housing Investment Support Centres are to be established in eight regions to provide expert support to municipalities for rental housing investments through the dissemination of investment know-how, methodological support, and liaising with local experts. For the efficient implementation of these institutions, some preliminary issues might be considered:

- Establish concrete mechanisms and communication channels to ensure that the national and regional centres take a cross-sectoral perspective. The Ministry of Regional Development might consider piloting both institutions over 2024-2026. While their special focus is on the housing sector, it is important to recognise that at the territorial level, housing cannot be seen in isolation. Planned rental housing investments need to be accompanied by other sectorial investments: transport, roads and connectivity, education, water and sanitation, health facilities etc.. Both the national and regional centres need to put this cross-sectoral perspective up-front when selecting and supporting project preparation. The Ministry of Regional Development needs to establish concrete mechanisms and communication channels to ensure that the national and regional centres have this cross-sectoral perspective.
- Avoid duplication of tasks by the national and regional centres and instead create complementarities and synergies in the support they provide. This will require daily co-ordination, starting from setting the criteria for selecting projects to receive support from both centres and how they target the support. While support can be focused on appraisal and project preparation, it is also important to provide expertise and technical assistance in areas such as financial modelling and business case development.

There are also some online platforms to support project preparation and management that provide easy-to-use documents. They usually provide a comprehensive map of all aspects to consider for the preparation of sustainable infrastructure projects and model documents. For example, multilateral development banks have developed SOURCE to provide a complete range of documents to support infrastructure planning and investment processes (OECD, 2022[38]). In the same spirit, municipalities would also strongly benefit from accessing framework agreements established at the national level with larger contracting authorities. For frequently purchased goods, services and works, a framework agreement can reduce administrative burdens for contracting authorities and suppliers by allowing simplified ordering processes once the agreement is in place (see Chapter 2).

With the renewed interest in the use of PPPs, especially for affordable housing, special support for cities and municipalities will be essential. Czechia is currently developing national guidelines for the development of affordable housing through PPPs (see Chapter 2). PPPs are not risk-free and require careful consideration and implementation by subnational governments. Maximising their benefits and minimising their downsides requires substantial public sector capacity, especially at the subnational government level.

A PPP Unit at the national level with dedicated and technically sound expert teams (in-house and/or contracted) can strengthen subnational governments' capacity in undertaking PPPs. Most PPP Units are national, but some countries also have PPP Units at the subnational level. Although their specific role varies, PPP Units tend to perform a combination of five main functions: policy formulation and co-ordination, gate keeping and quality control, technical assistance, education and capacity development, and PPP promotion (OECD, 2022[38]).

Regions and municipalities could also benefit from framework agreements and resources such as grants for project design and preparation (e.g. environmental impact assessments, technical feasibility studies). Chapter 2 provides some examples of how support from the Ministry of the Environment and the State Environmental Fund could be enhanced, by considering two-round calls, with the first-round funding project preparation and design or reimburse preparation costs after construction approval.

Summary of key recommendations

Given the challenges of implementing a full suite of reforms, Czech authorities could consider sequencing the recommendations made above. By grouping recommendations according to the time horizon needed to implement them effectively (short term, and medium to long term), Czech authorities could allocate resources to reforms in a way which would provide incremental benefits. A potential sequencing is included below.

Short-term reforms

1. **Identify capacity gaps in all types of regions and municipalities.** In order to properly target assistance and capacity building at the subnational level, it is crucial to have a clear picture of which capacities are missing and where. With a proper diagnosis, assistance and capacity building can be better targeted and tailored to a group a regions or municipalities in a systemic and sustainable way, rather than offering technical assistance or building capacity on a case-by-case basis. This will involve two complementary and parallel measures:

- Develop a comprehensive database on subnational public employment that captures not only the number of public employees, but also other crucial characteristics such as gender, education level, hierarchy, etc. This would provide a useful database of subnational public staffing and its evolution over time, helping to identify key capacity gaps.
- Conduct surveys or consultations with regions and municipalities to better understand regional and municipal gaps in public administration and management and find common challenges. This diagnosis could be led by the Ministry of Regional Development or the Ministry of the Interior.

2. **Strengthen national and regional support and assistance to plan, prepare and implement infrastructure investments at the local level**. As the national and regional levels often have greater capacity than small municipalities they can provide direct support, instead of training, to small municipalities for preparing investment projects.

3. **Embed a cross-sectoral and multi-level perspective within capacity-building activities** to help in breaking down silos. Proper co-ordination among the National Advisory Centre and the Regional Housing Investment Support Centres could be a way forward:

- Establish concrete mechanisms and communication channels to ensure that the national and regional centres take a cross-sectoral perspective. Use the 2024-2026 period to pilot both institutions with a special focus on the housing sector, but while taking a broader view when selecting and supporting project preparation. The State Fund for Investments Promotion, with the assistance of the Ministry of Regional Development needs to establish concrete mechanisms and communication channels to allow the national and regional centres to take this cross-sectoral perspective.

- Avoid duplication of tasks by the national and regional centres and instead create complementarities and synergies in the support they provide. This will require daily co-ordination.
- Use the pilot period as an opportunity to collect proper data at the territorial level or identify data gaps for assessing infrastructure needs across all sectors. This will require a co-ordinated effort not only involving the National Advisory Centre and the Regional Housing Investment Support Centres, but also all sectors and institutions developing or collecting data.

4. **Provide special resources and tools for regions and municipalities to better prepare and procure infrastructure projects.** One of the major bottlenecks for quality infrastructure at the subnational levels is the preparation phase. To strengthen these processes, some different measures can be taken:

- Complement technical assistance provided by the Ministry of Regional Development and the national and regional centres with specific resources by including project preparation in eligible costs – cities and association of municipalities might particularly benefit from these. For this, ministries and state funds could consider two-round calls, with the first-round funding project preparation and design or reimburse preparation costs after construction approval.
- Promote the use of online platforms to support project preparation and management. These online tools usually provide a comprehensive map of all aspects to consider in preparing sustainable infrastructure projects, as well as model documents.
- Make sure that regions and municipalities can access framework agreements established at the national level with larger contracting authorities. For frequently purchased goods, services and works, a framework agreement can reduce administrative burdens for contracting authorities and suppliers by allowing simplified ordering processes once the agreement is in place.
- Provide special support for regions and cities to use PPPs given the renewed interest in this tool. PPPs require careful consideration and implementation by subnational governments. A PPP Unit with dedicated and technically sound expert teams (in house and/or contractual) established at the national level could strengthen subnational governments' capacity in undertaking PPPs.

5. **Leverage the role of the national and regional governments and the associations of municipalities to build capacities at the local level**. It is important to provide co-ordinated capacity-building activities to enable municipal administrations to better plan, prepare and deliver infrastructure projects. Capacity building can include classroom training, guidelines and training materials, or formative activities delivered by experts to subnational officials. Some important considerations include:

- Target trainings to a group of regions or municipalities facing similar challenges or focus them on specific issues such as technical, economic, environmental areas, or social analysis to support investment appraisal.
- Ensure that training activities are structured and sustainable over time so that knowledge is retained at the institutional level in spite of the turnover of government officials.
- Work together with regional governments and the associations of municipalities to identify needs, and define the scope, targeted audience and content of training. The future Regional Centres could also facilitate the training.
- Leverage inter-municipal co-operation arrangements to pool expertise across local governments and promote peer-learning, in particular taking advantage of the experience of the Shared Service Centres. Regional centres – in co-ordination with associations of municipalities – could also act as hubs to gather good practice across municipalities and organise peer-learning exchanges among local authorities to tackle specific and common issues within the region.

- Strengthen the administrative capacities of Voluntary Associations of Municipalities (VAMs) through systemic financial support so that VAMs have sufficient personnel and administrative capacities to implement investment activities.

3.6 Funding and financing subnational infrastructure investment

In OECD countries, subnational governments often face infrastructure funding and financing challenges due to their limited revenue sources. Funding, which is essential to pay for infrastructure investment, operations and maintenance, mainly comes from a mix of grants and transfers from upper-level government, as well as subnational own-source revenue such as taxes, user-charges and property income. Funding may also come from specific user-charges collected by a private operator of public infrastructure (e.g., through a concession agreement). Access to financing instruments – i.e. money from private or public financiers – is also crucial for subnational infrastructure as it helps subnational governments meet the high up-front costs of infrastructure investment, which could otherwise be unaffordable or may place substantial pressure on subnational government budgets. The appropriate use of finance can increase the ability of subnational governments to undertake needed investments and spread the burden of payment across future beneficiaries. In most countries, the 'golden rule' applies, meaning that financing for subnational governments is only permitted to cover investment needs and cannot be used to cover current expenditure. Opportunities for subnational governments to mobilise financing mainly relate to the use of debt (loans, bonds), but may also involve equity and guarantees if certain conditions are met (OECD, 2022[38]).

While financing can help cover up-front investment costs, by spreading costs over time, it will always need to be repaid by funding. Funding is also required for infrastructure maintenance and operation costs during the investment lifecycle. This means that unlocking funding for the infrastructure lifetime is essential to unlock investment, support maintenance and avoid creating a fiscal burden for future subnational governments. To increase infrastructure investment, subnational governments can harness a range of existing and innovative funding and financing instruments. Even well-known approaches (e.g. grants and subsidies, taxes, and user charges and fees) are often under-utilised by subnational governments (OECD, 2021[48]).

Increase subnational government funding capacity

The high reliance of Czech regions and municipalities on central transfers, as well as their limited tax autonomy, challenge subnational infrastructure funding. Czechia's regions and municipalities strongly depend on central grants and subsidies – mostly aimed at funding state delegated functions. Grants and subsidies represent 46.7% of subnational governments revenue, which is in line with OECD countries where on average almost 50% of revenue comes from transfers from the national government. While transfers include hundreds of subsidy schemes, which are mostly earmarked, grants for infrastructure investments often come from different state funds – especially the State Investment Support Fund, the State Fund for Transport Infrastructure and the State Environmental Fund (Box 3.17). State funds are also responsible, in most cases, for handling transfers from EU funds for investments. Subnational governments in OECD countries usually access a mix of unconditional and earmarked grants – the latter are usually provided to encourage them to undertake certain investments that align with national policy objectives. The United Kingdom government, for example, has rolled out a funding programme to support local authorities to develop electric vehicle charging infrastructure as a policy measure to achieve its fully zero emission agenda (OECD, 2022[38]).

Tax revenues also represent a significant source of subnational government revenue in Czechia, especially for municipalities. However, municipal tax autonomy is limited as taxes are mostly shared; subnational governments have control over just 1.2% of total tax revenues (OECD, 2016[39]). Regions do not collect their own taxes and the property tax on land and buildings is the only tax levied by municipalities apart from income tax from companies, which represents a tiny share of municipal revenue (OECD, 2023[18]). Limited tax autonomy together with a strong dependence on central transfers challenge the capacity of regions and municipalities – especially small ones – to fund, co-fund, and finance infrastructure investments. Consequently, regions and municipalities strongly depend on EU funds to invest. This dependence means that municipalities need to meet the eligibility criteria to access those funds, which are not necessarily aligned with the basic infrastructure needs of some municipalities.

Box 3.17. Czechia's state investment funds

The **State Investment Support Fund** (SPI) is an independent legal entity under the Ministry for Regional Development. The fund supports municipalities, cities and regions in housing and tourism investment, but in accordance with the Housing Strategy 021+, the fund's activities primarily focus on the availability, stability and quality of housing. The mission of the SFPI is to co-create quality conditions for housing development, whether this means the quality of buildings intended for housing, or the public spaces near these buildings and in their wider surroundings, as well as the motivation of entities operating in the housing market to take care of the housing stock, at the national and regional level.

The **State Fund for Transport Infrastructure** mainly finances road and rail infrastructure of national importance through national resources and EU funds.[3] The fund also contributes to research, capacity building, and relevant expert support linked to transport infrastructure. It allocates resources from EU funds, road taxes, a percentage of the excise duties on hydrocarbon fuels and lubricants and the surplus raised by fees on certain motorways. The fund is administered by an elected committee composed of nine members, and headed by the Minister of Transport. The committee's responsibilities include appointing and dismissing the Director, approving proposed budgets, scheduling income and expenditures, setting timetables for the floating of tenders in accordance with legal requirements, and releasing funding for approved projects.

The Czech **State Environmental Fund** provides direct or indirect financial support to subnational governments and other beneficiaries through subsidies, soft loans, or a combination of both. The fund primarily co-finances projects to improve quality of water, air, waste management, protection of nature and the countryside, environmental education, utilisation of renewable energy and measures to improve the energy performance of buildings. It is responsible for administering financial resources from the EU, namely the Cohesion Fund, the European Regional Development Fund and The Next Generation EU Fund. It also administers resources from the state budget, and from fees collected from polluters – including wastewater discharge fees, fees for reclassifying agricultural land, air pollution fees and fees under the Waste Act.

The subsidies provided by the fund are designed to support the public sector, businesses and households, and can be used to improve heating systems, energy savings measures as well as funding green infrastructure in cities and municipalities. In May 2022, the government announced an additional CZK 4.75 billion (194 million EUR) in funds for 2022 for operating support related to the development of new renewable and other supported energy sources. Importantly, the Act on Promoted Energy Sources (Act No. 165/2012) was amended in 2022 to provide additional support for existing and new power plants with renewable energy sources. A key feature of the legislation was to move away from existing feed-in-tariffs and to introduce competitive bidding and auctions for renewable power generators and to offer green bonuses, also for heat generation. The revised legislation opens the door for support to renewable sources that has largely been lacking since the end of 2013.

Source: (State Environmental Fund of the Czech Republic, n.d.[65]) (State Fund for Transport Infrastructure, n.d.[66]) (OECD, 2023[67]) (State Investment Support Fund, n.d.[68])

There are several avenues for increasing Czech subnational governments' funding capacities. OECD analysis suggests that subnational tax revenues can be increased by revising the tax-sharing formula and making better use of the property tax. Other OECD analyses have highlighted that the current tax-sharing formula, which allocates revenue from personal and corporate income tax and VAT based on several determinants among which the population size, implicitly sustains municipal fragmentation, by encouraging very small municipalities to remain small because on average they receive significantly more tax revenue per inhabitant that way. Given the need for more intermunicipal co-operation, the reports note that this formula could be better structured to acknowledge the differences in revenue-raising capacity among municipalities in order to enhance horizontal equity (OECD, 2021[20]).

In addition to the issue of tax sharing, the OECD has long held the position that Czechia is not using the property tax to its full advantage. Property taxes are often a key source of revenue for subnational governments in OECD countries and the revenue raised from these taxes has a direct link to the quality of local infrastructure and public services. Property taxes have numerous merits: they are a stable tax base, they have solid return on tax collection, they prevent vertical tax competition, and they have a direct link to infrastructure provision (OECD, 2022[38]). Various OECD studies have therefore suggested that the tax autonomy of Czech local governments could be strengthened by encouraging municipalities to raise more revenue from the property tax. Collecting higher levels of property tax may not only strengthen the local fiscal base, but may also act as a counter-cyclical revenue source that provides stability for local revenues (OECD, 2020[17]) (OECD, 2023[18]). For this, property tax evaluation should be based on regularly updated estimates of property value rather than the size of the property, as it is today. This has been the path adopted by several countries that calculate the value of the property based on the rental value or the market value.

To address demographic and territorial inequalities' challenges that Czechia is facing, the OECD has also recently highlighted that there is a growing pressure for horizontal revenue redistribution across subnational governments. For this, many OECD countries resort to fiscal equalisation. There are a wide variety of fiscal equalisation models. Most can be classified depending on whether they equalise fiscal capacity or expenditure needs, or a combination of both; whether they are funded by vertical or horizontal grants; and whether they pursue a full or partial equalisation goal. However, many combine multiple features and some issues are relevant to all systems (Dougherty et al., 2022[69]) (OECD, 2023[18]).

Adopt innovative financing instruments to boost subnational infrastructure investment

Mobilising finance is essential to help subnational governments meet the high up-front costs of infrastructure investment and to spread those costs across the future beneficiaries of an investment (OECD, 2022[38]). Subnational governments mainly finance infrastructure investment through debt in the form of loans and bonds. While regions and municipalities access loans to finance infrastructure, their level of indebtedness is very low. Czech regions and municipalities can borrow from different sources, including commercial banks, the State Environment Fund or international donors such as the European Investment Bank. Subnational governments may also issue bonds with the approval of the Ministry of Finance (around 9% of municipalities issue bonds).

National governments can regulate subnational borrowing by introducing effective borrowing controls in the form of administrative or regulatory rules to preserve fiscal discipline. Since 2017, regional and municipal gross debt must remain below 60% of a four-year average of revenue (Act No. 23/2017). If the debt target is not respected, central authorities may cut revenue to a municipality or region by 5% of the difference between its amount of debt and the 60% target. This suspended revenue can only be released to gradually repay subnational government debt obligations made before the year in which the suspension occurred. As a result, subnational government debt in Czechia is well below the OECD average (3.5% of GDP and 7.5% of public debt vs. 27.9% and 20.2% respectively). Financial debt, which accounts for 43.7% of subnational government outstanding debt, is primarily made up of loans (85.6% of financial debt in 2020) while bonds account for only 14.4% of subnational government financial debt. In 2019 approximately 550 municipalities (9% of the total number) had a debt higher than 60% of their revenue and the regions had no debt exceeding this threshold.[4]

Subnational governments can also mobilise equity or guarantees provided by upper-level governments or multilateral development banks. While the use of guarantees needs to be carefully considered, this instrument can be an effective tool to improve access to finance for quality infrastructure investment by subnational governments, particularly where a project is economically and financially viable but includes risks that financiers would have little control over or may not be willing to bear (OECD, 2022[38]).

OECD countries are increasingly using more innovative financing instruments, including green, social, climate and sustainability bonds or loans (Box 3.18). Green bonds, for example, are gaining traction for financing green projects that deliver environmental benefits. Green bonds share the same financial characteristics as conventional bonds, with the exception of the ring-fencing or earmarking of proceeds required by the green label. They are usually issued by large cities or groups of cities that pool together their financing and human capacities. For green bonds to be successful, governments need to develop a pipeline of quality, bankable projects (OECD, 2020[31]). The use of innovative financing instruments in Czechia is very limited. No green bond has been issued at the subnational level and there is still low use of private capital to finance public investment. Following the example of France's Île-de-France region (Box 3.18), regions or big cities in Czechia could explore resorting to innovative financing instruments to make better use of existing opportunities to finance their infrastructure needs, especially for social housing and complementary infrastructure.

Box 3.18. Innovative financial instruments used by subnational governments in OECD countries

France's **Île-de-France** region has made climate finance a trademark for its investors. It has been a frequent and regular issuer in the green and sustainable bond market since 2012, with eight transactions. Its 6th Green and Sustainable Bond Issuance, launched in June 2018, amounted to EUR 500 million. As part of the process and under the supervision of the region's finance directorate, each sectoral department in the region is asked to identify priority projects with a high environmental and social impact and within a certain budget. The finance directorate then consolidates the information across departments and finalises the budget allocation by sector. Nine eligibility criteria have been established to guide the purpose and management of the projects (e.g. environmental responsibility, social and societal responsibility, economic responsibility and governance). Looking at the funds received from the green bond during the 2014-18 period, half went to public transport and sustainable transport projects. Social housing and facilities for education and leisure accounted for 16% and 15% respectively. Minor shares of funding were also allocated to projects related to biodiversity (5%), economic and socially inclusive development (7%), support to vulnerable groups (5%) and energy efficiency (2%).

The first municipal green bond in the **Nordic countries** was issued in 2013 by the City of Gothenburg, Sweden, to fund energy, transport, water management and waste management projects. It has renewed the experience almost annually since then. To support its green bond strategy, the city has developed its own Green Bond Framework, which specifies terms and conditions for the selection of eligible projects, follow-up and transparency requirements. Nordic local government funding agencies, such as *Kommuninvest* (Sweden) and Municipality Finance (Finland), are also regular issuers of green bonds. In general, Nordic green bond issuers rely extensively on the use of external reviews and second party opinions to support their green bond issuances, which confirms compliance with the Green Bond Principles and the climate components of the proposed investments.

In 2014, eight local municipal water utilities in the **Veneto region in Italy** joined together to raise finance through a 'hydrobond'. To achieve this, the municipal companies pooled mini bonds into a Special Purpose Vehicle (SPV) and jointly issued a EUR 150 million bond on the capital market. This has financed 728 individual infrastructure investments in the region's integrated water system from 2014 to 2017 (with an estimated value of EUR 300 million). These investments included new water mains and sewer pipes, upgrading facilities and network maintenance.

Source: (OECD, 2020[31])

Subnational governments in OECD countries are also increasingly innovating in the type of investment approach that they use. When delivering an investment, a subnational government might evaluate different options, including traditional and more innovative public procurement of infrastructure, the use of a public-private partnership or harnessing a state-owned enterprise (e.g., a municipal company). Various models exist to build public-private co-operation and leverage private investment, and new forms of collaboration are emerging. While the PPP market has seen some decline in recent years, there are other innovative partnership models involving national and local authorities in which there is a long-term vision and risks and rewards are shared over time. One form of emerging model of public-private collaboration is the regulatory asset-based model, which already exists for supporting private investment in some industries (energy, water, etc.), but is increasingly being explored for use in new sectors (OECD, 2022[36]). To support more inclusive investment, they may also explore the use of different procurement innovations such as green or social procurement. Green public procurement supports environment-friendly policies and investment strategies by integrating environmental and social considerations into the procurement process. In Europe, they have taken the form of Green Deals – generally, voluntary agreements between private partners, civil society and the national and/or regional government to establish a joint green project (OECD, 2020[31]).

PPPs can be attractive for a number of reasons (see Chapter 2), especially because they can be an efficient way of accelerating infrastructure investments at the regional and local levels. Taking advantage of the renewed momentum for PPPs, Czechia could envisage large municipalities engaging in PPPs. However, it is extremely important to closely assess financial commitments to ensure that the sequence of subsequent payments is compatible with the financial situation of subnational governments. This requires highly skilled, competent, and experienced teams, given the complexity of the financial, technical and legal frameworks of PPP projects. Such expertise is generally not available outside the bigger cities. Czechia could thus envisage appointing a special team within a National PPP Unit that is responsible for developing and reinforcing regional and municipal capacity to effectively engage with the private sector through PPPs. The UK model of the Private Finance Initiative (PFI) programme or the French "public-private partnership contracts" could be followed.

Summary of key recommendations

Given the challenges of implementing a full suite of reforms, Czech authorities could consider sequencing the recommendations made above. By grouping recommendations according to the time horizon needed to implement them effectively (short term, and medium to long term), Czech authorities could allocate resources to reforms in a way which would provide incremental benefits. A potential sequencing is included below.

Short-term reforms

1. **Increase subnational governments' funding capacities.** This can be implemented through several complementary avenues:

- Revise the tax-sharing formula to avoid encouraging municipal fragmentation. The formula could be better structured to acknowledge the differences in revenue-raising capacity among municipalities in order to enhance horizontal equity. For this it would be important to raise the weight of factors linked to economic activity (number of employees) and income.
- Consider designating the municipal income tax as own-source only for certain types of municipalities or large cities, as small municipalities do not necessarily reach an optimum size to collect taxes efficiently.
- Make better use of the property tax. Property tax evaluation should be based on regularly updated estimates of property value rather than the size of the property, as it is today. This has been the path adopted by several countries that calculate the value of the property based on the rental value or the market value.

Medium to long-term reforms

1. **Adopt innovative financing instruments to boost subnational infrastructure investment.** Mobilising finance is essential to help subnational governments meet the high up-front costs of infrastructure investment and to spread those costs across the future beneficiaries of an investment. They can be either an alternative or a complement to subsidies, depending on their conditions and investments needs:

- Encourage the use of innovative financing instruments, including green, social, climate and sustainability bonds or loans. In the first instance they could be targeted especially at social housing and complementary infrastructure.
- Provide expert support for subnational governments to guide them in the use of innovative instruments. The Union of Towns and Municipalities could provide expert support, especially for medium or small municipalities. Bigger cities could aim at integrating this expertise directly in their administration. This could also take the form of a special task force bringing together stakeholders from all government levels, as well as from the financial sector, to develop a methodology, pilot and implement it to make innovative instruments accessible and attractive for subnational governments.

2. **Explore wider engagement in public-private partnerships by regions and cities as an option to accelerate infrastructure investments**. PPPs can be a tool for reforming public procurement and public service delivery, and not just a means of leveraging private sector resources. For this it would be of utmost importance to have a special team within a national PPP unit responsible for developing and reinforcing regional and municipal capacity to effectively engage with the private sector in PPPs

Notes

1 The NUTS classification (Nomenclature of territorial units for statistics) is a hierarchical system developed by the European Union for dividing up the economic territory of the EU and the UK. NUTS 1: major socio-economic regions; NUTS 2: basic regions for the application of regional policies; NUTS 3: small regions for specific diagnoses.

2 https://www.risy.cz/cs/

3 With the establishment of regions in 2000 and the subsequent transfer to their purview of Class II and III roads, the fund's tax revenues were reduced as funds for lower class roads were transferred to local governments in the form of tax budgeting.

4 The structural fiscal balance rule was amended in 2020 to allow the central government to deal with the COVID-19 crisis and to implement fiscal support.

References

Bakoš, E. et al. (2021), "The perception of inter-municipal cooperation by local officials and managers", *Central European Journal of Public Policy*, Vol. 15/1, pp. 1-14, https://doi.org/10.2478/cejpp-2021-0002. [53]

Council of the European Union (2021), *Council implementing decision on the approval of the assessment of the recovery and resilience plan for Czechia*, https://data.consilium.europa.eu/doc/document/ST-11047-2021-INIT/en/pdf. [154]

Czech National Bank (2022), *Financial Stability Report: Spring 2022*, Czech National Bank, Prague, https://www.cnb.cz/export/sites/cnb/en/financial-stability/.galleries/fs_reports/fsr_2022_spring/fsr_2022_spring.pdf. [174]

Czech Statistical Office (2021), *Ownership structure of houses (database)*, Czech Statistical Office, Strašnice, https://www.scitani.cz/ownership-structure-of-houses#skupina-54463. [175]

Czechia (1969), *Act No. 2/1969 Coll., on the Establishment of Ministries and Other Central Authorities of the State Administration of Czechia*, https://www.zakonyprolidi.cz/cs/1969-2# (accessed on 10 June 2023). [137]

CzechInvest (2023), *Annual Report 2022*, CzechInvest, Prague, https://www.czechinvest.org/getattachment/03a24875-7757-4fe8-bc6e-ddbd6516aed7/Vyrocni-zprava-2022. [185]

CzechInvest (n.d.), *Services for Municipalities (in Czech)*, CzechInvest, Prague, https://www.czechinvest.org/cz/Sluzby-pro-municipality/Uvod (accessed on 10 June 2023). [186]

De Barbieri, E. (2018), "Urban Anticipatory Governance", *Florida State University Law Review*, Vol. 46/1, https://ir.law.fsu.edu/lr/vol46/iss1/3. [45]

Demmou, L. and G. Franco (2020), "Do sound infrastructure governance and regulation affect productivity growth? New insights from firm level data", *OECD Economics Department Working Papers*, No. 1609, OECD Publishing, Paris, https://doi.org/10.1787/410535403555. [117]

Department of Public Expenditure, NDP Delivery and Reform (2023), *Circular 06/2023: Update of the Public Spending Code Capital Spending Requirements*, https://assets.gov.ie/251585/daa5c0b1-4165-4a49-8668-d3137ac6e124.pdf. [118]

Department of Public Expenditure, NDP Delivery and Reform (2021), *National Development Plan 2021-2030*, https://assets.gov.ie/200358/a36dd274-736c-4d04-8879-b158e8b95029.pdf. [77]

Department of Treasury and Finance Victoria (2021), *Victorian Infrastructure Plan 2021*, https://www.dtf.vic.gov.au/sites/default/files/document/Victorian%20Infrastructure%20Plan%202021.pdf. [87]

Dobbs, R. et al. (2013), *Infrastructure productivity: How to save $1 trillion a year*, https://www.mckinsey.com/capabilities/operations/our-insights/infrastructure-productivity. [112]

Dougherty, S. et al. (2022), "Going beyond fiscal equalisation: Institutional and fiscal tools to fight territorial inequalities", https://www.oecd.org/tax/federalism/going-beyond-fiscal-equalisation-note.pdf. [69]

ESPON (2021), *Cross-fertilisation between spatial planning and EU Cohesion Policy in the Czech Republic*, ESPON, https://www.espon.eu/cohesion-policy-and-spatial-planning. [22]

ESPON (2021), *IMAGINE - Developing a metropolitan-regional imaginary in Milan-Bologna urban region*, ESPON, https://www.espon.eu/imagine (accessed on 2 June 2023). [34]

ESPON (2021), *New spatial imaginaries need*, https://polimi.maps.arcgis.com/apps/dashboards/09a3b36b3d4d409f9d0bb461a453362c (accessed on 2 June 2023). [35]

European Commission (2023), *2014-2020 Cohesion Policy Overview*, European Commission, Brussels, https://cohesiondata.ec.europa.eu/cohesion_overview/14-20 (accessed on 22 July 2023). [160]

European Commission (2023), *2023 Country report - Czechia*, European Commission, Brussels, https://economy-finance.ec.europa.eu/system/files/2023-05/CZ_SWD_2023_603_en.pdf. [146]

European Commission (2023), *Cohesion Data*, https://cohesiondata.ec.europa.eu/countries/CZ/21-27 (accessed on 25 May 2023). [6]

European Commission (2023), *Cohesion Open Data Platform*, https://cohesiondata.ec.europa.eu/countries/CZ/14-20 (accessed on 22 July 2023). [152]

European Commission (2023), *Cohesion Open Data Platform*, European Commission, Brussels, https://cohesiondata.ec.europa.eu/countries/CZ/21-27 (accessed on 21 July 2023). [153]

European Commission (2023), *NextGenerationEU: Questions and Answers on REPowerEU and on the revision of national recovery plans*, European Commission, Brussels, https://ec.europa.eu/commission/presscorner/detail/en/qanda_23_2489 (accessed on 7 July 2023). [157]

European Commission (2022), *Cohesion in Europe towards 2050: Eighth report on economic, social and territorial cohesion*, European Commission, Brussels, https://ec.europa.eu/regional_policy/information-sources/publications/communications/2022/cohesion-in-europe-towards-2050-8th-cohesion-report_en. [150]

European Commission (2021), *Analysis of the recovery and resilience plan of Czechia*, https://eur-lex.europa.eu/legal-content/EN/TXT/PDF/?uri=CELEX:52021SC0211. [73]

European Commission (2021), *Analysis of the recovery and resilience plan of Czechia*, European Commission, Brussels, https://eur-lex.europa.eu/legal-content/EN/TXT/PDF/?uri=CELEX:52021SC0211. [155]

European Commission (2021), *Analysis of the Recovery and Resilience Plan of Czechia*, https://eur-lex.europa.eu/legal-content/EN/TXT/PDF/?uri=CELEX:52021SC0211. [10]

European Commission (2021), *NextGenerationEU: European Commission disburses €915 million in pre-financing to Czechia*, https://ec.europa.eu/commission/presscorner/detail/en/ip_21_4912. [156]

European Commission (2020), *ProcurCompEU Implementation in Slovenia*, [94] https://commission.europa.eu/system/files/2021-04/procurcompeu-slovenia-en_1.pdf.

European Commission (2020), *ProcurCompEU: European Competency Framework for Public Procurement Professionals*, https://commission.europa.eu/system/files/2020-12/procurcompeu-ecf_for_pp_en.pdf. [93]

European Commission (2020), *ProcurCompEU: Study on professionalisation of public procurement in the EU and selected third countries*, https://commission.europa.eu/system/files/2020-12/procurcompeu-study_prof_pp_en.pdf. [62]

European Commission (n.d.), *Cohesion Policy Instruments*, European Commission, Brussels, https://www.dotaceeu.cz/en/evropske-fondy-v-cr/programove-obdobi-2004-2006-(1)/nastroje-politiky-soudrznosti (accessed on 19 July 2023). [148]

European Commission (n.d.), *Czechia's recovery and resilience plan*, https://commission.europa.eu/business-economy-euro/economic-recovery/european-semester/czechias-recovery-and-resilience-plan_en (accessed on 25 May 2023). [9]

European Commission (n.d.), *Open Data Portal for the European Structural Investment Funds*, https://cohesiondata.ec.europa.eu/2014-2020_cohesion_overview (accessed on 1 June 2023). [110]

European Commission Joint Research Centre (2022), *Handbook of Territorial and Local Development Strategies*, Publications Office of the European Union, https://doi.org/10.2760/57919. [64]

European Development Agency (n.d.), *Local Action Group Mezilesí*, European Development Agency, https://euda.eu/local-action-group-mezilesi/. [50]

European Investment Bank (2021), *The state of local infrastructure investment in Europe: EIB Municipalities Survey 2020*, European Investment Bank, https://www.eib.org/attachments/efs/eibis_2020_municipality_en.pdf. [52]

Global Infrastructure Hub (2020), *Water Height and Flood Management System*, https://www.gihub.org/infrastructure-technology-use-cases/case-studies/water-height-and-flood-management-system/ (accessed on 5 April 2023). [102]

Global Infrastructure Hub (2019), *Leading Practices in Governmental Processes Facilitating Infrastructure Project Preparation*, https://cdn.gihub.org/umbraco/media/2344/gih_project-preparation_full-document_final_art_web.pdf. [82]

Government of Czech Republic (2019), *National Energy and Climate Plan of the Czech Republic*, https://energy.ec.europa.eu/system/files/2020-03/cs_final_necp_main_en_0.pdf. [16]

Government of Czechia (2023), *Resolution of the Government of Czechia No 448*, Government of Czechia, Prague, https://www.odok.cz/portal/services/download/attachment/2023/448/pdf/. [196]

Government of Czechia (2022), *Policy Statement of the Government of Czechia*, https://www.vlada.cz/assets/jednani-vlady/policy-statement/Policy-Statement-of-the-Government.pdf. [123]

Government of Czechia (2022), *Policy Statement of the Government of Czechia*, Government of Czechia, Prague, https://www.vlada.cz/assets/jednani-vlady/policy-statement/Policy- [162]

Statement-of-the-Government.pdf.

Government of Czechia (2020), *Statute of the State Investment Support Fund*, Government of Czechia, Prague, https://sfpi.cz/zakladni-dokumenty/. [183]

Government of Czechia (2019), *National Investment Plan of Czechia 2020-2050*, http://www.vlada.cz/assets/media-centrum/aktualne/Narodni-investicni-plan-CR-2020_2050.pdf. [124]

Government of Czechia (2017), *Strategic Framework Czechia 2030*, https://www.vlada.cz/assets/ppov/udrzitelny-rozvoj/projekt-OPZ/Strategic_Framework_CZ2030.pdf. [126]

Government of Czechia (n.d.), *Advisory and Working Bodies*, Government of Czechia, Prague, https://www.vlada.cz/en/pracovni-a-poradni-organy-vlady/ (accessed on 10 June 2023). [142]

Government of Czechia (n.d.), *Annex to the Government Resolution of 21 June 2023 No 448*, Government of Czechia, Prague, https://vlada.gov.cz/assets/ppov/strategicke-investice/priloha_usneseni_2023_448_1_statut.pdf. [195]

Government of Czechia (n.d.), *Members of the Government*, Government of Czechia, Prague, https://www.vlada.cz/en/vlada/ (accessed on 10 June 2023). [135]

Government of Czechia (n.d.), *Working Committees*, Government of Czechia, Prague, https://www.vlada.cz/cz/ppov/lrv/pracovni-komise/ (accessed on 10 June 2023). [136]

Huerta Melchor, O. and J. Gars (2020), "Planning mobility in a fragmented metropolitan area: The case of Prague and its suburbs", *OECD Regional Development Papers*, No. 08, OECD Publishing, Paris, https://doi.org/10.1787/4cdf2d31-en. [100]

IEA (2021), *Czech Republic 2021 Energy Policy Review*, IEA Energy Policy Reviews, OECD Publishing, Paris, https://doi.org/10.1787/fd01b443-en. [170]

IEA (2021), *Czech Republic 2021 Energy Policy Review*, IEA Energy Policy Reviews, OECD Publishing, Paris, https://doi.org/10.1787/fd01b443-en. [201]

Infrastructure and Projects Authority (2021), *Assurance Review Toolkit*, https://www.gov.uk/government/collections/infrastructure-and-projects-authority-assurance-review-toolkit (accessed on 17 April 2023). [89]

Infrastructure and Projects Authority (2020), *About the IPA*, https://assets.publishing.service.gov.uk/government/uploads/system/uploads/attachment_data/file/973834/About_the_IPA_2020_12.03.21.pdf. [99]

Infrastructure Victoria (2021), *Victoria's Infrastructure Strategy 2021-2051*, https://www.infrastructurevictoria.com.au/wp-content/uploads/2021/08/1.-Victorias-infrastructure-strategy-2021-2051-Vol-1.pdf. [85]

International Energy Agency (2022), *Czech Republic Climate Resilience Policy Indicator*, https://www.iea.org/articles/czech-republic-climate-resilience-policy-indicator. [29]

ITF (2023), *ITF Transport Outlook 2023*, OECD Publishing, Paris, https://doi.org/10.1787/b6cc9ad5-en. [164]

ITF (2023), "Transport infrastructure investment and maintenance", *ITF Transport Statistics* (database), https://doi.org/10.1787/g2g55573-en (accessed on 7 July 2023). [163]

ITF (2022), *Broadening Transport Appraisal: Summary and Conclusions*, ITF Roundtable Reports, No. 188, OECD Publishing, Paris, https://doi.org/10.1787/a0e2e0a6-en. [121]

ITF (2021), *Developing Strategic Approaches to Infrastructure Planning*, ITF Research Reports, OECD Publishing, Paris, https://doi.org/10.1787/d8d6651c-en. [101]

Ježek, J. (2015), *Critical analysis of strategic planning of municipalities, cities and regions in Czechia*, Vydala Západočeská univerzita v Plzni, https://dspace5.zcu.cz/handle/11025/22570. [145]

Kim, J., J. Fallov and S. Groom (2020), *Public Investment Management Reference Guide*, Washington, DC: World Bank, https://doi.org/10.1596/978-1-4648-1529-4. [120]

Madsen, B. (2021), *The Covid-19 legacy: More Resilient Procurement Strategies?*, https://www.oecd.org/gov/public-procurement/infrastructure-and-public-procurement-webinar-series-2021.htm. [83]

Maier, K. (2020), "Planning of Bohemian regional centres in the period of their industrialisation and modernisation: Pilsen and Hradec Králové", *Architektúra & urbanizmus*, Vol. 54/1-2, https://doi.org/10.31577/archandurb.2020.54.1-2.5. [59]

Malik-Kapler, E. (2021, Unpublished), *Support for problem areas in Poland*. [63]

Marine Information and Data Centre (n.d.), *Marine Information and Data Centre*, https://www.informatiehuismarien.nl/uk/about-us/ (accessed on 5 April 2023). [104]

Ministry of Environment (2023), *Operational programme Just Transition (OPJT) 2021-2027*, https://www.mzp.cz/en/operational_programme_just_transition (accessed on 25 May 2023). [8]

Ministry of Finance (2023), *Approved Sort Budget for Expenditures: Central Government*, Ministry of Finance, Prague, https://monitor.statnipokladna.cz/statni-sprava/schvaleny-rozpocet/vydaje-druhovy?rad=t&obdobi=2312 (accessed on 7 September 2023). [139]

Ministry of Finance (2023), *Convergence Programme of the Czech Republic*, Ministry of Finance, Prague, https://commission.europa.eu/system/files/2023-04/Czechia-CP-2023_EN.pdf. [147]

Ministry of Finance (2023), *State Final Account of Czechia for the Year 2022*, Ministry of Finance, Prague, https://www.mfcr.cz/cs/rozpoctova-politika/statni-rozpocet/plneni-statniho-rozpoctu/2022/statni-zaverecny-ucet-za-rok-2022-51132. [138]

Ministry of Finance (2022), *Ministers agree on the distribution of EUR 20 billion from the RePowerEU package, the Czech Republic will get about CZK 16.7 billion*, Ministry of Finance, Prague, https://www.mfcr.cz/en/news/press-releases/2022/ministers-agree-on-the-distribution-of-e-48940/ (accessed on 7 July 2023). [158]

Ministry of Finance (n.d.), *About the ministry*, Ministry of Finance, Prague, https://www.mfcr.cz/cs/o-ministerstvu/zakladni-informace/hlavni-cinnosti (accessed on 10 October 2022). [184]

Ministry of Industry and Trade (2020), *The National Energy and Climate Plan of Czechia*, https://www.mpo.cz/en/energy/strategic-and-conceptual-documents/the-national-energy-and- [129]

climate-plan-of-the-czech-republic--252018/.

Ministry of Industry and Trade (2015), *State Energy Policy of Czechia*, https://www.mpo.cz/assets/en/energy/state-energy-policy/2017/11/State-Energy-Policy-_2015__EN.pdf. [130]

Ministry of Industry and Trade (n.d.), *Authority of the Ministry*, Ministry of Industry and Trade, Prague, https://www.mpo.cz/dokument1926.html (accessed on 10 October 2022). [171]

Ministry of Labour and Social Affairs (2019), *Responsible Public Procurement: European Practice*, https://sovz.cz/wp-content/uploads/2019/10/responsible-public-procurement-european-practice.pdf. [108]

Ministry of Labour and Social Affairs (2017), *Socially Responsible Public Procurement in Czechia: Selection of Best Practice Case Studies*, https://sovz.cz/wp-content/uploads/2017/08/sovz_case_studies_en_komplet.pdf. [131]

Ministry of Regional Development (2024), *Spatial Development Policy of the Czech Republic (as amended, in effect on 1 March 2024)*, Ministry of Regional Development of the Czech Republic, Institute for Spatial Development, https://mmr.gov.cz/cs/ministerstvo/stavebni-pravo/koncepce-a-strategie/politika-uzemniho-rozvoje-ceske-republiky. [194]

Ministry of Regional Development (2023), *Info page IROP 2021-2027*, https://irop.mmr.cz/cs/irop-2021-2027 (accessed on 25 May 2023). [7]

Ministry of Regional Development (2023), *National Standing Conference*, https://mmr.cz/cs/microsites/uzemni-dimenze/stale-konference/nsk (accessed on 25 May 2023). [26]

Ministry of Regional Development (2022), *Strategy Database - Strategic document portal of the Czech Republic*, https://www.databaze-strategie.cz/cz/oblastni-dokumenty (accessed on 26 May 2023). [23]

Ministry of Regional Development (2021), *Housing Concept of Czechia 2021+*, https://mmr.gov.cz/getmedia/30528174-7e61-421e-a058-5f39aa4f09c9/KB-2021-_komplet-web(C)_max.pdf.aspx?ext=.pdf. [197]

Ministry of Regional Development (2021), *Spatial Development Policy of the Czech Republic (as amended, in effect on 1 September 2021)*, Ministry of Regional Development, Prague, https://mmr.gov.cz/getmedia/d081772b-2d7e-4454-9fef-478a70c788e6/Spatial-Development-Policy-of-the-CR_recent-version-from-September-2021.pdf.aspx?ext=.pdf. [24]

Ministry of Regional Development (2019), *Regional Development Strategy 21+*, https://mmr.cz/getmedia/a9985cb6-b672-4a97-a92c-c4c68bea2925/EN-III_ma_SRR-prac_doplneni-schemat-a-map_kontrola.pdf.aspx?ext=.pdf. [5]

Ministry of Regional Development (2019), *Regional Development Strategy of Czechia 2021+*, Ministry of Regional Development, https://mmr.cz/getmedia/a9985cb6-b672-4a97-a92c-c4c68bea2925/EN-III_ma_SRR-prac_doplneni-schemat-a-map_kontrola.pdf.aspx?ext=.pdf. [132]

Ministry of Regional Development (2019), *Regional Development Strategy of the Czech Republic 2021+*, https://mmr.gov.cz/getmedia/4023f194-31f3-4269-83ef-0e2c86255e92/SRR21- [21]

brozura-A5-tisk-EN-9_12_2019-(002).pdf.aspx?ext=.pdf.

Ministry of Regional Development (n.d.), *Ministry of Regional Development*, Ministry of Regional Development, Prague, https://www.mmr.cz/cs/ministerstvo (accessed on 5 July 2023). [180]

Ministry of Regional Development (n.d.), *Programming period 2004-2006*, Ministry of Regional Development, Prague, https://www.dotaceeu.cz/en/evropske-fondy-v-cr/programove-obdobi-2004-2006-(1) (accessed on 21 July 2023). [149]

Ministry of Regional Development (n.d.), *Programming period 2007-2013*, https://www.dotaceeu.cz/en/evropske-fondy-v-cr/programove-obdobi-2007-2013 (accessed on 22 July 2023). [151]

Ministry of Regional Development (n.d.), *Programming period 2007-2013*, Ministry of Regional Development, Prague, https://www.dotaceeu.cz/en/evropske-fondy-v-cr/programove-obdobi-2007-2013 (accessed on 22 July 2023). [159]

Ministry of Regional Development (n.d.), *Strategy Database: Portal of Strategic Documents in Czechia*, https://www.databaze-strategie.cz/cz/info (accessed on 10 July 2023). [127]

Ministry of the Environment (n.d.), *Climate Policy of the Czech Republic*, Ministry of the Environment, Prague, https://www.mzp.cz/en/climate_policy_of_the_czech_republic (accessed on 3 July 2023). [188]

Ministry of the Environment (n.d.), *Lean public administration*, https://www.mzp.cz/cz/setrna_verejna_sprava (accessed on 5 May 2023). [109]

Ministry of the Interior of the Czech Republic (2020), *Strategic Management and Municipal Planning – Study Guide for Municipal Representatives*, Ministry of the Interior of the Czech Republic, Prague. [44]

Ministry of the Interior of the Czech Republic (2018), , https://eu.eventscloud.com/file_uploads/e9093b29069afb13593f6ac3e0b70cd8_TUEPublicadministrationVazaAdam.pdf. [61]

Ministry of the Interior of the Czech Republic (2018), *Public Administration in the Czech Republic*, 2nd edition, Ministry of the Interior of the Czech Republic, Prague, https://eu.eventscloud.com/file_uploads/e9093b29069afb13593f6ac3e0b70cd8_TUEPublicadministrationVazaAdam.pdf. [19]

Ministry of Transport (2021), *ŘSD will turn into a state-owned enterprise, the government approved savings and speeding up construction*, Ministry of Transport, Prague, https://mdcr.cz/Media/Media-a-tiskove-zpravy/RSD-se-zmeni-na-statni-podnik,-uspory-a-urychl-(1). [167]

Ministry of Transport (2021), *Transport Policy of Czechia for the period 2021-2027, with an outlook until 2050*, https://www.mdcr.cz/getattachment/Dokumenty/Strategie/Dopravni-politika-a-MFDI/Dopravni-politika-CR-pro-obdobi-2014-2020-s-vyhled/Dopravni_Politika_CR_ENG.pdf.aspx. [128]

Ministry of Transport (2018), *Departmental Guideline for the Evaluation of Economic Effectiveness of Transport Construction Projects*, https://www.sfdi.cz/soubory/obrazky- [105]

clanky/metodiky/2017_03_departmental-methodology-full.pdf.

Ministry of Transport (2010-2022), *Transport Yearbooks Czechia*, Ministry of Transport, Prague, https://www.sydos.cz/cs/rocenky.htm. [140]

Mizell, L. and D. Allain-Dupré (2013), "Creating conditions for effective public investment: Sub-national capacities in a multi-level governance context", *OECD Regional Development Working Papers*, No. 2013/4, OECD Publishing, Paris, https://doi.org/10.1787/5k49j2cjv5mq-en. [55]

National Development Bank (n.d.), *About the bank*, https://www.nrb.cz/en/about-the-bank/ (accessed on 10 October 2022). [187]

National Infrastructure Commission (2022), *Cambridgeshire and Peterborough leaders inform national infrastructure advisers' fact-finding tour*, https://nic.org.uk/news/cambridgeshire-and-peterborough-leaders-inform-national-infrastructure-advisers-fact-finding-tour/. [32]

National Infrastructure Commission (2022), *West Yorkshire leaders engage on region's infrastructure goals*, https://nic.org.uk/news/west-yorkshire-leaders-engage-on-regions-infrastructure-goals/. [33]

OECD (2023), "Delivering environmentally sustainable and climate-resilient infrastructure", in *Government at a Glance 2023*, OECD Publishing, Paris, https://doi.org/10.1787/2387658e-en. [115]

OECD (2023), *Housing Sector Country Snapshot: Czech Republic*, https://www.oecd.org/housing/policy-toolkit/country-snapshots/housing-policy-czech-republic.pdf. [173]

OECD (2023), *Housing Tenure Distribution*, https://www.oecd.org/els/family/HM1.3-Housing-tenures.xlsx (accessed on 18 December 2023). [176]

OECD (2023), *OECD Economic Surveys: Czech Republic 2023*, OECD Publishing, Paris, https://doi.org/10.1787/e392e937-en. [67]

OECD (2023), *OECD Economic Surveys: Czech Republic 2023*, OECD Publishing, Paris, https://doi.org/10.1787/e392e937-en. [198]

OECD (2023), *OECD Public Governance Reviews: Czech Republic: Towards a More Modern and Effective Public Administration*, OECD Public Governance Reviews, OECD Publishing, Paris, https://doi.org/10.1787/41fd9e5c-en. [18]

OECD (2023), *OECD Public Governance Reviews: Czech Republic: Towards a More Modern and Effective Public Administration*, OECD Publishing, Paris, https://doi.org/10.1787/41fd9e5c-en. [199]

OECD (2023), "OECD Regional Outlook - Country profiles", *OECD Regional Outlook 2023 - The long standing Geography of Inequalities*, https://doi.org/10.1787/92cd40a0-en. [14]

OECD (2023), *OECD Regional Outlook 2023: The Longstanding Geography of Inequalities*, OECD Publishing, Paris, https://doi.org/10.1787/92cd40a0-en. [13]

OECD (2023), "Professionalising the public procurement workforce: A review of current initiatives and challenges", *OECD Public Governance Policy Papers*, No. 26, OECD Publishing, Paris, https://doi.org/10.1787/e2eda150-en. [92]

OECD (2023), *Public Investment in Bulgaria: Planning and Delivering Infrastructure*, OECD Public Governance Reviews, OECD Publishing, Paris, https://doi.org/10.1787/b73ef3b4-en. [114]

OECD (2023), *Public spending on support to social rental housing as % GDP*, https://www.oecd.org/els/family/PH4-1-Public-spending-social-rental-housing.xlsx (accessed on 18 December 2023). [177]

OECD (2023), *Public spending on support to social rental housing as % GDP*, https://www.oecd.org/els/family/PH4-1-Public-spending-social-rental-housing.xlsx (accessed on 18 December 2023). [178]

OECD (2023), "Stakeholder participation in infrastructure decision making", in *Government at a Glance 2023*, OECD Publishing, Paris, https://doi.org/10.1787/59c7c2b2-en. [116]

OECD (2023), "Strengthening environmental considerations in public investment in Ireland: Assessment and recommendations", *OECD Public Governance Policy Papers*, No. 35, OECD Publishing, Paris, https://doi.org/10.1787/83b97aca-en. [119]

OECD (2023), *Subnational Governments in OECD countries: Key data*, https://www.oecd.org/regional/multi-level-governance/NUANCIER%202023-3.pdf. [11]

OECD (2023), *Subnational governments in OECD countries: key data, 2023 Edition*, https://www.oecd.org/regional/multi-level-governance/NUANCIER%202023-3.pdf. [144]

OECD (2022), *Addressing territorial disparities in future infrastructure needs in the wake of the COVID-19 crisis: A G20 perspective*, OECD Publishing, Paris, https://doi.org/10.1787/e246f50f-en. [2]

OECD (2022), *G20-OECD Policy Toolkit to Mobilise Funding and Financing for Inclusive and Quality Infrastructure Investment in Regions and Cities*, OECD Publishing, Paris, https://doi.org/10.1787/99169ac9-en. [38]

OECD (2022), "Making the most of public investment to address regional inequalities, megatrends and future shocks", *OECD Regional Development Papers*, No. 29, OECD Publishing, Paris, https://doi.org/10.1787/8a1fb523-en. [36]

OECD (2022), *OECD Regional Statistics: Regional Demography, Population density and area, large TL2 and small TL3 regions*, OECD Publish, https://stats.oecd.org/Index.aspx?DataSetCode=REGION_DEMOGR# (accessed on 25 May 2023). [3]

OECD (2022), *OECD Regional Statistics: Regional Economy, Gross Domestic Product, Small regions TL3*, OECD Publishing, https://stats.oecd.org/Index.aspx?DataSetCode=REGION_DEMOGR# (accessed on 25 May 2023). [4]

OECD (2022), *OECD Regions and Cities at a Glance 2022*, OECD Publishing, Paris, https://doi.org/10.1787/14108660-en. [30]

OECD (2022), *Regional Governance in OECD Countries: Trends, Typology and Tools*, OECD Multi-level Governance Studies, OECD Publishing, Paris, https://doi.org/10.1787/4d7c6483-en. [42]

OECD (2022), *Survey on the Governance of Infrastructure - Part I: Ensure transparent, systematic and effective stakeholder participation*. [134]

OECD (2021), *Better Governance, Planning and Services in Local Self-Governments in Poland*, OECD Publishing, Paris, https://doi.org/10.1787/550c3ff5-en. [57]

OECD (2021), *Brick by Brick: Building Better Housing Policies*, OECD Publishing, Paris, https://doi.org/10.1787/b453b043-en. [172]

OECD (2021), *Economic Policy Reforms 2021: Going for Growth: Shaping a Vibrant Recovery*, OECD Publishing, Paris, https://doi.org/10.1787/3c796721-en. [202]

OECD (2021), *Housing Affordability in Cities in the Czech Republic*, OECD Urban Studies, OECD Publishing, Paris, https://doi.org/10.1787/bcddcf4a-en. [20]

OECD (2021), *OECD Implementation Handbook for Quality Infrastructure Investment: Supporting a Sustainable Recovery from the COVID-19 Crisis*, https://www.oecd.org/finance/OECD-ImplementationHandbook-for-Quality-Infrastructure-Investment.htm. [1]

OECD (2021), *OECD Implementation Handbook for Quality Infrastructure Investment: Supporting a Sustainable Recovery from the COVID-19 Crisis*, OECD Publishing, https://www.oecd.org/finance/oecd-implementation-handbook-for-quality-infrastructure-investment.htm. [81]

OECD (2021), *OECD Regional Outlook 2021: Addressing COVID-19 and Moving to Net Zero Greenhouse Gas Emissions*, OECD Publishing, Paris, https://doi.org/10.1787/17017efe-en. [15]

OECD (2021), "Procurement strategy in major infrastructure projects: Piloting a new approach in Norway", *OECD Public Governance Policy Papers*, No. 06, OECD Publishing, Paris, https://doi.org/10.1787/38996343-en. [98]

OECD (2021), *Unlocking infrastructure investment: Innovative funding and financing in regions and cities*, OECD Publishing, Paris, https://doi.org/10.1787/9152902b-en. [48]

OECD (2020), *Delineating Functional Areas in All Territories*, OECD Territorial Reviews, OECD Publishing, Paris, https://doi.org/10.1787/07970966-en. [46]

OECD (2020), "Infrastructure Governance Review of Argentina", *OECD Journal on Budgeting*, https://doi.org/10.1787/f2574b7b-en. [88]

OECD (2020), *OECD Compendium of Policy Good Practices for Quality Infrastructure Investment*, OECD Publishing, http://, www.oecd.org/finance/oecd-compendium-of-policy-good-practices-forquality-infrastructure-investment.htm. [74]

OECD (2020), *OECD Economic Surveys: Czech Republic 2020*, OECD Publishing, Paris, https://doi.org/10.1787/1b180a5a-en. [17]

OECD (2020), *OECD Economic Surveys: Czech Republic 2020*, OECD Publishing, Paris, https://doi.org/10.1787/1b180a5a-en. [161]

OECD (2020), *Policy Actions for Affordable Housing in Latvia*, https://issuu.com/oecd.publishing/docs/latvia_housing_report_web-1. [84]

OECD (2020), *Recommendation of the Council on the Governance of Infrastructure*, https://legalinstruments.oecd.org/en/instruments/OECD-LEGAL-0460. [72]

OECD (2020), *Regional Policy for Greece Post-2020*, OECD Territorial Reviews, OECD Publishing, Paris, https://doi.org/10.1787/cedf09a5-en. [58]

OECD (2020), *Supporting Better Decision-Making in Transport Infrastructure in Spain : Infrastructure Governance Review*, OECD Publishing, Paris, https://doi.org/10.1787/310e365e-en. [70]

OECD (2020), *Survey on the Governance of Infrastructure*, https://qdd.oecd.org/subject.aspx?Subject=GOV_INFRA. [133]

OECD (2020), *The Future of Regional Development and Public Investment in Wales, United Kingdom*, OECD Multi-level Governance Studies, OECD Publishing, Paris, https://doi.org/10.1787/e6f5201d-en. [31]

OECD (2019), *Effective Multi-level Public Invesment - OECD Principles in Action*, https://www.oecd.org/effective-public-investment-toolkit/Full_report_Effective_Public_Investment.pdf. [54]

OECD (2019), *Effective Multi-level Public Investment: OECD principles in action*, OECD, https://www.oecd.org/effective-public-investment-toolkit/Full_report_Effective_Public_Investment.pdf. [27]

OECD (2019), *Effective Multi-level Public Investment: OECD Principles in Action*, OECD Publishing. [43]

OECD (2019), *Effective Public Investment across Levels of Government: Implementing the OECD Principles*, OECD Publishing, https://www.oecd.org/effective-public-investment-toolkit/OECD_Public_Investment_Implementation_Brochure_2019.pdf. [51]

OECD (2019), *Effective Public Investment across Levels of Government: Implementing the OECD Principles*, OECD, Paris, https://www.oecd.org/effective-public-investment-toolkit/OECD_Public_Investment_Implementation_Brochure_2019.pdf?_ga=2.19617528.1599561827.1664860525-807839953.1630415883. [56]

OECD (2019), *The Path to Becoming a Data-Driven Public Sector*, OECD Digital Government Studies, OECD Publishing, Paris, https://doi.org/10.1787/059814a7-en. [75]

OECD (2018), *OECD Environmental Performance Reviews: Czech Republic 2018*, OECD Environmental Performance Reviews, OECD Publishing, Paris, https://doi.org/10.1787/9789264300958-en. [47]

OECD (2017), *Getting Infrastructure Right: A framework for better governance*, OECD Publishing, Paris, https://doi.org/10.1787/9789264272453-en. [200]

OECD (2017), *Making Decentralisation Work in Chile: Towards Stronger Municipalities*, OECD Multi-level Governance Studies, OECD Publishing, Paris, https://doi.org/10.1787/9789264279049-en. [40]

OECD (2017), *Multi-level Governance Reforms: Overview of OECD Country Experiences*, OECD [41]

Multi-level Governance Studies, OECD Publishing, Paris, https://doi.org/10.1787/9789264272866-en.

OECD (2017), *Recommendation of the Council on Open Government*, https://legalinstruments.oecd.org/en/instruments/OECD-LEGAL-0438. [97]

OECD (2017), "Strategic practices for the effective use of framework agreements in Chile", in *Public Procurement in Chile: Policy Options for Efficient and Inclusive Framework Agreements*, OECD Publishing, Paris, https://doi.org/10.1787/9789264275188-6-en. [79]

OECD (2017), *The Governance of Land Use in the Czech Republic: The Case of Prague*, OECD Regional Development Studies, OECD Publishing, Paris, https://doi.org/10.1787/9789264281936-en. [71]

OECD (2016), *OECD Economic Surveys: Czech Republic 2016*, OECD Publishing, Paris, https://doi.org/10.1787/eco_surveys-cze-2016-en. [39]

OECD (2016), *The Korean Public Procurement Service: Innovating for Effectiveness*, OECD Public Governance Reviews, OECD Publishing, Paris, https://doi.org/10.1787/9789264249431-en. [80]

OECD (2014), *Effective Public Investment across Levels of Goverment: Principles for Action*, https://www.oecd.org/effective-public-investment-toolkit/Effective-Public-Investment-Brochure.pdf. [25]

OECD (2014), *Manual for Framework Agreements*, https://www.oecd.org/gov/ethics/manual-framework-agreements.pdf. [78]

OECD (2012), *Recommendation of the Council on Principles for Public Governance of Public-Private Partnerships*, https://legalinstruments.oecd.org/en/instruments/OECD-LEGAL-0392. [96]

OECD (n.d.), *Ireland: National Development Plan 2021-2030*, https://infrastructure-toolkit.oecd.org/wp-content/uploads/Ireland_NDP.pdf. [76]

OECD (forthcoming), *Regional Outlook 2023*. [49]

OECD/UCLG (2022), *Country Profile - Czech Republic*, https://www.sng-wofi.org/country-profiles/. [28]

OECD/UCLG (2022), *Country profile: Czech Republic, World Observatory on Subnational Government Finance and Investment*, https://www.sng-wofi.org/country-profiles/. [12]

OECD-CoR (2015), *Results of the OECD-CoR Consultation of Sub-national Governments: Infrastructure planning and investment across levels of government: current challenges and possible solutions*, https://portal.cor.europa.eu/europe2020/pub/documents/oecd-cor-jointreport.pdf. [60]

OECD-UCLG (2022), *World Observatory on Subnational Government Finance and Investment*, https://www.sng-wofi.org/country-profiles/. [143]

Office of Projects Victoria (n.d.), *Victorian Major Projects Pipeline*, http://www.opv.vic.gov.au/Pipeline (accessed on 17 April 2023). [86]

Plaček, M., D. Špaček and F. Ochrana (2020), "Public leadership and strategies of Czech [37] municipalities during the COVID-19 pandemic: Municipal activism vs municipal passivism", *International Journal of Public Leadership*, Vol. 17/1, pp. 108-117, https://doi.org/10.1108/ijpl-06-2020-0047.

Railway Administration (2023), *Annual Report 2022*, https://www.spravazeleznic.cz/documents/50004227/156465524/V%C3%BDro%C4%8Dn%C3%AD+zpr%C3%A1va+2022/06df59a1-94fa-4360-85b7-a0c7dc6bc129. [169]

Railway Administration (n.d.), *Company profile*, https://www.spravazeleznic.cz/web/en/about-us/our-activities. [168]

Rijkswaterstaat (n.d.), *Rijkswaterstaat Publication Platform*, https://open.rws.nl/ (accessed on 5 April 2023). [103]

Ruiz Rivadeneira, A. and P. Mcmaster (2023), "Mapping institutional arrangements for infrastructure governance in OECD countries", *OECD Working Papers on Public Governance*, No. 62, OECD Publishing, Paris, https://doi.org/10.1787/31825d0d-en. [122]

Schwartz, G. et al. (eds.) (2020), *Well Spent*, International Monetary Fund, Washington, D.C., https://doi.org/10.5089/9781513511818.071. [111]

SIGMA (2016), *Division of Contracts into Lots*, OECD Publishing, https://www.sigmaweb.org/publications/public-procurement-policy-brief-36-200117.pdf. [107]

State Environmental Fund (2023), *Management Report of the State Environmental Fund of Czechia for 2022*, State Environmental Fund of the Czech Republic, Prague, https://www.sfzp.cz/o-sfzp-cr/vyrocni-zpravy/detail-vyrocni-zpravy/?id=55. [192]

State Environmental Fund (n.d.), *About us*, State Environmental Fund of the Czech Republic, Prague, https://www.sfzp.cz/en/about-us/ (accessed on 3 July 2023). [189]

State Environmental Fund (n.d.), *Advisory Board*, State Environmental Fund of the Czech Republic, Prague, https://www.sfzp.cz/en/about-us/advisory-board/ (accessed on 4 July 2023). [193]

State Environmental Fund (n.d.), *What we do*, https://www.sfzp.cz/en/about-us/what-we-do/ (accessed on 4 July 2023). [190]

State Environmental Fund (n.d.), *What we do*, State Environmental Fund of the Czech Republic, Prague, https://www.sfzp.cz/en/about-us/what-we-do/ (accessed on 3 July 2023). [191]

State Environmental Fund of the Czech Republic (n.d.), *Advisory Board*, https://www.sfzp.cz/en/about-us/advisory-board/. [65]

State Fund for Transport Infrastructure (2022), *Budget of the State Fund for Transport Infrastructure for 2023 and the medium-term outlook for 2024 and 2025*, https://www.sfdi.cz/soubory/obrazky-clanky/rozpocet/2023_rozpocet_text-rozpoctu.pdf. [113]

State Fund for Transport Infrastructure (2022), *Budget of the State Fund for Transport Infrastructure for 2023 and the medium-term outlook for 2024 and 2025*, State Fund for Transport Infrastructure, Prague, https://www.sfdi.cz/soubory/obrazky-clanky/rozpocet/2023_rozpocet_text-rozpoctu.pdf. [165]

State Fund for Transport Infrastructure (2010-2022), *Annual Reports and Financial Statements*, [141]

State Fund for Transport Infrastructure, Prague, https://www.sfdi.cz/rozpocet/vyrocni-zpravy-a-ucetni-zaverky/.

State Fund for Transport Infrastructure (n.d.), *General information*, State Fund for Transport Infrastructure, https://www.sfdi.cz/en/ (accessed on 4 July 2023). [166]

State Fund for Transport Infrastructure (n.d.), *Homepage*, https://www.sfdi.cz/en/. [66]

State Investment Support Fund (2023), *2022 Annual Report and Financial Statements for 2022*, State Investment Support Fund, Prague, https://sfpi.cz/vyrocni-zpravy/. [182]

State Investment Support Fund (n.d.), *Rental housing*, State Investment Support Fund, Prague, https://sfpi.cz/najemni-bydleni/ (accessed on 30 June 2023). [179]

State Investment Support Fund (n.d.), *SFPI*, State Investment Support Fund, Prague, https://sfpi.cz/sfpi/ (accessed on 10 June 2023). [181]

State Investment Support Fund (n.d.), *Základní dokumenty (in Czech)*, https://sfpi.cz/zakladni-dokumenty/. [68]

The Housing Agency (2022), *Annual Report 2021*, https://www.housingagency.ie/sites/default/files/2023-01/The%20Housing%20Agency%20-%202021%20Annual%20Report%20English.pdf. [106]

The Housing Agency (2022), *Strategic Plan 2022-2024*, https://www.housingagency.ie/sites/default/files/2022-01/Housing%20Agency%20Strategic%20Plan%202022-2024%20online.pdf. [95]

Union of Towns and Municipalities of Czechia (2020), *Examples of Good Practice in Voluntary Associations of Municipalities*. [125]

World Bank (2021), *Infrastructure Governance Assessment Framework*, https://thedocs.worldbank.org/en/doc/96550c14d62154355b6edc367d4d7f33-0080012021/infrastructure-governance-assessment-framework-december-2020. [91]

World Bank (2020), *Infratech Value Drivers*, World Bank, https://openknowledge.worldbank.org/entities/publication/675dc4d5-56fb-535d-9c32-d6d2b17e0dd0. [90]

www.ingramcontent.com/pod-product-compliance
Ingram Content Group UK Ltd.
Pitfield, Milton Keynes, MK11 3LW, UK
UKHW051503290926
15471UKWH00008B/1394